Mosul: Story of Hope

Palewell Press

Mosul: Story of Hope

Ahmed Zaidan

From Mosul: Story of Hope
First edition 2025 from Palewell Press,
https://palewellpress.co.uk
Printed and bound in the UK
ISBN 978-1-911587-96-5

All Rights Reserved. Copyright © 2025 Ahmed Zaidan. No part of this publication may be reproduced or transmitted in any form or by any means, without permission in writing from the Author. The right of Ahmed Zaidan to be identified as the author of this work has been asserted by him in accordance with the Copyright, Designs and Patents Act 1988

The front cover photo is Copyright © 2025 Saad Salem, https://1x.com/saadsalem and abosuaood@yahoo.com
The cover design is Copyright © 2025 Camilla Reeve
The photo of Ahmed Zaidan on the back cover is Copyright © 2025 Rewan Kakil
A CIP catalogue record for this title is available from the British Library.

Dedication

This book is dedicated to the victims of wars around the world.

To the city of Mosul, which endowed me with the seeds of fire to ignite my revolution.

To the Old Town - the cradle of memories - turned by bombs into a flock of letters travelling across the globe, casting a story of resilience and hope.

To my mother, the courageous breeze that carried life stealthily into an ominous land.

To my father, the peaceful trench amidst the rain of bombings.

To my grandmother, who inspired me to divert the moon from the folds of pain.

To all my friends mentioned in this book.

To the victims of wars around the world.

To the brave soldiers who sacrificed their lives to liberate the city, and to the noble commanders whose names the people of Mosul will remember forever.

Acknowledgements

Thanks are extended to my friend, the poet and playwright Andy Willoughby, who edited and revised the book - an inspiring companion throughout my journey.

I would like to express my sincere thanks to Iraqi journalist Ali Ayad for kindly facilitating the interviews.

Special thanks go to Petri Tähtinen for his encouragement, urging me to keep writing despite the gusting challenges.

I would also like to thank my friends in Finland, who have been a window through which I drew the power of the present, spanning the writing trek - amidst the tornado of memories and the distant past that often drifted me away from the now.

I am grateful to the Kone Foundation for funding this project. In 2013, when I first came to Finland, I noticed the Kone logo on machines - especially lifts and escalators. Later, as I stepped into the Finnish literary scene, I often overheard colleagues mention Kone. Once, at the Book House in Turku, I was fortunate enough to meet people whose projects were funded by Kone. That encounter gave me the courage to continue as an artist in Finland.

As my knowledge grew, the meaning of Kone began to transcend the world of steel and machinery. To me, the name no longer resonated only with elevators and mechanical parts, but with something far more profound; where gear wheels spin dynamically, helping entire worlds to move: the worlds of research, of art, of human connection.

To me, the Kone Foundation is like a forest growing at the edge of the industrial era, absorbing what the machines exhale, then expanding to restore a delicate balance where the sky can glitter and lakes can glint.

This is how I see the Kone Foundation through my poetic lens. It gave me a platform to share my own story, with the belief that by telling others' stories, we can make the world a better place. This springs from Kone's conviction that, despite long distances and razor-wire borders, we are all human - connected.

As an immigrant, I would say that my relationship with Finland is defined through my cultural endeavour and involvement, where I've created authentic friendships and inspiring memories and cultural events have become gates through which I conjure a memory or title a year. It is, I believe, the most meaningful way to become part of this society - and to help this society remain connected to the world beyond.

Contents

Introduction 1
Editor's Foreword 4
1988-2002: My Earliest Memories 7
2003-2022 Political and Military Overview 21
    Years leading up to ISIS 21
    Mosul "handed over to ISIS" 23
    10 June 2014 - The ominous day of the conquest.. 29
    Mosul lay outside the world 32
2014–2016: ISIS Occupation of Mosul 35
    Assault on Nineveh 35
    The Yazidi Genocide 36
    Personal Accounts of ISIS seizing Mosul 37
        The Author's Own Memory of 4-10 of June 2014. 37
        Testimony of Um Umar, a grandmother living in Mosul 42
        Poem: In wars, women are stronger 43
        Um Umar continues her testimony 43
        Poem: To my brothers and sisters 44
        Testimony of the Author's Younger Uncle 44
        The Author's Interview with his Younger Brother 46
        The Author's Other Relatives 47
        Poem: Let us hold a funeral procession for Arabhood 51
December 2016 - Liberation of Mosul Begins 53

Author's Personal Investigation 53
A man on his knees 55
A Survivor's Account. 56
US-led attack on ISIS-held Mosul 56
Testimony by Abu Omar 58
The impact of ISIS on Mosul 59

2017 - Eve of Western Mosul's Liberation 63

Breaking the silence 63
Final battle to clear Eastern Mosul of ISIS, June 27 2017 63
What is happening at Al Manasah (Platform) Street in Eastern Mosul? 65
The eve of ISIS facing defeat 66
Eye witness Accounts of the Liberation 67
  Um Umar - feeling forced to leave 68
  Um Umar - escaping the abyss 69
  Um Umar - getting separated from her son 71
  Poem: Humans can kill a fly for fun! 72
  Um Umar - still trying to escape 73
  Ahmad - journeying on alone 73
  Ahmad - trapped in the Old Town 76
  Ahmad - seeking shelter from strangers 79
  Ahmad - whether to stay or move on 82
  Um Umar and the family keep trying to escape . 85
  Um Umar - recalling her neighbour's son, Mahir 89
  Um Umar - queuing at the security checkpoint .. 91

- Um Umar - everyone's fear of secret informants 94
- Um Umar - worrying about Ahmad 95
- Um Umar - reunited with her son 96
- The Author's Close Family 97
  - The Author's Uncle 97
  - The Author's Father... 98
  - The Author's Close Family is Liberated.......... 100
- Interwoven Stories.. 111
  - Sahar and Taha 111
  - Sahar - hearing of the start of the liberation Oct 16 2016... 113
  - Sahar - discovering husband's secret journalism 115
  - Sahar - watching video of Mosul under ISIS ... 118
  - Sahar - implications of Taha's secret journalism 122
  - Muhammad Talal - a writer secretly in touch with Taha.. 123
  - Muhammad Talal - ISIS persecuting musicians 126
  - Muhammad Talal - ISIS targeting journalists.. 130
  - Poem: Looking for interstellar home 134
  - Muhammad Talal - whether to leave Mosul 134
  - Sahar - discovering more of Taha's secrets 136
  - Sahar - watching a secret poetry film 139
  - Sahar - confronting Taha about his secrets 143
  - Sahar - thinking about the risks Taha ran 146

- Sahar - hearing of how Buthaina met Abu-Hamza 147
- Buthaina - after Abu Hamza was killed 152
- Buthaina and Muthanna - sharing a wish for revenge 153
- Buthaina - Muthanna's memories of sectarian violence 157
- Buthaina - hears Yazidi girls are being marketed by ISIS 159
- ISIS lyrics known by extremists who fought in Syria and Iraq 162
- Yazidi girl, Suzaan, tells Buthaina her story 163
- Yazidi girls escape, helped by Buthaina 164
- Yazidi student shares her sister-in-law's story. 166

2017–2021: Citizen Heroes 171

- Maha - leading her family's escape 171
- Maha - planning the escape from Old Town 172
- Maha - heading for the Al-Refai neighbourhood 176
- Maha - a new escape plan 178
- Poem: We dealt with life that was stripped of accessories 181
- Maha - more preparations for the escape 182
- Suruur - Corpse Clearing and Women's Cycling. 199
- Suruur - life under ISIS occupation 200
- Poem: In every book there are secret gates hidden in the lines 203
- Suruur – losing touch with her loved ones 203
- Surrur - the journey into voluntary work 209

Suruur - becoming a volunteer 213
　　　Suruur - the Corpse Clearing Team 214
　　　Suruur - challenges to the Corpses Team led by a girl 216
　　　Suruur - a new kind of voluntary work 220
　　　Suruur - the price of her victory 221
　　　Suruur - a women's cycling team for Mosul ... 223
　　Naqam - a Human Rights activist 227
　　　Naqam - working as a citizen journalist 231
　　　Naqam - life after liberation 233
　　Anfal - an artist from the heart of Mosul 235
　　　Anfal - volunteering and work life 239
　　　Poem: A New Morning 241
　　　Anfal - writing as a way to explore the world . 243
　　　Anfal - women need to be financially independent 246
　　　Poem: Reunifying with herself 247
　　Marwa - founding a team of volunteers 248
　　　Marwa - Marriage of Minors in Iraq 249
　　　Marwa - life after separation 254
　　　Marwa - women and financial independence .. 254
Mosul - A Better Tomorrow 257
　　Abu Omar - Mosul is reclaiming its spirit 258
　　Um Umar – now feeling optimistic 258
　　A Gleam of Hope 259
　　Poem: Story of Hope 260
　　A New Era 261

Conclusion..263
Author's Biography - Ahmed Zaidan....................................265

Introduction

This book defies stereotypes and crosses borders, venturing beyond the safety of familiar territory. It is a vessel in which I have chosen to preserve what I can salvage from the depths of oblivion.

You are not just reading a book, you are taking a tour in the corridor of a great prison, where every page is a cell and every story is a window bidding you to find the way to the outside world. Welcome inside! beyond the walls of the media and the razor-wire of stereotypes.

This is the story of a man who resembles the story of the earth in the multiple birth of its features. It's set in a gloomy neighbourhood called the Valley of the Stones (which isn't a valley and there aren't any stones) – which apparently gained some truth to its misleading name after the war.

My name is Ahmed Zaidan and I am a writer from Mosul. I fled my hometown due to threats to my life as a journalist there, and I now live in Finland. But I have, of course, kept a close eye on events in the town of my birth. This book seeks to bring together the concealed dimensions of the story and the general image when it's looked at from another angle. This is my testimony about a significant era in the history of the Middle East in one of the most populated cities, the metropolis of ancient civilisations and the most civil society in Iraq that was turned overnight to the capital of the so-called "Islamic State."

I decided to break silence in order to share my narrative with the world. It begins with my earliest memories: from the Second Gulf War through the International Embargo imposed on the Iraqi People, lifted after the war of 2003 that ousted the regime of Saddam Hussein, the development of events in the "New Iraq" that became a fertile ground for terrorists and death squads to rampage day and night all over the country, resulting in large scale exodus and displacement after the ISIS conquest in 2014. It examines how society has been changed and discovers a brighter part of this story of deep torment.

I am a needle lost in the hay,
perforating the thumb of the oblivious farmer
I am the rake that clears your way

As a man who resides in Finland but originally comes from Mosul, I also project my own experience before departing from the city towards my new homeland and the journey to get there. How does it feel seeing one's mother town being gutted by flames, starting from pre and post ISIS? Can this earthquake lead to a more stable society that benefits from prior mistakes? Can a society be rinsed clean in the shower of hard experience?

This book also focuses on the stories of diverse social elements. I chose to listen to other people bearing witness and to transform their stories into migratory words that would fly beyond the walls of the siege and the fence of borders, crossing all cultural boundaries. Here on the horizon of humanity, suffering is eloquent and love speaks the language of the soul.

I called this book *Mosul – Story of Hope* because, after liberation from ISIS, ordinary people volunteering, journalists and artists, and feminist movements lit up the city of Mosul. Testimonies from a series of people whom I interviewed online, and during a research visit back, reveal what the situation is and was really like on the ground. Here, against all odds we find stories of survivors engaging in bold initiatives that soar beyond the social heliosphere, resisting the gravitational power of religions and some of the local heritage crushing down on the chest of freedom.

Getting rid of the shackles of the past and extending a hand to the world are an essential step that comes from the flare of experience – no matter how hard that experience is – but they require the fusion of concepts and reshaping of values. Trusting the outside world hasn't been easy in Mosul. But it seems possible now that shells from the battles have demolished the thick walls, permitting the caravans of the world to infiltrate into the razed heart in the form of civil organisations and so on… to resurrect the city.

My old city, and its residents, were abandoned, conquered, liberated and finally forgotten after the flames of war and tears of international tragedy left their streets. They need to be heard once again – as inspiration for man's desire for common good and ordinary equality.

Through this book, I share the stories of a city that once tossed me away into the dark ages but would eventually shake off the dust and move forward; its citizens who never lost hope; and its artists who sing for love so peace may finally prevail in this world!

Among the stories to be told are:
- The poet of Mosul who didn't stop writing poetry in Mosul when ISIS was conquering the city, tried to flee and was so near to the end, arriving in Europe to narrate his story via poetry.
- The musician - ISIS broke into his house and destroyed his instruments, but he never surrendered, he kept fighting to the last minute by composing and recording while the war was howling outside.
- The women who challenged society, from young single women volunteering through to a courageous grandmother, each sharing the story of liberation from ISIS from her own point of view.

The Mosul I grew up in would be scattered and reassembled in the form of poems and art pieces, in the form of pictures travelling around the world, in the forms of refugees living with their hearts split between here and there, between the nightmares of the past and the shining future.

Ahmed Zaidan

Editor's Foreword

I am indebted to Andy Willoughby, poet and playwright, the first person to edit and revise this manuscript. He helped Ahmed Zaidan prepare it for submission to Palewell Press. Once we had accepted it for publication, I began offering my own editorial suggestions but Andy generously stayed in touch with the process. Ahmed describes Andy as being "an inspiring companion throughout my journey."

The book is an extraordinary work of memoir, reportage and storytelling. It begins with the author's earliest years growing up in Mosul, then charts the city's capture and occupation by ISIS, that group's eventual defeat, and the city's post-liberation rebirth.

The story unfolds through the poignant eyewitness accounts of many different people. Ahmed places these accounts in context, writing sometimes as a journalist and social historian and, at other times, by providing his personal recollection of events.

It was really important to clarify who the narrator was at every point. The approach I have adopted is as follows: Ahmed's words are in a regular typeface except where he is providing context to eyewitness accounts. At those points, his words are in italics. Also shown in italics are the poems included in the book and transcriptions of radio broadcasts.

Following the eyewitness accounts, Ahmed presents Interwoven Stories, a chapter based on composite characters, sharing narratives that, for reasons of people's safety, could not be told in any other way.

It has been a privilege publishing *Mosul – Story of Hope*. Few people whose home city has been ravaged by an invader are capable of focusing on the re-emergence of hope. Ahmed shares a core value with Palewell Press: by telling others' stories, we can make the world a better place. I hope you find the stories in this book as engaging and inspiring as I have.

Camilla Reeve

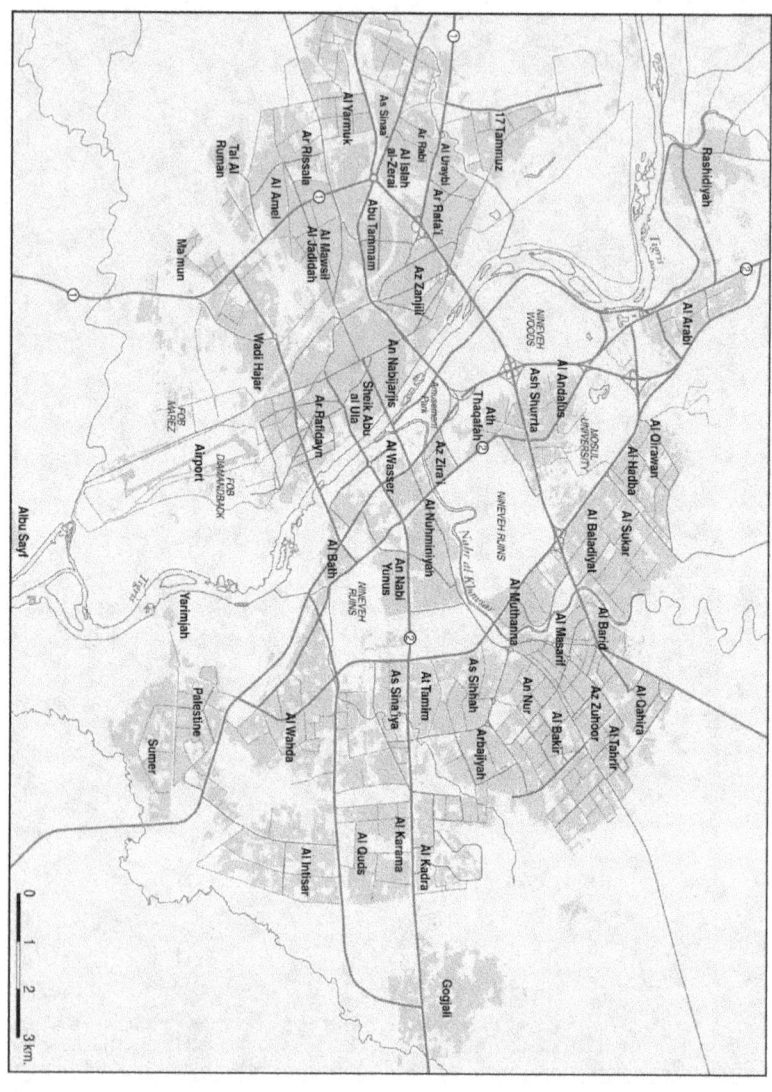

Map of Mosul, downloaded from ISW Institute for the Study of War

1988-2002: My Earliest Memories

In 1988, the 1st Gulf War ended after eight years of fierce fighting between Iraq and Iran causing the death on both sides, of a million people, with many still missing.

Two years later, Saddam Hussein would vow that his men would have their breakfast in Kuwait, the 19th province as he claimed it to be. Yes, the guys had their breakfast there, but unfortunately that was the most expensive breakfast in history. Iraq is still paying the bill for that breakfast to its southern neighbour, the State of Kuwait.

According to the army officers who were deployed in Kuwait: "The president ordered our commanders, whatever happens, even if you hear me on radio ordering you to withdraw, never do that!"

Yes, Kuwait was looted, and the Iraqi markets were flooded with the spoils from the petroleum country. Well, Iraq is a petroleum country too. One of the most famous goods was the Kuwaiti VCR "Video Driver" that thrived in the 90s. It was one of the most well-known goods that acquired its name from where it was stolen.

After the 2nd Gulf War, Iraq was in declined, drowning in a stagnant pond of corruption. From time to time, the country was plunged into a new crisis, starting from the gas crisis to the medical crisis and deprivation of basic needs.

That was the time of the early 90s during the war, when my family had to flee from Mosul to the village where my grandmother lived. It was northwest of Mosul, close to the Syrian border from the west, and the lake of Mosul Dam from the east. During wars, the lucky ones were those with relatives or friends living in the suburbs or villages. My grandmother's family isn't from the city; this is where I realised that diversity is a strength and a wider world.

Let me tell you my earliest memory: the picture looks like a dream drained of its colours or like a foggy flicker stripped from an old film, my younger brother is chasing the chickens, many people are crammed in one room, the mud is staining everything and there was a man with thick moustache and shaved, toasted face wearing rural clothes mentioning Mosul: "Who would want to go back to Mosul?" he cried. So, I first heard the name "Mosul" outside Mosul, from someone who is not from Mosul, and I didn't know what it meant. Back then, just the most repeated word of all words...

Mosul is not such an open city according to historians. The city of Mosul itself has been exposed to many atrocities over the years, causing locals to be more careful when dealing with the outsiders. You can probably see that clearly just before 2003; how people of Mosul, Muslims and Christians lived next door to each other, without any regard for the religious aspects if their ancestors lived together peacefully. It made it difficult for outsiders to dwell in the Old Town.

As a kid, I enjoyed being in the village, for me it was like a picnic. I would have said "summer cottage" but it was a cold winter, however I would call it our "war cottage."

As we returned from our war cottage to Mosul, the International Embargo was being imposed over the country to ruin the regime. I remember my younger brother got intimidated when he saw white bread. Perhaps this doesn't sound funny, but it was for us. My uncle was holding a loaf of bread towards my younger brother, causing the kid to back away.

Until this time, I was not able to understand: what was so scary about white bread? Dark bread was commonplace because it was the cheapest.

Yes, in the early 90s, all Iraqis except the elite, were underdogs. One of the friends reminisced about that day when he was ill, and his mom asked him to wish for just anything for breakfast: He thought it was his chance to ask for a great breakfast, an unprecedented one. "Mom, I would like to eat one full half-boiled egg, without having to share it with my sister." What a big wish.

Do you want to know how the international resolution was viewed by us: "the siege"? I thought it was a giant man who was barring everyone wanting to deliver aid to us, the Iraqi people, from reaching. Later, when I was sure that giants belonged in the past, not in our time, I started to picture the siege as a great gate. When it opened, the marvels of things we hadn't heard and seen, would flow into the country.

While I was growing up, the concept of siege had been growing up with me, until the true concept of siege was revealed as a malignant political action, imposed on the whole nation to punish just one person – the head of state, who lived a life as far as possible from deprivation. All people in the target country endured the international sanctions, except the ruling family.

Unlike the desired outcome, hatred towards the international community surged, and it seemed to prove what the president was telling us in every speech, almost every day: the whole world wanted us to suffer.

International sanctions led us to develop some bad habits as indispensable instruments to survive in everyday life. Let me put it in a practical way here: Teachers were given extremely low salaries that could barely cover a few days of the month. Only 2 euros per month. Often, they worked as taxi drivers or in construction during the afternoon.

Otherwise, people had to literally live on the ration. In the 90's, the state had allocated a food ration for every family that was awarded monthly. Food rationing excited people at that time, they eagerly awaited the news that rations had arrived. In every alley, there was a rations agent who would distribute the food according to the national ration card. Some of the people could sell some items from their rations if they were in financial tension. They would survive anyway.

Gas was given, based on the national ration card. From 2000 on, as the situation began to improve, eggs and chickens were being sold at a lower price for the nationals. Those two items that had been hard to obtain during the 90's, became available. If crowds of people were blocking the stalls, you could tell what was going on – chicken or eggs were being distributed. People started to adapt as the government started to spoil the nation by feeding it what had been scarce in the past years.

My mother used to tell us stories about how things were lavish before the siege was imposed: "We used to buy apples and bananas every day!"

I couldn't believe that bananas really belonged to our world. We only saw them on TV in the form of cartons and so on...

In the mid-90s, some of the high-level grocery stores started to sell actual bananas. One of my friends told me that a friend of his saw bananas on sale, and he asked his grandfather to buy him one. The grandfather promised him: "Son, this banana as you can see, it is bent, I will buy you one later when it becomes straight," and he succeeded in convincing the insistent kid.

In the nineties, the international embargo was imposed on Iraq as a bid to punish the regime after the 2nd Gulf War. If you lived in Iraq during the international embargo, you lived in one of the most isolated countries in the world, not just being banned from travelling but also not allowing people in at all. Foreign goods were rarely seen in the country.

I was fortunate enough to have inherited old toys from my younger aunt and, in the late 80s right before the international siege, my dad could have bought me good quality toys. Still there was an issue, I needed to share all that I had with my younger siblings. In that time, you didn't own anything, it was just like a mini version of communism that the situation entailed.

The bottle of homemade Pepsi became the logo of luxury; the homemade luxury... While we were on a visit to my grandfather's house (the grand house of the family) my uncle came back in the afternoon, grinning. He thought that what he'd brought would be unprecedented for us: a glass bottle containing a dark drink. It seemed to me like date's syrup which was common and easy to obtain. But when he put that bottle in the fridge, I thought it could be something else... It was something else!

Believe it or not, all the family members shared that bottle; the bottle of Pepsi that Iraq started to produce in a step to cover the lack of international imports and to cope with the global siege. Small shots it is called in Iraq (Estikan, a traditional glass cup for serving tea which is curved and small), so the whole family would take a shot of that new product after the deprivation followed the 2nd Gulf War in a country used to living a lavish life, according to what they said.

The first time I went to the kindergarten in a worn-out bus affiliated to the state, I saw that beautiful toys were tossed on the floor. I thought I could take some of them with me, and stacked two pieces in my bag. I went home exclaiming: "I have got these toys from the kindergarten!"

My mom explained that what I had done was unrighteous. I insisted that they were tossed on the ground, and nobody really cared. I saw other kids were throwing the toys in something like a bin!

Anyway, my dilemma was how to return them to the kindergarten without anyone noticing. My mother told me to take them out of my pocket and slide them down with the other toys. The mission was accomplished.

In the nineties, (Baba Saddam) the Iraqi former president was everywhere, his pictures, his sayings, and his ghost. In kindergarten, if they wanted us to restrain ourselves and to be quiet, they just needed to say: "Hey, Baba Saddam is coming here soon! Or Baba Saddam is waiting to meet you at the dining room!"

Every time those sentences were being said, we believed them.

I liked to draw. I used to be the painter of the classroom because one day what I did was so popular, I drew Al-Aqsa Mosque in the primary school under a large caption "Jerusalem is for us." I knew that no one dared to say a word against my art, even if it wasn't good enough, it was something of the president's interests.

I felt honoured to see my art hung on the wall of the classroom. And my name was affixed below.

In the fourth grade, we started to get involved in military training, teaching us the love of the president and how to fight in case the Americans attacked us, we were called the "Cubs of Saddam." I used to wear my uniform even in the classroom, it was something like a privilege helping us earn the respect of teachers – those teachers who were always angry.

In class, I practised my bad habit; the habit that everyone had warned me to stop, I enjoyed drawing on the curriculum's books. Sometimes, I would make a rocket on the verge of the pages, falling, while the pages were flipped swiftly. It was the first form of animation in motion.

Every schoolbook started with a picture of the president laughing or with his uniform on, on the first page. One time, I tried to secretly draw the president's face, but I failed, I couldn't show my bad quality version of Saddam to anyone, because I knew it was a great sin. It might cause me to get expelled from the school and my father could even lose his life for not teaching me how to respect the picture of our president.

The class was so boring, so I decided to mess with the picture of the president. Nobody would see me and if they saw me, my uniform would always stand for me, acquitting me from any charges. I started with moustaches, I used my pencil to prolong them down to his chin, and then I thought, now I should make a beard for him. He would definitely look like a heroic figure from the movies, I painted a beard for him – that was how he looked like when he was captured by the Americans in Dec 2003, when they pulled him out of his den – I drew small warplanes approaching his cheeks, and a rocket passing by his forehead. I was enjoying messing with his picture, I had seen no one doing that.

Then I got smacked on my shoulder. "You should feel ashamed of yourself, bad kid!" the teacher barked.

She was so pretty, petite, almost the prettiest of all the teachers I've ever seen. She slapped me in the face and asked one of the older students to take me to the headmaster of the school, the most loyal man to the president, he got a high rank in the Baath Party. I used to see Saddam in his gaze, his voice, the way he addressed us and the speech he delivered to our parents on every occasion.

On the way to him, I was sobbing. Meanwhile, the student who guided me downstairs, couldn't have said anything. I felt that he was so sorry for me, but he couldn't say it out loud. Also, he looked at me as if I was a stranger; like he was feeling horrible inside to see his classmate sliding towards the abyss. What a big sin, Ahmed!

On the way to the headmaster, I felt like a lamb being escorted to the butchers.

My classmate reported, "He was caught by the teacher while he was messing with the picture of the president in class."

The headmaster's eyes widened. He leapt out of his chair and stood up on hearing the name of president "Saddam Hussein." It took him a while to comprehend what I had done. I might've been the first student accused of defacing the picture of Saddam Hussein.

"How dare you, you stupid kid!"

I heard his assistant saying, "Oh My God!"

By then, I realised I'd gone beyond the limit of help. No one would be kind and say: "He is just a 10-year-old kid who didn't know what he was doing, just forgive him for his unprecedented sin."

But luckily, another teacher sitting on the couch said, "It is so dangerous to leak this case out of the school, they might say that the school has taught him to do so. Think of the reputation of the school and your history of struggle in the Party."

The headmaster stood as a bewildered statue staring first at my weeping face and then at the wise teacher who was nodding to him that he should just punish me, nothing out of the ordinary.

I stopped being able to hear anything. I felt that the noise of my thoughts had blocked my ears. I just heard him yelling and reproaching me. "Don't you feel ashamed of your military outfit that you are wearing, idiot!"

Then, the wise teacher interfered again, asking me to stretch my hands, so the headmaster could beat my palms with his famous stick.

I felt that I was the luckiest one on earth to get beaten, so I stretched my hands with love, feeling gratitude after every hit.

Then the wise teacher asked the headmaster to refrain: "Headmaster, let him go back to his class, we don't want him to miss the lesson."

So, he dismissed me. I was thankful for them being so generous to me. It was the first time I willingly walked back to the class. I was just like a fish returning to water, listening to the teacher with all my senses, clutching onto the edge of the ordinary world that I had been about to lose just a minute earlier.

I received shaming glances from hard-working students, while the ones who sat in the last row were mocking me. From then on, I stopped practising my favourite hobby. Drawing became political for me. The headmaster had informed the teacher of art to keep an eye on me during the lesson. I could feel that by glancing at the teacher who frequented my desk from time to time, then nodded before heading back to her preferred seat. That was in the corner, where the single stove donated to the school by some well-off folk was conducting warm whispers to the teacher, not the students. For us the classroom was so cold.

We say in Iraq that fire is the fruit of winter. During the 90s, we could neither obtain fruit nor fire except the flare of wars. The country was suffering; however, everybody knew that the ruling family members and the officials were living a luxurious life.

I often thought that the world must be more beautiful beyond the border of my neighbourhood. I envied pupils from distant districts. I was fascinated by their speech about the countryside. Whereas I could actually see my home from the window of the classroom.

Most of the teachers knew my mother and grandmother at a personal level, which made it easier for them to control my behaviour. In 1994, I remember my first day in the school and my mother cramming a piece of bread and one tomato into the bag that I inherited from the prior pupil in the family, my aunt who attended the intermediate school.

My backpack was faded but still usable. In the years of siege, people would keep re-using their belongings till they fell apart. Most of our clothes had been repaired over and over. One item would play multiple-roles; oil cans could play the role of trash bins and proper containers that would be in service for years before decommissioning into homemade lanterns for outside-illuminating purposes by plunging in a flammable strip of fabric soaked into oil.

The school years were a struggle that we couldn't have sensed. It became our normal, fusing into everyday life. That was the only hidden bliss that made our lives move within an ordinary pace. Or perhaps life is made of levels, where going up is a privilege while relapsing to a lower level is a disadvantage. But the difference of levels could be sensed only in the transitional process, thereafter people would encounter the same sufferings that hold different titles. People of the lower level clutched more eagerly at life because they believed going to the upper level would endow them with paradise. That thought itself is called hope. People at the bottom absorb it while those at the top are busy preserving their position and sustaining their critical standing on the tip of the pyramid. Up there, the brisk breeze smacks the quiet, where falling takes longer before ramming into the rigid ground.

It was through the toughness of those times that I acquired my resilience.

Remembering my early classmates, I see them in their worn-thin jackets shivering in the winter sun. As they swarm to the sunny spot of the school yard, I can remember the colour of their jackets. I often wonder why I remember the colours. The answer is as simple as our life in that era: our families couldn't afford to buy us new clothes every season; we just kept repairing the same clothes for many years.

My early classmates were Nazhan, Arshad, Yussif and Anas.

Nazhan had been my close friend who would accompany me to school by interrupting my slack breakfast near the stove and dragging me to walk in those foggy mornings all the way to school, where heavy rules burdened us alongside the slogans of ruling party on walls and in the lobby. You could tell that you are in the most primary part of the school from the density of the pictures of the president and slogans. For a moment you feel that school was built for that purpose.

We grew up just reading slogans on the walls until the 3rd grade. From then on, every Thursday morning, we had what we called the flag-salute, where teachers and pupils alike would be unified by repeating the anthem and slogans of the party.

In the second grade, one of my female colleagues misinterpreted what I said to her when I made small pieces of paper and distributed them to all my classmates who were inside the classroom saying to each one: "Please keep this letter until tomorrow morning! I will take it back from you by the morning."

I didn't know if I wanted to share something with my early peers to build the first bridge of trust through this simple activity of giving something and restoring it the next day? To be honest, even now, I don't know. But what I am sure about is that I didn't mean anything bad. Those pieces of paper weren't love letters as one of the female pupils accused me and I was summoned by the principal of the school. When I entered her office, it felt warm and pleasant, but it wasn't comfortable to me. It wasn't part of our natural environment!

The principal was holding a piece of paper and she was grimacing and staring at me and yelling: "Do you know what this is?"

Well, this piece of paper looks familiar, I said to myself.

"How dare you? Love letter! Do you know what a love letter is?"

I kept silent, because I truly didn't know what she was talking about.

Anyway, she punished me and demanded the attendance of my mother.

Luckily my father took it lightly and said: 'Great that my son has grown up to write love letters!'

I desperately tried to make them believe that it wasn't a love letter; just a piece of paper, an innocent letter, nothing more! It took me many years to believe that love letters are something good. But what to do? It wasn't a love letter.

In the third grade, they made a decision to separate males from females.

The airport is close to the neighbourhood of the Valley of Stones "Wadi Hajar" where I lived with my family. On the opposite side of the runway, Ghazlani Military Base bordered the south west Mosul, indicating the end of the residential area at the edge of the Valley of Stones – the closest location for military folks to hang out, obtain their groceries and socialise with locals. Back to Intermediate school that entailed us crossing from the railway to reach it.

One day, I thought to myself: why not go to Baghdad by walking on the railway towards the south. I suggested the idea to my friend while we were on the way back home, carrying our school bags and teenage curiosity. We just have to walk, aligning the railway, as simple as it is. The distance from Mosul to Baghdad is about 400 km. We believed we would make it to the capital back and forth on the same day, so our families wouldn't get worried. I was the captain of that trek. As we commenced the walk, we reached new terrains that denoted we had exceeded our borders; the borders drawn by our families. We reached the military base, the first sign that the city had ended for us.

We ate from the berries tree and then got back to the neighbourhood.

Before 2003, while I was in intermediate school, I lost my earliest school friend, Nazhan. I learned that he quit studying to provide for his family, since his father was martyred in the war. Nazhan worked as a blanket smuggler, carrying them on his back on the Turkish border. One day, he was spotted by the border guards, he tried to escape by attempting to cross the river. He jumped into the river, he tried to keep himself floating but in vain, the blankets were tied to his body, and they became soaked with water which made it difficult for him to go on.

The boy drowned in the cold river. He couldn't save himself nor his purchase. It might look insane to think of those blankets in that way. However, he knew that the value of those blankets was identical to his soul, at least this is what he had been told. I felt so sorry that Nazhan couldn't make it to see what was going to happen after 2003; the remarkable overthrow of the Iraqi regime.

But the first victim of the events following 2003 was Yussif who got killed in a random mortar shell in my neighbourhood.

On one of those hellishly hot Iraqi afternoons, while I was walking home, I sensed something unusual. I was startled and a movie tape rolled in my mind, starting from the years of the Gulf Wars, the international siege, the Desert Storm War, and the turmoil that led to the current situation. When a man is afraid, time will stop for him as though falling into a blackhole, he sees all his life events floating around randomly. Only time holds our life's events together, permitting us to peer from one angle, what we call the present moment, otherwise what has happened and will happen is simultaneous.

I wondered if perhaps it was the end. Should I have listened to my mother when she warned me frequently that I should stop writing and quit my job as a TV presenter and reporter?

My father, the former army officer, didn't say much: *You are an adult, and one day you will face the consequences of your choices!*

In a moment like that, you wish that your parents' advice could materialise in the form of walls between you and the imminent danger rattling a few steps ahead. I saw my future dreams mocking me, grinning like ghosts, while I perched on my knees trying desperately to dismiss them.

A bullet could end this absurd play now, just when I have reached the zone of fate; a miserable fate... As I turned desperately to the right, death was death... I saw a swarm of house sparrows rambling, splashing in the pond, causing a noise that sounded to me like the rattle of death...

Instead, I left the country, and that bullet would penetrate my uncle's head, the chests of many friends, the whole city of Mosul.

2003-2022 Political and Military Overview

"When we move in the right direction, the shadow of our past doesn't show up. Future is an upcoming moment hidden in our current choices, let's enjoy the best of it."

I believe that true nations are born from turmoil after experiencing torment, and getting over such situations; they become stronger and more resilient.

Mosul is a vivid example for those who want to witness how humans are capable of coping with life at its lowest level and in its most horrific form; there at the bottom, where people have undergone hunger and an acute lack of all reason to live. During the war of liberation 2016-2017, people would be shown on TV, ashen and intimidated, being thwarted attempting to flee their homes. They looked as though they had risen from the grave, haunted, striving in any way to survive.

Years leading up to ISIS

Since 2003, Mosul, the second largest city in Iraq, had been slowly sliding to the abyss. I can say that as one of its citizens. After the US-led invasion of Iraq, Mosul lost its leading role in the country, being accused of being the main pillar shoring up the former regime via its largest contribution to the Iraqi army, among all Iraqi cities. And the new government accused it of being the centre of opponents that rejected the toppling of the Iraqi regime. Although the city had its palpable role in founding the first cell of the Iraqi army back in the '20s of the past century, this didn't repel these charges.

The city was exposed to turmoil triggered by the constant conflict between the political blocs competing to get into power. Violence was present in daily life, materialising in the fight between the US army and the so-called Islamic State (Al Qaida). Life was difficult for locals. Curfew between 8 pm and 6 am was a daily practice, turning the city to literally a city of ghosts in the night. In short, the night was fully diminished, and the vibrant streets that once thrived with lights and people, road restaurants and cafés, were emptied. For example, if it happened that you needed to move from a neighbourhood to another during curfew, you would need to ignite all your senses, and walk carefully, avoiding all the police checkpoints. Any voice denoting that a military vehicle was approaching would be deemed a warning alarm, and should be responded to by stepping back, as a bid to conceal yourself, otherwise you would be treated as a potential enemy.

I call the years following 2003 the dismal years; no nightlife, no entertainment, no freedom even at its lowest level, no life in general. Even life on Earth needs a "Goldilocks Zone", the suitable distance between the planet and its star. Whereas the Goldilocks Zone on Earth is security. Life cannot bloom when the element of security is being omitted. Thus, what happened in 2014 was that the city had reached the bottom of the abyss; it was tumbling like a ball, nearing the bottom gradually. The city was conquered by ISIS who murdered tens of thousands throughout the two years of their control. This was in addition to the cultural demolition and altering of identity they perpetrated.

The battle had cast its dark shadow on the city as well. The vibrant heart of the city was ruthlessly hit, while infrastructure was purposely destroyed, as well as the lives lost, whether among the civilians or the Iraqi soldiers. My mother said, "When I saw our quarter for the first time after the battles, I was shocked seeing the magnitude of destruction, I wouldn't have recognized it."

This is indeed, what most locals said, describing the scene after the battles of liberation. And the UN listed Mosul as the most inhabited city to be destroyed, since the 2nd World War.

Mosul "handed over to ISIS"

In August 2014, President Obama authorised U.S. airstrikes on ISIS in Iraq to prevent them from moving on the Kurdish city of Erbil and to protect tens of thousands of refugees in northern Iraq. Obama described the airstrikes as "limited" to assist Iraqi forces in reaching refugees and to protect American forces who were advising the Iraqi troops.

The U.S. airstrikes targeted vital facilities of ISIS. The campaign was intended to reinforce and deliver the needed support to Iraqi forces on the ground before the actual battle.

The international military support, came very late, after a time in which ISIS had established a great force on the ground. By that time ISIS had demolished most of the significant archaeological sites in Mosul. The air raids had been effectively targeting the important sites affiliated to ISIS such as the Media Centres spread in Mosul, and the heavy military vehicles seized by ISIS after the Iraqi army had left its weapons behind and escaped in 2014. The International Airstrikes operated as the blade that had always been trimming the growing power of ISIS.

It must have been a plot. It wasn't clear who was the major conspirator in the Mosul Downfall of 2014. But, according to the testimonies given by several soldiers deployed in Mosul at that time, the orders "to withdraw" were given by the highest ranks! One soldier appeared on YouTube in the aftermath, describing the catastrophic situation as the "shameful escape of the military commanders." The high-ranking officers were apparently the first ones to evacuate their barracks.

Unfortunately, ISIS got to occupy the city of Mosul on the night of 9th of June. People in Mosul had been barred from leaving their abodes in what was thought to be a security technique known as a curfew. On the 6th of June, there was news of victory over a group of militants who wanted to take over Samarra, northern Baghdad. Amid a scene full of obscurity and vagueness, people in Mosul didn't know what was really going on. They were scared of the possible arbitrary bombardments like those going on in Syria at that time.

On the 7th of June, the malignant plot of handing over Mosul to ISIS completed with the decommissioning of two competent military commanders and the arrival of substitutes who, the next day, would order soldiers to put down their weapons and flee. There had been a fierce fight in northwestern Mosul by that time, the insurgents managed to take over the first neighbourhoods in Mosul adjoining the well-known "Al Mosul Hotel" lying on the western bank of the Tigris. Many residents of that zone had fled for fear of random bombardments, which did happen on the 8th of June.

Meanwhile the Iraqi army deployed its elements spanning the North-Eastern bank of the Tigris River in a bid to bog down any advance waged by the insurgents. So no one was sure who exactly they were. Their deployment seemed to be an attempt to defend their military base a few kilometres from the frontline.

Atheel Al Nujifi, the governor of Mosul at that time, appealed to the military commanders to "arm the civilians" so they could defend their neighbourhoods in case the military forces had collapsed. But his request was declined. Al Nujifi didn't have any authority over leading the combat in Mosul, though he appeared in the local media carrying his Kalashnikov, roaming in the old neighbourhoods of Mosul in what seemed to be a warning alarm.

He claimed he had warned responsible politicians in Baghdad beforehand that a large-scale "armed assault" and Mosul's takeover was looming. And he claimed the officials didn't take him seriously; the military commanders in Mosul were complacent, pretending that everything was under control.

According to a local policeman from Mosul, "the weakest side in the game", said that federal police and the army had been repeatedly refusing to arm "us" in what seemed to be a distrust crisis between the troops sent from Baghdad and the local police in Mosul that most of its elements were originally from Mosul and its suburbs. The federal police and the army were politicised in favour of the former Prime Minister Nouri Al Maliki who was the commander in chief, at that time.

Local people were trapped in their homes, and didn't realise the fall of their city till the next morning. Then it was starkly true that the city was left alone to face the evil of the new invaders that would later be called the "Islamic State."

Was it a coincidence that only 300 insurgents had managed to push three military divisions out of the second largest city in Iraq? A few days later, the 300 insurgents would grow into thousands, and ISIS head Abu Bakr Al Baghdadi would appear for the first time to proclaim his alleged Caliphate "succession."

ISIS were left in peace for so long. They got to organise themselves as a power in the city, by that time, all sorts of atrocities and carnage would be carried out systematically against the civilians who couldn't leave the city.

Just from one district called Wadi Hajar, thousands of men were arrested in one day, and to this day most of them have never come back. Wadi Hajar is located in southwestern Mosul adjacent to the airport of Mosul. From the same neighbourhood were the highest number of the security personnel in Mosul who had once made up the security forces belonging to the city. After the occupation, those people were asked to attend one of the biggest mosques in Mosul to show their repentance and regret as a remission of their past. They were asked to hand over to the Islamic State their weapons, otherwise they would be fined the estimated price of the weapon. They had no other chance, only to do so, just to secure their lives and the lives of their families. Months after ISIS's pledging not to hurt them, they were all detained anyway and collected at schools in their neighbourhood, and then taken away to unknown destinations.

Their families were told that everything would be fine after just a small interrogation. But the claim was never true. The pace of murdering people of Mosul by ISIS peaked when the battle of retaking the city was imminent, at the gates of the Mother of Two Springs, Mosul. ISIS had tremendous concerns that the former Iraqi security personnel could turn against them with the approach of the Iraqi fighting squads that were advancing towards Mosul from the east. Also, there was a big concern that those folks were sending information to their possible colleagues that might have been working with the Iraqi Forces outside Mosul. There was also a vengeance that ISIS wanted to take on them due to the years preceding Mosul's fall.

Zakar from the Wadi Hajar neighbourhood, a father of five, used to work among the "local police" in Mosul after 2003. In 2011, Zakar witnessed an assault with a silencer gun targeting one of his colleagues on the street. Zakar, being off duty, was sitting on the doorstep of the house. He couldn't stay calm. He hauled out his pistol and went after the perpetrator, chasing and shooting from time to time, until he wounded his target in the leg. He handed him over to the Iraqi police.

Brave Zakar, stayed in Mosul after 2014, so he was the first one to be taken away by ISIS in Wadi Hajar district. Before June 2014, the security situation in Mosul was on the way to being brutally unleashed. Lawyers had been killed in their offices, journalists like the famous TV presenter Wathiq Al Qathanfari, known as "the Guard of the memory of Mosul", were assassinated, in what was supposed to be a secure zone controlled by the Iraqi army, eastern Mosul.

On the 6th of June 2014, the remarkable modifications that occurred in the security formula in Mosul were just the start of the staged falling. Nouri Al Maliki belonged to the Islamic Dawa party, as an opponent to Saddam's regime. Al

Maliki had taken office from 2006 to 2014, being politically chosen twice as prime minister, in the Iraqi parliamentary elections. The long period he spent in office had given him more power to enlarge his authority and to reestablish the Iraqi forces loyal to him. Despite that, the second round in 2010 came as a result of political compromises rather than polling outcomes. The Al Iraqi bloc led by the secular Ayad Alawi had gained more votes. The reason why Alawi didn't become the Iraqi prime minister indeed, was that Iran had always intercepted any change led by figures adopting the policy of anti-Iranian intervention in Iraq. Alawi was ousted from effective Iraqi decision making, while Al Maliki became the commander in chief again. Al Malki had managed to strip the guns from the Iraqi Shia militias deployed in the south and Baghdad after 2006. He managed to have the fighting power frozen, or perhaps he postponed the tasks of militias to the right time. ~~Since~~ No one in Iraq's political scene dared to limit the enlarging power of militias. It is known that some of the militia groups were sourced from Iran as an extension to the Iranian Islamic revolution. But what if someone belonging to this ideology was actually the legal leader of Iraq?

In a short while, the situation in Iraq was fully controlled up to 2009, at least in the southern provinces, and parts of Baghdad, where the militia members were known to be based.

But the situation in the Sunni provinces was completely different. Considering the region was opposed to Iran's role in Iraq, Sunni provinces were simplistically thought to belong to Saddam's regime. Things were deteriorating only as a result of the political defect in not having an equal role in leading the country, instead that seemed to be a one-sided policy in favour of the pro-Iranians.

In 2011, after the American withdrawal, the Iraqi authority in Baghdad had escalated its hostile course against Sunnis, by discriminating against the citizens on all levels, specifically the tremendous lack in having an equal opportunity in security-making. Many people had been detained, some falsely, on terrorism related charges. The international humanitarian organisations like Amnesty and the international court abstained from recognizing the Iraqi judicial outcomes. Corruption was the main factor in that era. Many terrorists were released after they paid bribes, while many innocents stayed in jails for years without even a trial.

It was a time when Sunnis had to rise above all that. Protests took place between 2011 and 2014, starting in December 2011 in the city of Ramadi, which is the capital of Anbar province in western Iraq. From there the spark of the protest spread to other major Sunni cities, including Fallujah, Tikrit, Mosul, and Kirkuk demanding reform and the release of their children who had been detained on fabricated allegations. The Iraqi government had purposely ignored over and over these demands, describing the protesters as Saddam's remnants and terrorists.

In Al Hawija near Kirkuk, SWAT forces launched live ammunition on the unarmed protesters. Since then, the situation went slightly in another direction. Iraqi authorities facilitated Al Qaida militants to emerge amidst the peaceful demonstrations, vowing that they would reach Baghdad sooner or later. Just before the events of 2014, Abu Ghraib prison was opened for the dangerous inmates to flee and they found their way to the so called "squares of freedom and dignity" overshadowing the scene of the legal demonstration that had lasted for nearly 3 years. Everything overlapped, and the people of these cities couldn't have a clear view.

In Mosul, the situation was gradually sliding into the abyss. For a long time, Iraqi forces that arrived from Baghdad were practising all sorts of tightening on the people of Mosul; such as installing dense security check-points that would bog down the flow of everyday life; detaining innocent people for financial or personal reasons attributed to terrorism charges; blackmailing the families of detainees and business men.

Abd Al Quni Al Asadi, the Chief Commander of the Terrorism Counter Forces in Iraq, recently claimed that "corruption of the security forces before 2014 in Mosul was the reason to push the city of Mosul to fall. The officers were blackmailing even the seller who owned a Falafel stall." Three military divisions couldn't prevent the terrorist activities that had been on the rise. Mined cars and road bombs harvested the lives of many civilians.

The ongoing murders targeted all society disciplines like security personnel, lawyers, journalists. In fact, more than 50 journalists were killed in Mosul between 2003 and 2014. Mosul was the biggest city in Iraq to vote against Al Maliki in both 2010 and 2014. That could be added to the package of reasons why the situation was deteriorating, which cast the Mosuli individual in the category of opposition that the administration seemingly wanted to take revenge on, to trim the wings of locals.

10 June 2014 - The ominous day of the conquest

Before ISIS controlled the city in June 2014, the Insurance Bank was one of the highest buildings in Mosul. After that ISIS sought to terrify people there in different ways by practising on locals all sorts of carnage and atrocities, carried out for different reasons, such as smoking or drinking alcohol.

On the 10th of June 2014, people woke up to see that the Iraqi flag had been taken down everywhere, and new flags were soaring in the air; black and big, flapping sinisterly. On the roofs of buildings, on Toyota vehicles roaring in the streets back and forth to declare that the sole victor is the one who holds the ground, three days of a fierce fight concluded in favour of the extremists; the ones who'd been prepared to fight to the death, meanwhile the Iraqi troops had retreated, leaving their barracks full of ammunition and tanks as extra logistics for the new invader.

The picture wasn't clear at that time what the victors would do and how the central government in Baghdad would react. The Iraqi prime minister had already sent backup troops to Spiecher Air Base in Tikrit. Most of the fighters sent by the Iraqi government to the airbase were young and inexperienced in how to handle such a fight. Many of them were underage, didn't know how to use guns, if there were even enough guns distributed to every man who came voluntarily to fight.

The Iraqi government sought to disperse the troops to northern Baghdad while the US president Barack Obama announced limited air-strikes would be implemented to target ISIS vehicles as a bid to keep the evil forces contained within the map; not to overpass the border of Baghdad in the south and Erbil in the North as a method to protect the American diplomatic presence.

Based on a religious resolution issued by the main spiritual leader for the Shia in Iraq "Ali Al-Sistani" everyone capable of carrying guns was bound to go and fight ISIS which had devoured 60 percent of the territory in a short time. It was a one-way ticket where the chance to survive was slim.

Soon those inexperienced men would be captured by ISIS, a mass genocide would be organized and filmed to widen the void between Sunnis and Shia, so the fight against ISIS would take a sectarian dimension to justify the displacing, abducting, killing of the locals of that region seized by ISIS, many of them would be banned from entering the capital of their country, Baghdad for terrorism related charges.

People in Mosul were not allowed to leave the city

By the summer of 2014, ISIS had completed its plan of enlarging the gap between Christians and Muslims who had lived in Mosul hand in hand, for so long. ISIS announced that all Christian priests should attend the meeting within two days, otherwise they would face the judgement of the prince of faith, the leader of ISIS, Al Baghdadi.

The meeting was to discuss the situation of the Christian minority living in Mosul, the city that had become the capital of the Islamic State extended to Syria in the west and to northern Baghdad in the south. The leaders of the Christian community agreed on declining the invitation. They came up with the idea of fleeing Mosul and leaving everything behind rather than attending the meeting. They had previous experience to distrust such circumstances. Everything might be staged, and the meeting might be an ambush. No one would trust ISIS elements who were always lurking to carry out their crimes against people.

Instead of going to the alleged meeting, Christians sought to leave the city. They refused to pay Al-Jiziyha (tribute) to such a criminal group. And again, a mass exodus targeting a basic ethical component in Mosul in particular had taken place before the eyes of the world. Previously, hundreds of thousands of Muslims had chosen to flee Mosul, the moment ISIS conquered the city. Those folks were mostly government employees, and the individuals who were already under the threat of ISIS before the city's fall.

According to ADF, in 2003 the Christian population in Iraq was estimated at 1.4 million, while by 2016, this huge number was sharply lowered, estimated at only 275,000. Most of the Christians in Iraq lived in Mosul and its surroundings. When ISIS conquered Mosul in 2014, it caused 100,000 Christians to flee.

For nearly 2000 years, the hymns and the church bells of Mosul hadn't been drowned out, as they were in 2014. A year later, ISIS declared that people in Mosul were completely prohibited to leave the capital of the Islamic State, and a severe punishment would ensue if they disobeyed the orders in any form. The next phase of the plan seemed specifically to get the people trapped inside Mosul. As the battle of liberation was approaching, ISIS would use people as human shields, two years later.

ISIS got more frenzied when it became obvious that people in Mosul were eagerly waiting for saviours to retake Mosul from the grip of their savagery. Throughout the time ISIS were grabbing Mosul, countless numbers of people were massacred and tossed on the roads while they were trying to flee. While others were brutally dumped from the roofs of high buildings, accused of being gays or alcoholics. Others appeared to have been handcuffed in high quality videos projected in public places and distributed to locals on CDs. The content of those videos was super-terrifying, aiming to deter simple locals, warning them not to commit any similar offences. Having any internet connection, considered at that time to be a big crime, meant you could be tried to death.

Some of the videos showed victims wearing orange clothing, seized in a cage that was slowly descending into a pool of water. Victims would be submerged underneath water for minutes. The high-quality cameras would capture the horrific footage of how the victims would die drowning, second by second, human beings inside a cage awash in the pool, craving for air. Other videos showed a group of people, crammed in a car that had been charged with explosives, then ISIS would blow up the car with them in it. The beheading videos were considered a very basic way of killing used by ISIS in the normal cases of the death industry, now seemed very primitive compared to the new ways of death ISIS practised on the people of Mosul during the years of conquest.

Mosul lay outside the world

ISIS barred people from having any access to the internet, after it had erased the cell phone networks. The private use of the internet services was prohibited; but people could to go over to the internet cafés and talk with their loved ones who had left the city before. The people of Mosul realised that internet connection was under ISIS surveillance. People were cautioned not to mention anything regarding the Islamic State's existence.

On the other side of the story, courageous connections had been conducted behind the scenes, and a huge network of resistance had been formed in a bid of supplying information to the liberating troops. A certain number of people decided to be the eyes that would observe all ISIS movements and then convey them to the Iraqi Forces beside the International Coalition led by the US. Despite many innocents being accused of espionage in favour of Iraqi forces and sentenced to death in horrific ways, it couldn't prevent sacrifices being made, and courageous stories being written in blood.

2014–2016: ISIS Occupation of Mosul

Assault on Nineveh

The summer of 2014, started with ISIS conquering the largest territory ever seized by a terrorist group in modern times. The black map of the Islamic state had extended from Western Syria to 60 percent of the Iraqi territory, causing major cities like Mosul and Ramadi with the vast desert to be out of control of the Iraqi government. Within months, Islamic State was bordering the autonomous region of Kurdish provinces in northern Iraq, sweeping out the disputed areas in Ninawa inhabited by ethnic minorities such as Yazidi and Christians.

Nineveh's disputed areas were under the authority of Kurdistan, though it was administered nominally by the Provincial Council of Ninawa (Nineveh) in Mosul. According to eyewitnesses, ISIS waged a large-scale assault on Nineveh after being provoked by the Peshmerga by launching mortar shells on a drug factory north of Mosul; this claim has not been verified yet. The importance of the Nineveh plane comes from its being the biggest home for diversity in Iraq. Declaring the Islamic state in that area meant thousands of non-Muslim Iraqi citizens were either displaced or massacred. The Iraqi government aside, the Kurdish authority had seemingly underestimated the magnitude of the likely disaster before ISIS waged the assault.

In August 2014, ISIS managed to take over vast areas of Nineveh plain, pushing back the Peshmerga forces to the former territory of before 2003. The same scenario that had happened in Mosul, repeated itself in Nineveh, the formal troops put down their weapons and ran away. All the Christian families had to join an exodus with the approach of the Islamic State's Toyota's cars. A few other families couldn't get out of their historical home and decided to stay. Twenty days after ISIS occupation, the remaining families were asked to convert into Islam or they would be deported after their property being confiscated to the Islamic State. Though paying AL-Jiziyha (tribute) had been an option, people got to study the message very well.

On the Western side of Nineveh, the largest area on Earth inhabited by Yazidis spread out in separate residential complexes and villages spanning North-West Iraq up to the Sinjar District. These territories were under the control of the Peshmerga affiliated to the Kurdistan Government (KRG). After the fall of Saddam Hussein's regime in 2003, the KRG took advantage of Iraq's political vacuum to expand its presence and assert authority over several regions - collectively known as "the disputed areas."

Although disputed areas suffered from being neglected throughout the years following 2003, no real devolvement had happened compared with the Kurdish cities and their suburbs. In the end, these areas were left alone to face the swords of the Islamic State. A smooth withdrawal of the Peshmerga had happened, bringing to mind how Iraqi forces abandoned Mosul three months ago in that summer.

The Yazidi Genocide

Yazidi, one of the most ancient religions in the world, has been exposed to genocides throughout history. They might know how to handle that kind of situation; they knew how to survive as they did in the previous times. They immediately ran away to take shelter in the mountain of "Sinjar" adjoining their villages and towns. They knew how to get there faster than their oppressors. As a result of ISIS taking over those areas, many families were caught, detained in the schools, crammed in what once were governmental facilities. Women and children were separated from men. Mostly men were killed, some of them were killed in front of their families, whereas women and children were taken as slaves.

Months after the obscene, catastrophic invasion, a video seemed to have been purposely leaked from ISIS elements, showing an auction of Yazidi girls. They appeared in the video distributing what they'd obtained after battles. The shocking video was filmed in Mosul in what seemed to be an enormous hall made of marble. ISIS insurgents were sitting on the sofas, and a man with beard and long hair was videoing the attendees and saying "Today is the marketing of the enslaved girls, our rights." The man was offering to buy any girl belonging to the fighters. He also asked them, one by one, if someone needed a girl.

ISIS elements were also selling and buying Yazidi girls on social media, such as in closed groups and "WhatsApp" groups, according to testimonies advanced to Iraqis forces. The price of a girl ranged from thousands of dollars to hundreds or to tens in some cases. The criteria on which the prices varied was age, physical health and appearance.

The ISIS oppression of the Yazidi is covered in more detail near the end of the chapter called Interwoven Stories.

Personal Accounts of ISIS seizing Mosul

The Author's Own Memory of 4-10 of June 2014.

At that time, I was living in Finland, in the reception centre of Punkalaidun. There were some Iraqis at the same camp. In February 2014, I heard for the first time the term Daesh, which refers to ISIS in Arabic. I didn't know what it meant. One Iraqi asylum-seeker explained to me that they were a new terrorist group who had appeared in Eastern Syria and they were controlling the city of Al Raqqa. I thought it might have been to work with the tribes. I didn't expect that they would take over the city of Mosul for two reasons:

How was it possible for a newborn organisation to conquer a big city like Mosul, which was swarming with three military divisions and its local police, when in the meantime, Al Qaida had failed to conquer it?

Surely the US, which had a security agreement with the Iraqi government, would not allow the second largest city in Iraq to fall into the hands of terrorists?

On March 4th, I received an unexpected call from a relative who also was my Facebook friend saying: "My condolences, Ahmed! Was he your uncle or your brother?"

I didn't have a clue what he was talking about. "What do you mean? Who has passed away?"

He apologised for telling me what my family was trying to hide from me.

"Ok, please spit it out. Please, I am in shock."

Then he said, "The lawyer."

I realised he meant my uncle. I phoned my younger brother. "Is it right what I have just heard regarding our uncle?"

"Yes. I am sorry! We didn't know how to deliver such horrible news to you. We thought we could protect you, since you live in Finland alone. You know no one there to comfort you."

Unable to cry, I just went out of the asylum-seekers' reception centre on that cold evening into the middle of the Finnish fields. I walked faster and faster until I was running along the country road with all my energy, as though I wanted to exceed the barrier of space and time to prevent something from happening. I kept running, trying to escape the reality that was chasing me like a pack of hungry hyenas. My nose was running and my body was sweating, while my face became a mask of cold, rigid pain, like an ominous comet hurtling through the desolate tracks of loneliness. I reached what appeared to be a small town. It was then I realised how limited and helpless I was like an extinguished star hapless, watching its last batch of light hurtle through space, marking the location of a fading moment; a memory of a cherished human.

Just as I gave up on buying an energy drink to fuel the journey back to where I was dwelling, alongside all those asylum seekers, I knew that everyone had a story that forced them to leave everything behind and to come to share with the others here at the same time.

I had learned from my brother that my uncle was killed by the terrorists. My first reaction when I saw the first Muslim group, I refrained from greeting them with Peace Be Upon You! I just hated everything related to the religion of Islam. I informed one of the reception centre employees. Her eyes moistened and she said that she felt so sorry for me.

By the next day, I started to restore my logic. I felt that it was too unfair to boycott all Muslims. Those people had fled from the same enemy that forced me to leave and that killed my uncle, so I thought that what had happened had nothing to do with ordinary people with their everyday religion. We just happened to be born in the wrong time and place. I thought to myself that in a country like Iraq that was plagued with tyrants and then an invasion that led all terrorists around the globe to gush into a country without borders; I would be surprised if Iraq was safe! It's like a wealthy dying person, and everyone wants to take some of the inheritance, everyone wants to loot and walk away.

Muslims are being killed and displaced by other Muslims. Even my grandmothers, who are devout Muslims, would cry when they saw the suffering of people on TV, regardless of their beliefs. Evil has no identity; it can emerge and exploit the human dimension, whether it be a belief or ideology that reaches into the depths, where the seas of our emotions interact to shape who we are.

It took me several days to adapt to the new situation; a world without my wonderful uncle. The artist who got me to enter the world of music through his Oud instrument. The spiritual man who taught me that life is not forever, so share with the others what you have. My uncle who enlightened my mind by his new thoughts: God cannot be a criminal avenger.

My uncle gave me the keys to a larger realm; where all people regardless of their beliefs are equal, and where love is unconditional. He was a poor lawyer. I often wondered why this man wasn't as wealthy as his counterparts. The answer was incarnated in his office, once when I saw him refusing to take his fees from one of his clients. I asked him, why did you do that:

"Life is not only about money. There is a deeper pleasure acquired by advancing assistance to the others, the ones that are in need of it."

My uncle was a lawyer, a musician and a physician of alternative medicine. He'd spent his life learning new helpful things. Life goes on, but the departure of kin will stay painful however we have tried to be oblivious of the fact.

A month later, in April 2014, Wathiq Al Qathannfari, the well-known TV presenter was killed in Mosul.

Before this, in 2010, I began working at Al Mosulia Channel. Several months later, Wathiq would join us to present his famous TV Program, called Bel Maslawi, (in Mosuli dialect). The show was successful and became popular, since it brought the focus on all details of the Mosuli lifestyle.

The killing of Wathiq Al Qathannfari marked the last chapter of the story of Mosul; a city that had been totally silenced. The escalation of killings, especially targeting of celebrities and lawyers, generated a tidal wave of fear that engulfed the Mosuli street especially since the last month of 2013 which witnessed the killing of Nawras Al-Nnuaimi, who was the only young female TV show presenter at Al Mosulia Channel. She was once my workmate. I held her in high regard for being a determined person who went against the tide.

After Wathiq Al Qathannfari's death, the city of Mosul became frightful and gloomy. On a personal level, I thought it could be the end of the Mosul that we knew. I felt that it couldn't be worse than it was; Mosul had reached the bottom or the summit, it had to tumble down from the other steep slope, to a new horizon, to a new era.

In June 2014, I started to witness on social media unprecedented security measurements taken by the authorities in Mosul. I called my friends and family members. They all assured me that the situation had reached the point of no-return; what was called peaceful demonstrations had received empowerment from Al Naqshabandi, Islamic Resistance Movement that was founded as an armed resistance against the US Invasion. People didn't hold a very bad attitude towards that movement, since the movement didn't target Iraqis as other armed groups did.

The Governor of Mosul was thought to have a good relationship with Al Naqshabndi, that was the talk on the Mosuli street. People of Mosul all believed that Al Naqshabndi was going to unite with the "Tribes Rebels" to put control on the city of Mosul that was suffering from arbitrary actions carried out by the Iraqi Security Presence in Mosul.

I would describe my pre-conquest image of Mosul as "fuzzy." I didn't have a clue exactly what was going on. My aunt told me on the phone that the cars of the Rebels had been seen in a rural district North West Mosul.

On the 7th of June 2014, a general curfew was imposed on the city of Mosul. I saw pictures on social media of a group of young people playing football in the empty streets. Meanwhile, the battles were ongoing at the western gate of Mosul.

People of the western edge of Mosul marched to the depth of the city to seek shelter. Explosions and clashes had been heard by the locals.

People felt uncertainty, they didn't have clarity on the situation and what was going on Western Mosul.

On the evening of 9th of June, people heard a series of big explosions. Plumes of smoke escalated from Western Mosul, adjacent to the Mosul Hotel.

At night, on Mosul TV, the governor of Mosul appeared with a group of his guards roaming the streets in the centre of the city, carrying a Kalashnikov pledging he would fight for his city. At that moment people of Mosul realised that the defensive line of western Mosul had been penetrated. People were asked to stay at home.

Testimony of Um Umar, a grandmother living in Mosul

Um Umar peered out the window before closing her eyes as if she wanted to retrieve part of her soul that stayed trapped in the old house that became rubble. Then she began narrating the story of conquest that brought to life the grinning ghosts of past years.

ISIS was just a tool; someone must bear the responsibility! The city was systematically destroyed, and locals were the fuel of that war. The true doers who ordered the suspicious withdrawal of the Iraqi forces, they got away with it. The commanders who tossed their ranks to be trampled by the boots of the invaders, have reverted to their offices, in the meanwhile the government stands paralyzed to resurrect the no man's land; barren and the odour of death permeated the air.

When the city of Mosul was plagued with ISIS that went after many young people who once had worked with the Iraqi government and the suspected ones until the battle of liberation when young people got killed for any reason, women from Mosul used to hide their boys to prevent ISIS from getting access to them. In one incident, a woman from western Mosul would risk her life to hide her two teenage boys in the debris and she had to find the way back to her house that ISIS broke into in search for her boys. However, she repelled them and they threatened to kill her and the family if they found out that her boys were around.

Poem: In wars, women are stronger...

empowered by the emotion endowed by the universe
She eyed the oppressor and steadily said:
If you take me throat, you will not confiscate my voice
If you take my life, you cannot guarantee that I will not be born again
You can take everything, but you can't take my child
I fight to death to protect my family
I dig under the rubble, despite the explosive, to find the favourite toy of my little daughter
I cross the most dangerous floating bridge, swinging between death and life,
Against the current, I chose to walk back to the battlefield
Against the storm, I went to save my family who were buried in the cellar of the house that had collapsed
The policeman shouted: You must be crazy! You are walking to the point of no return!

Ahmed Zaidan

Um Umar continues her testimony

The next day, we realised that we were left alone. My daughter, who was 30 years old, phoned me, telling me that we should get out of the town as soon as possible, the Iraqi government might wage a large-scale offensive to retake the city of Mosul before ISIS has stationed itself well in the town. Intuitively, we would think that way, based on what we saw in Aleppo, and how the Syrian government was bombing the city ruthlessly and randomly using barrels charged with explosives instead of smart bombs. We already knew that civilians were the weakest party in that game. The bomb has a price if it can doom entire families at once. Unfortunately, in the Middle East we live in a cheap way, suffering from the absence of basic life infrastructure, and we die in a cheap way, but we will be remembered by our loved ones for a long time.

We sought to leave the house despite hearing comforting messages from the new invader via speakers fixed on the cars roamed the residential neighbourhoods. Like any of the prior conquerors, ISIS claimed that it came to liberate Mosul from the sectarian government that had been discriminating against locals based on their belief. Mosul is deemed to be the biggest city inhabited by Sunni in Iraq, in addition to the diverse community that thrived in the city over the years. We couldn't believe that they were true liberators, all they wanted was an Islamic State that served their own agenda, while the ordinary people looked for an authority that could attain social justice on the ground.

Poem: To my brothers and sisters

Brothers and sisters, stay as calm as the dead!
We are the black crows coming from the sacred graveyard
We didn't infiltrate through the borders,
We found our way out of the radical books repeatedly open,
We had been confined in those books for centuries
We are every word in the books of hatred;
We turned into bats that were launched from the lines
We will swarm the sun and manipulate the light
We will alter the shades, and highlight hate
The branches tossed on the ground are venomous
When the flowers are absent, thorns will be prevalent
And life is bleak.

Ahmed Zaidan

Testimony of the Author's Younger Uncle

My younger uncle works as a high school teacher. He supported me throughout my writing journey. He is the kind of person that young people need in their lives to shine, and I feel blessed to have such a person in my life. In Iraq, finding such individuals is a rare gift.

In that night, we couldn't sleep, we heard via radio that the military armed forces withdrew. Rumours were rampant, I got a call from a friend informing me that Mosul was taken over by the Ba'ath party, and sometimes another friend would call and say that Mosul was taken over by the tribes, others would surmise that it was Naqshbandis. No one anticipated that they were ISIS.

Those rumours served the invaders' agenda. Fear was the master of the situation. There was a TV channel called (Change) that misled a large number of people into believing what was going on was a revolution carried out by the rebellious tribes who rose up against the corrupt government.

We really didn't have a clue what the truth was, but we were sure that the defence lines of the Iraqi armed forces had collapsed. We stayed awake exchanging phone-calls with our relatives and friends until we came to a conclusion that the city of Mosul was no longer safe for us. We had to seek refuge in the suburbs of the city, since we knew that the reaction of the Iraqi government to bring back the city could be ruthless. We saw how the Syrian government had reacted to the fall of Aleppo: by barrels of death being tossed on the city randomly, barrels stuffed with explosives.

We thought that that was the end of the city. A friend of mine called me at 5 am informing me that they would evacuate from the city of Mosul to the village.

My sister who lived in Eastern Mosul made a phone-call. She asked us to head to the house of a relative of her husband who lived in Tel-Kaif, a suburb located a few kilometres north of Mosul.

We were resigned to the idea; we knew we had no choice left except saving our family from the unknown future.

At 7 am, we commenced our journey to the shores of safety, in Tel-Kaif. We saw the first signs that proved one of last night's multiple stories: the escape of the Iraqi troops.

Military clothes were tossed along the street. Ranks were on the pavement. We knew that military commanders had run away. On the fourth bridge, we saw a military vehicle set on fire, while the security checkpoints that once had choked the city, had been deserted.

Pillars of smoke were everywhere and no presence of the Iraqi armed forces was seen on the street.

In Eastern Mosul, at Mosul woods, I saw the first member of the new invaders. He looked weird with his outfit that denoted that the man belonged to Islamists, not the tribes nor the Naqshbandis, he was carrying the black banner of ISIS. We realised that ISIS were the ones coming. Personally, I felt horrible seeing that those monsters become the new rulers of the city. I knew they were the worst of the fighting groups in Iraq.

On the road, I saw an Iraqi soldier changing his clothes, replacing his military uniform with civilian clothes. I learned later that local people had provided the Iraqi soldiers with clothes, just to camouflage their enemy, so that they could make it back to their cities safely. We reached Tel-Kaif, my nephew had received us outside. There were about 30 people crammed in that house.

The Author's Interview with his Younger Brother

My younger brother was 24 years old at the moment of the city's collapse seven years ago. He was working as a pharmacist at Mosul Hospital in 2013 and 2014, then he was forced to leave the city several months after the ISIS conquest as a result of being at risk of airstrikes at the hospital that was controlled by ISIS. He had to take an epic journey to get to Turkey across Syria. He departed from the city of Mosul stealthily in the summer of 2015 in one of the most dangerous treks one may take.

It was a good chance to meet other family members that we hadn't seen in a long time ago. I remember how safe we felt, it was just calm, unlike the last days we spent in Mosul that was charged with blasts and armed clashes. Since it was summer, we slept on the roof of the house. In Mosul, in a long time we couldn't have done so for fear of the random rounds and bullets. I was lying on the mattress staring at the night sky that was so clear, the stars were blinking like a loving heart beating and sending their shine as though they wanted to comfort us. The situation down there was different. It was so far from clarity. An unknown future was awaiting us.

I wished I could seek shelter in the city of the night-sky. I wished I could fly distantly from the inferno of Earth. I couldn't believe that elsewhere life was flowing smoothly, just as the Tigris River that kept gushing onto rocks splitting the city of Mosul into two parts, in the meanwhile the time was casting despair on the banks of that river, people's hopes were withering and their beautiful dreams were weltering, while the chamomile would still bloom despite all what was going on.

The Author's Other Relatives

One of my uncles was in the targeted group for working briefly as a member in Mosul District, which made him wanted by the new invader.

One of my cousins and my childhood friend worked for a short while in the Higher Committee of Election in Iraq. in the summer of 2014, most of those folks got detained by ISIS.

They all agreed to escape to Turkey across Eastern Syrian soil. The way to Turkey had been challenging since all the territory along the road had been under ISIS control.

Luckily, in Syria, people weren't barred from leaving the land of the Islamic State, which made the dangerous peak at the border of Iraq, and then at the border of Turkey.

The three refugees (my younger brother, cousin and uncle) who wanted to get to Turkey, couldn't make it smoothly through Syria, they were intercepted by the Turkish Border Guards and got detained for nearly a month suffering inhumane conditions. My brother told me that many people were crammed in one hall, they had to wake up so early and queue up for the toilet, while even having a quick shower was flanked by challenges.

They faced the risk of deportation to Baghdad which was full of militias that saw people from Mosul as potential enemies. However, some detainees of the Turkish camp found it more merciful to be deported than living on the very edge suffering from poor life conditions.

Personally, I sent many appeals to distinct social media pages and journalists to bring their issue to the public. I thought they were left alone in the shade of death and they could perish even without anybody noticing it. A group of Iraqi politicians took action and responded to our appeal. Then, my brother, cousin and uncle were sent back to Baghdad.

My uncle found a friend in Baghdad and stayed living there for two years, while my brother and cousin flew back to Erbil in northern Iraq and then made it again to Turkey.

My brother wanted to settle down in Turkey by starting to look for a job. He had lived for a while with my relative who moved to Turkey at the beginning of the conquest for fear of being killed by ISIS, since their children worked as security personnel before the conquest. He moved to a shared apartment with other guys from Mosul. Life in Turkey was not easy for him to continue. He found work at a farm, but he couldn't have survived more than one day, because simply the work was based on exploiting people from Iraq and Syria by turning them to work for so many hours with little or no pay.

Eventually, my brother agreed with a group of young people who also wanted to resume their life in a natural way, a life which has certainty, so they made it across the sea of uncertainty, putting their lives at risk, to Europe.

My family members had spent two days in Tel-Kaif, the city of freedom, at least for me. Before I left Iraq I used to practise part of poetic ritual in meadows of Tel-Kaif, the city was relatively safer than Mosul, it was inhabited mainly by the Christian community. Back in the day, my friends and I went on picnics there, sipping on beers that we bought without having to fear the extremists outside the liquor stores when in Tel-Kaif. At that time, drinking alcohol was a risk in the city of Mosul. For us the ceiling of freedom was to drink so that we could still feel that we were in life; in which people live all the phases of their life out of the patterns.

When I heard that my family took shelter in Tel-Kaif, I thought to myself that five years before, I also used to take shelter in that town, just to reunify with my missing self; the self that I would renounce at the borders of Mosul. I often believed that living in Mosul made it like a jail for me, or a mass grave even then.

Mosul after 2003 had no night life at all, with the sunset, the story of the day would be wrapped up, unfolding another story of killing and kidnapping rampaging in the darkness, would be revealed upon the first rays of sunlight. Simply, people would wake up to see new corpses on the streets. Often when I was going to school, I used to see a swarm of people, then I knew it was a new corpse that had been tossed in a dumpster or on the pavement.

I thought that I belonged to a larger entity. On every New Year's Eve, I would isolate myself in my small room to watch TV and share with the world the joy of the new year. In Mosul at that time, the New Year wasn't something to celebrate. A few people would go to Erbil if they wanted to watch the fireworks. The road to Erbil was so dangerous, it wasn't worth taking the gamble.

Honestly, I found that loneliness is a way to interact with the absent part of myself. Believe it or not, in the city of Mosul people couldn't become fully their entire selves. Musicians were giving lessons secretly and poets were limited, because the price of the irresponsible word was a bullet slammed in the back of the head!

I still remember when I was at the first stage at faculty of arts in 2007, I didn't know my limits. Some people learn their limits through severe experiences, I didn't listen to my family who advised me to be careful in what I was writing, I thought that I would bring change through my writings. I didn't know that I was just a tiny straw trying to travel against the torrent.

    I was influenced by all the bold Arabian poets who tried to liberate the Arab world from the burden of the heavy legacy, so it can lightly move towards the door of freedom and catch up the train of civilization. I posted one of my earliest poems entitled Curse from Heaven, criticising everything about the religious leaders who made our life as absurd as their thoughts. They stone lovers to death while under the umbrella of their divine authority they would bless an old man getting married to an underage girl. The poem was full of rage that would reflect my early rebellious thoughts. Luckily, I have one picture of that poem sent by a friend. Here is a translation:

Poem: Let us hold a funeral procession for Arabhood

Let us bury the wars in a coffin made by America
Let us lay to rest all daggers and swords
Let us mourn for Mutanabbi and the Caliph
Let us mourn for the pens and papers
Let us break the arrows and spears
Let us raise the white banner and declare peace

May heaven curse the tribe that eats raw meat in hunger
They see no difference between water and blood
They treat bread and women alike
May heaven curse our absurd fates and foolish thoughts
May heaven curse our pride in deserts, nights, and duels
May heaven curse our timid tongues
Our virgin legs that never leave our safe zones
Wandering among mosques, churches, the same streets,
Hanging in the holes, implanted in the place like palms

May heaven curse our religious leaders who stone lovers
Their explanation of our tragedy as the will of God
May heaven curse our glorious victors made of paper
Weltering under the rain of their own decay
May heaven curse our history full of tears
Our nations that accept submission to tyrants
Never daring to move forward or even to step back
They die at the place where the candles end.

Ahmed Zaidan

The next day, I headed to the "Wall of Creativity", a board on which students would hang their writings and paintings. However, the ceiling of freedom was lower than one would imagine. Poems about the love of the prophet or pure love without going into explicit detail were common. Female students often posted religious poems or replaced the pronoun "He" with "She" when addressing a boyfriend, so as not to give the impression that they were in love with a male colleague.

I must admit that I saw amazing pieces posted by female students, sometimes under nicknames or explicit names. However, I knew that I was given more freedom to express my feelings and address my lover by using the pronoun "she." Exceeding the known boundaries, however, was a problem. I felt that the only way for me to shine and bring about change was by provoking people's minds and examining the rotten values. Many of my colleagues warned me, but I did not take them seriously or did not have the capacity to realise that what I was posting could lead to my end.

This realisation came crashing down on me when I went to see if my poem "Curse from Heaven" was still pinned on the board, only to find it replaced with a paper threat:

To those who try to inject the conservative society with their poisonous thoughts, the Islamic State warns them for the last time, otherwise they will face judgement from God (Death).

My brain couldn't take everything in. A mixture of feelings engulfed me; happiness, worries and fear. I felt that my poem had been responded to by someone who managed to understand the message and estimate the power of it. Probably I had thought before publishing it that nobody would be interested.

December 2016 - Liberation of Mosul Begins

Author's Personal Investigation

The following report is based on my personal investigation in December 2016 into the challenging situation before the liberation of the western part of Mosul, also known as "the right side of the city."

- According to the Iraqi Prime Minister, Eastern Mosul has been successfully liberated.
- Since the military campaign began, approximately 180,000 people have been displaced from their homes.
- About 90 percent of governmental buildings in Eastern Mosul have suffered significant damage.
- The international coalition bombed the five bridges spanning the Tigris River in the city.
- Eastern Mosul, despite being densely populated, was the last stronghold of ISIS in Iraq.
- Mosul is gradually recovering, particularly in the district of Al Rashydia, where the final battle successfully cleansed the area of ISIS fighters.
- Rumours circulated in western Mosul that ISIS had dispatched 200 suicide bombers to carry out attacks in the recently liberated eastern part of the city.
- Additionally, ISIS attempted to convince the people of western Mosul that the Iraqi forces were persecuting locals based on their religious beliefs.
- The battle in Mosul is rapidly progressing towards the river, and a flood of stories is emerging from there. However, the same cannot be said for the untouched western part of the city. Many untold stories and atrocities remain hidden. Despite this, we managed to reach the town and discovered that the people have grown accustomed to war.

- The rhythm of daily life is disrupted by mortar shells, and locals share tales of terrifying killings taking place in public areas, fuelling fear among families who worry they could be the next victims. Another source of fear is the international bombardments, which have often resulted in mistakes and the accidental targeting of civilians. Numerous innocent lives have been lost due to airstrikes aimed at ISIS vehicles or small media stalls that are interspersed among crowded marketplaces filled with civilians.
- Iraqi forces have encircled Mosul from all directions, with popular mobilisation troops blocking the route to Syria from the west. The city has been under embargo for months, making it impossible for goods to reach the area. The imminent threat of famine looms over every family in western Mosul.
- Locals have reported a lack of reasons for life in the area. The dominant food sources are limited to flour, radishes, and potatoes, which have become increasingly unaffordable for the majority due to high prices. Fleeing ISIS families from the recently liberated eastern Mosul have increased the population density, while missile bases are being established in residential areas.
- In contrast, the eastern part of Mosul has seen victory after victory as Iraqi special forces drive out ISIS from a city with a population of 1.5 million. The battle for Mosul's liberation from the grip of the so-called Islamic State began over three months ago, with the Iraqi Prime Minister declaring October 10th as the starting date. Despite attempts to delay the battle, the Prime Minister remained resolute, vowing to eradicate terrorism from all of Iraq by the end of 2016.
- The international community has repeatedly expressed concern that the battle in Mosul may lead to an unprecedented humanitarian crisis. Civil society organisations have warned that ISIS may use the large

population of Mosul as human shields. The Iraqi government claims to be prepared for the potential consequences, with displacement camps established by the UN. Over the past three months, approximately 180,000 people have been forced to leave their homes in Mosul, as reported by the International Organization for Migration.
- The majority of the population remains trapped in districts where combat continues, making living without shelter a constant risk due to the mortar shells launched by ISIS. Each car bomb sent by ISIS has the potential to alter the course of the battle, as it disregards civilian casualties and targets Iraqi troops in densely populated areas. The people of Mosul have adhered to the instructions issued by the security forces before the battle and have remained in their homes.
- Reports indicate that American forces have directly engaged in the fight, standing shoulder to shoulder with the Iraqi special forces. In a joint operation, they successfully repelled an ISIS raid on the Al Zuhur neighbourhood in eastern Mosul, regaining control of the area according to witnesses.
- It is reported that ISIS has detonated over 700 car bombs since the operation to retake Mosul began.

A man on his knees

Earlier this month, a heartbreaking story circulated on social media about a man from the Eastern part of Mosul who had returned from the camps to check on his house. Despite the locals advising him not to enter the bombed house, he couldn't resist the urge to see it for himself. Ignoring the warnings, he forcefully pushed the door and rushed inside, only to be met with a sudden explosion. The man fell to his knees, pleading for help, but no one dared to enter the crumbling house to assist him. Within seconds, the house collapsed while he was still inside. The tragic story came to an end, as he had promised his family to return after inspecting the house, a promise he would never fulfil.

A Survivor's Account.

Another harrowing story came from a woman who recounted the aftermath of a traumatic event. The tale begins when Iraqi forces approached her neighbourhood, and the sounds of their clashes with ISIS and special forces reverberated through the air. Sensing danger, ISIS fighters rushed to her house, attempting to displace her family.

One of them warned us that the infidels were closing in and urged us to leave immediately. However, we chose to stay put. Frustrated, the fighter returned and fired at our door. My husband rushed to explain that the house was not yet empty. The fighter accused my husband of having connections with the special forces based on phone records.

Despite my husband denying the accusation, I overheard the fighter threatening to kill him. Desperate, I intervened, begging him not to harm us and pleading that we were just a family with two daughters inside. Reluctantly, he led us to another alley where numerous families were crammed into houses. We joined three families in a single house; all huddled in the guest room.

In a matter of minutes, a devastating car bomb exploded right in front of our house. The blast caused our home to collapse, taking the lives of my sister and her son, as well as the other family who sought shelter with us. My two daughters suffered grave injuries, adding to the unimaginable pain and tragedy of the situation.

US-led attack on ISIS-held Mosul

According to Stephen Townsend, the leader of the US coalition, more than 2,000 ISIS fighters have been killed or wounded during the US-led military operation in Mosul. However, an estimated 3,000 to 5,000 ISIS fighters still remain in the city, defending their positions. Townsend held a joint press conference with US Defense Secretary Ash Carter, who pledged to send an additional 2,000 troops to Syria to combat terrorism.

Meanwhile, in Baghdad, on the last day of 2016, a series of blasts resulted in a death toll of 27 and left 53 others gravely wounded. Two suicide bombers reportedly targeted a crowded marketplace and a popular restaurant where people were having breakfast at around eight o'clock in the morning. These suicide attacks occurred one day after the anniversary of Saddam Hussein's hanging. The American authorities had previously warned the Iraqi government about the potential increase in suicide attacks in the coming days.

Recent events in Baghdad have highlighted the ongoing instability and lack of safety in the city. One prominent incident that garnered attention was the hijacking of journalist Afrah Shawqi, which circulated widely on social media and was extensively covered by Iraqi media and newspapers. The incident has further fuelled tensions and accusations between political factions and militant groups within Baghdad, exacerbating the already precarious situation. Surprisingly, ISIS did not claim responsibility for the operation.

It appears that ISIS has reverted to its previous strategy of targeting Iraqi cities, aiming to inflict maximum casualties among civilians. While Iraqi forces have made significant progress in reclaiming territories previously captured by ISIS since 2014, their biggest challenge still lies ahead - driving ISIS out of Mosul. This undertaking is expected to be time-consuming, and the process may extend beyond the originally anticipated timeframe. The Iraqi prime minister has set a deadline for the total liberation of Mosul by the next spring, but it remains to be seen if this goal can be achieved within the specified timeframe.

Testimony by Abu Omar

Abu Omar, a Mosul resident vividly describes the atrocities and lack of mercy that were the norm during the ISIS era. Life under their rule was characterised by fear and a complete absence of tolerance. Even simple acts, like unveiling a woman's face or smoking cigarettes, could result in severe punishment.

Abu Omar recalls a heartbreaking incident where a young man was killed in his presence because he had a document proving his employment with the Iraqi election. The ISIS member justified the execution by accusing him of collaborating with the "infidels." This story serves as a stark reminder of the ruthless and indiscriminate nature of ISIS, where even those who had already suffered immense loss became targets.

During the intense battles in their neighbourhood, Abu Omar and his family sought refuge, hiding under stairs for days and enduring the chaos and danger surrounding them. Eventually, they managed to escape to a neighbouring house, where they spent additional days exposed to fire and danger. His wife narrowly escaped being shot, an incident that highlights the constant threat faced by everyone in Mosul under ISIS rule.

After a challenging journey, Abu Omar and his family reached the Saddam neighbourhood, a liberated district. Iraqi forces welcomed and assisted them in crossing the main street to safety, providing much-needed support and refuge.

Recent documents discovered by the Iraqi forces have shed light on the true nature of the so-called Islamic State. Widely circulated on social media, these documents confirm that ISIS was nothing more than a group of international gangs who manipulated religion for their own gain. In June 2014, they invaded Mosul, bringing destruction and displacing nearly a million residents. Abu Omar reflects on the day ISIS seized control of the city, when they falsely claimed to be saviours and protectors, promising to rescue the people of Mosul from a brutal army that had been arresting and mistreating them.

Under ISIS rule, Christians were coerced into feeling safe under their custody, but at a price. They were required to pay the Jizya tax according to Islamic Sharia law. The heads of the Christian community were summoned to attend an initial rally held by ISIS in Mosul, where they were faced with a difficult decision: leave and never return or flee for their lives. Ultimately, escaping became the best choice for the Christians, as their properties were looted and seized by ISIS militants.

The impact of ISIS on Mosul

Mosul, once a thriving city in Iraq, has experienced increasing damage over the past decade. The lack of international protection during the era of the fragile previous government has contributed to the city's devastation. As the battle to drive out ISIS intensifies, more people are displaced, gravely wounded, and killed. There is a looming danger that ISIS may become more aggressive in targeting civilians who express support for Iraqi troops on television or through social media.

The essence of Mosul lies in its coexistence between diverse communities. It is home to the largest Christian community in Iraq. To support the idea of ethnic diversity in Mosul, religious entities must take a new approach, advocating for reform at all levels, including unifying Friday sermons and adhering to community regulations. These sermons should promote pure coexistence, free from any violation of others' beliefs. Today, the people of Mosul understand better than ever before that building a stable community requires burying the seeds of hate-speech that provided fertile ground for ISIS to emerge. The first element of ISIS was a book found on Al Najafi street, promoting extremism and animosity towards other beliefs. Together, we must burn this book and its counterparts.

Yes, Mosul has suffered immense losses throughout its history. The city's 3,000-year-old monuments have been destroyed, and antiquities and artefacts have been looted and sold on the black market. This lucrative trade provided income for the perpetrators to acquire more weapons and commit further atrocities against humanity. Priceless statues of winged bulls and sculptures dating back to the Assyrians, the founders of the Assyrian Empire, were ruined. At one time, the Assyrian Empire extended from Persia in the east to Turkey, and even parts of South Europe and North Africa. For centuries, the empire relied on the forced labour of other kings to construct the palaces of the great Assyrian king, Ashurbanipal. Ashurbanipal sought to exert his power over other kings by subjugating them. The great king of Nineveh also established the most important library in history.

Today, there is nothing left of these monuments to serve as reminders to future generations of humanity's beginnings. Drones could have prevented ISIS from committing such acts, but the international community chose to allocate millions of dollars to explore the possibility of life on Pluto. Meanwhile, people march in the streets to protest whether Pluto should be classified as a planet or an asteroid. All the while, human civilization in Iraq and Syria was on the verge of vanishing during months of destruction.

Reports from Mosul, though unverified, indicated that two families were reportedly slaughtered in the recently liberated Al Tamim neighbourhood after an offensive carried out by ISIS fighters. As a result, other families abandoned their homes and fled to the eastern districts in an attempt to avoid such massacres. However, the Iraqi special forces swiftly managed to defeat the ISIS elements that had infiltrated the liberated neighbourhoods close to the front lines. The special forces have been patrolling the neighbourhoods, using speakers attached to military vehicles to reassure people and encourage them to feel safe.

The spokesperson for the Iraqi forces also announced that a few ISIS elements had managed to infiltrate the liberated areas due to the absence of air support caused by bad weather conditions. However, the special forces swiftly eliminated all of them, restoring stability once again. The displaced families were accommodated in the homes of strangers in safe areas, while others sought refuge with their relatives. One family reported that upon hearing about families in need of shelter, they quickly opened their doors to provide assistance.

2017 - Eve of Western Mosul's Liberation

Breaking the silence

In this book, I bring together stories of members of my family and other people I knew. We have already heard from Um Umar, a grandmother living in Mosul, who told me her story by phone right after liberation. There I was in Finland, sharing with friends the warmth of Christmas and bliss of being in a safe country, while listening to a grandmother narrating the siege and liberation.

I found it an act of betrayal to stay silent over what had happened in my city, people were contacting me and telling me their stories, they expected their stories to be heard, they expected I could tell all the people here how the people of Mosul had suffered, what price they had to pay as ransom, just to become part of the world after getting rid of the impish state.

I built this chapter based on multiple narratives from family members and friends alongside my own experience. For the purpose of privacy some names have been changed and some details were omitted. The chapter begins with two sections from the report I wrote on the eve of liberation.

Final battle to clear Eastern Mosul of ISIS, June 27 2017

- Tomorrow, activists are planning to stage the greatest popular rally in Mosul at Platform Street to celebrate the first Eid in Mosul following the defeat of the Islamic State. The Iraqi terrorism-counter force spokesman has announced that Mosul will be completely liberated within the next few days.
- Life is gradually returning to eastern Mosul; even as Iraqi forces continue to fiercely fight to recapture the remaining parts of the Old Town. Civil activists have

widely circulated a notice urging people to participate in this significant declaration of victory, as Mosul, once the de facto capital of the Islamic State, celebrates the defeat of the extremist group.
- However, recent events have shown that ISIS is still capable of causing havoc. The Nouri Mosque, along with its 850-year-old minaret, a symbol of pride for Mosul, was destroyed by ISIS. This heinous act is believed to be the last desperate message of the Islamic State, signalling its ultimate defeat. Some speculate that the destruction of this important landmark could also be seen as a revenge against the local population, who expressed their hatred for the terrorist group in Mosul.
- In recent days, ISIS has managed to instigate disorder in certain districts. In the Muthana neighborhood, a crowded market was targeted by a deadly suicide attack, claiming the lives of 12 civilians. In Zuhur market, however, another suicide bomber failed to detonate the explosives.
- On Sunday, Iraqi forces successfully confronted an ISIS raid in the liberated Nahrauan neighbourhood. The offensive was thwarted, resulting in the death and arrest of the attackers, according to the Iraq Federal Police. Additionally, on Monday, locals spotted ISIS militants attempting to sneak into Eastern Mosul and open fire on a security checkpoint. One of the attackers was killed by stabbing, while another was handed over to the police.
- Earlier this month, ISIS fighters managed to overrun the liberated Dannadan neighbourhood in southwest Mosul. As a result, nine houses were burned down, and families were forced to seek refuge in their basements. However, the Iraqi forces swiftly responded to address the situation, and within two days, people were able to return to their homes.
- In the Yarmja district of eastern south Mosul, the Chosen-Man (sheriff) of the neighbourhood was

reportedly killed by unidentified assailants. In the Intesar neighbourhood of eastern Mosul, a woman's body was found on the roadside. People have claimed that she had previously been arrested by the Iraqi security forces without any charges. As of now, the security forces have not released any official statement regarding the incident.

What is happening at Al Manasah (Platform) Street in Eastern Mosul?

- A group of civil activists has decided to convey their message to the world: that Mosul is determined to create a better future. Today, the first batch of reconciliation caravans from the southern Iraqi provinces is scheduled to arrive at the University of Mosul. This initiative comes after 90 percent of Mosul has been cleared of ISIS elements, although the major part of the Old Town is still under fire. It is estimated that around 400,000 people are still trapped within the battlefield.
- The activists state that the Iraqi flag will proudly fly at the summit as a symbolic banner that unites all Iraqis. Additionally, books are expected to be donated to the attendees, aiming to spread a new ideology after the dark ages brought upon by ISIS.
- Many Facebook users have expressed their admiration for seeing their city once again becoming part of the world, despite the damage inflicted on the infrastructure and the significant cultural losses suffered by the city. Mosul University, which is located near Platform Street, will open its gates to receive cultural delegations from Baghdad and other Iraqi cities. Local residents willing to participate in the event will need to register beforehand. It's worth noting that the location of this cultural celebration is next to the ruins of the devastated Assyrian civilization by ISIS in 2014.

- As a precautionary measure against any planned suicide attacks by ISIS, Iraqi security forces will secure the avenue and create a cordon.

The eve of ISIS facing defeat

The battle to retake the heart of the city began and ISIS got suspicious over everything. They started to arrest more people and question those who had worked for the government in any form. Many of the people who had been taken didn't go back.

Iraqi forces started to clear the southern villages and suburbs, hurtling towards the city of Mosul. ISIS couldn't have resisted for long on the open territories. ISIS came to realise that their survival was to get all the papers mixed up, just like a last bid to run away and get the civilians trapped for the last minute of the fight.

The first thing they did was to bury the hole of death in which they had tossed the corpses of the victims they killed. They dedicated a giant effort to hide all the traces of their crimes. Inhabitants of the adjoining village called (Al-Athba) woke up to an army of vehicles that worked all the time burying the hole of death located on the southern edge of Mosul.

The Iraqi armed forces were achieving a remarkable advance, recapturing suburbs and villages. Meanwhile, the UN had set up displacement zones, where an enormous number of tents were erected to shelter families who had recently been liberated. The families were marching towards the south, far from the heart of the town where the pillars of smoke were escalating and tails of flames were lurching like ghosts.

By the time, Iraqi armed forces were capturing the edge of the city, Southwest of the city. It was adjacent to the airport of Mosul where ISIS ruined the runway so neither the Iraqi forces nor the International Coalition would be able to use it during the battle. Many families from those areas got expelled from their houses and told to head to the Old Town. The city was teeming with the evacuee families. The families of ISIS didn't suffer a lot, because ISIS supplied them with whatever they needed to have a normal life.

Eye witness Accounts of the Liberation

During the liberation, battles crawled from door to door, targeting sequentially all districts in the city of Mosul. One of those who provided me with an account of the Liberation is Um Umar, a grandmother from the Old Town in Mosul. Everyone in the Old Town tried their utmost to escape life in a city that had turned into a battlefield. Um Umar and her family, alongside other locals, battled for survival in an epic journey. Her journey folds into that of her son Ahmad, who became trapped in the Old Town while he was trying to slip out to safety where the Iraqi armed forces swarmed the west exit of the old city.

Out of the 25 people crammed in her house, Um Umar was the best at describing the suffering. On the edge of the old Mosul and its narrow alleyways, Khzraj was a thriving neighbourhood that lay close to where Iraqi forces would have to begin the fierce fight to re-take the old Mosul from ISIS's firm fist of death. Um Umar was trying to fit into her new environment, distant from her childhood home where she had lived all her life, there in the depths of the old city, the narrow alleyways and cracked walls made for her the border of her world that she was forced to leave upon the destruction that was inflicted on the heart of Mosul, the Old Town.

During the liberation, many homes were turned into mass graves. The luckiest ones were those whose corpses would later be found by their beloved ones, if any of the beloved ones managed to survive. Um Umar saw various types of atrocity committed by the frenzied ISIS insurgents in their last days. Most of the massacres were of those who tried unsuccessfully to escape. Then, ISIS would massacre them in horrific ways to deter other locals.

At a time when ISIS wouldn't permit people to escape towards the Iraqi security forces, Um Umar's family was among thousands of families that did manage to slip out.

Um Umar - feeling forced to leave

It was raining shells and bombs in the Old Town. How dare they shower an inhabited neighbourhood with bombs and shells! ISIS fighters were popping up from time to time, and when a bullet was being broken out, the reply would be ruthless, regardless to the civilians' lives living in the quarter. God saved us.

She wiped her tears and spent a moment of silence when she recalled her neighbour's son.

He was an only child whom his parents wanted to save from imminent death. They didn't know that they were sending him to certain death. He was caught with a handful of young guys sitting on the boat, trying to cross the Tigris River to the liberated eastern Mosul. That part of the city had preceded Western Mosul in liberation. But according to a woman who witnessed the homicide. Al had been crying for a while, begging the militants to let him go, because of his parents who would really die after him, but ISIS insurgents had ignored his tears, and with no mercy they shot him in the head and dumped his corpse into the river.

I asked Um Umar: How did you dare to flee, disobeying ISIS members that were lurking for locals?

It wasn't my idea. I would rather have died at home than see ISIS members pull one of my sons out to kill before my eyes. We fled because of the escalation of bombing over us. I don't want to point the finger of accusation at the doer, but let the world investigate and find out.

In those days, my son Ahmad used to roam in the neighbourhood searching for any route to flee. We didn't know that Ahmad would agree with his friends on every detail. To take the next step of the epic escape, we would need to pass through a long argument on whether to take the gamble.

In that bleak evening, Ahmad returned ashen and intimidated, indicating the moment of truth: "Hurry up, hurry up! I found a way to escape," he whispered.

At first, as a mother, I was reluctant to take the risk. But when I saw everybody was happy and excited while getting themselves ready, I changed my opinion, and decided to follow them. I also realised it was almost impossible to stop them; I mean my family members. That was the last ray of hope looming in the frightful darkness flanking our alley with the roads we knew that had become the most dangerous roads in the world.

Um Umar - escaping the abyss

Dusk fell and we abandoned our house, leaving everything behind, our past and memories. The house where we'd been trapped in for months might turn to rubble. When the military operations in Mosul started, Iraqi military media distributed flyers informing us to stay at home waiting for the liberators. Our escape or exodus didn't resemble any of the traditional images because the situation was unprecedented and extraordinary.

We fled one by one, spanning the twisted alleyways in old Mosul. From door to door, there were specific houses where we would hide while trying to get out. Those houses had been the safe shelters for dozens of the families who shared with us the same longing for survival. We concealed ourselves in the houses of people whom we once saw in the neighbourhood and greeted, or perhaps we were at odds with them, but that night they were next to kin. We knew we must either to live or to die together. Children were crying from empty tummies. I didn't want to use up all the cookies in my purse slung on my tired shoulder, because I knew that the road would never be short. I knew that we could get trapped for several days in one of those houses, then, if I ran out of all the candies I had, I believed the chance of living would have been slim. At least this is what I thought.

It was raining in the gloomy neighbourhood, my black clothes got stained with mud and dirt, the rubble being conveyed by the water streams to form what appeared to look like muddy ponds spanning the walkway. We got bogged down somehow. Debris of the houses or the scattering of people's dreams littered the road with the rocks. A proof indicating that the world has not become yet a better place to live, while you might think it has.

In some phases of that horrible advance, we had to sprint when crossing the main streets because ISIS members were patrolling. I got stuck with my son Ahmad when everybody had crossed. That had happened after ISIS fighters popped into sight. We had to retreat somehow. Our folks looked at us in what seemed to be a farewell stare. We indicated that they should quickly vanish, in the meanwhile I walked with Ahmad who carried his infant between his arms, we disappeared in the darkness, cuddling the child so it wouldn't cry. Fifteen minutes rushed by, and Ahmad studied the situation again and when it was a chance to pass, we hurried like ghosts in the darkness crossing to the opposite side of the neighbourhood. We didn't have any idea where the others were crammed at that moment. We weren't even sure if they were still at large or doomed. I was intensely worried about the rest of the family. But we kept walking to our elusive dream.

Um Umar - getting separated from her son

I was distracted while following Ahmad whose sole compass was the experience he retrieved from childhood up to now when he used to roam with his friends in the neighbourhood. Then we heard footsteps penetrating the rain, tramping feet. Two men who seemed to be guarding the place, popped up. I was shocked, and would have done anything to hide Ahmad so they wouldn't kill him. They might understand that I am an old lady with a child. I had started walking when they intercepted me "Do you want to slip out, old lady?"

"No, but I am looking for my relative's house and I got lost because of the rain and darkness," I answered trying to veil the truth of escaping.

Their faces creased into laughter and they said "You have survived! We have been waiting for your arrival. We heard that you and your son have lost the way, welcome inside the house."

They escorted me to the entrance, where the rest of the family were there alongside other families. As I entered, I saw the rest of my family members, Ahmad's wife was waiting in tears. The moment she saw me coming in, she scooted next to me, pulling her infant to her chest, mumbling to him the loving angel's song, in the meanwhile hell was blazing outside, and a moment would pass before she would ask about her husband, "Ahmad; where is he?"

After I verified what the guys said, I realised it wasn't a trap installed by ISIS to hunt the escapees at the arena of death, I rushed out with the two guys in the hopes of finding Ahmad.

I knew that that house was the last station just before reaching the gate of the normal world, after a series of houses, aligned as shelters, mitigating our appearance while we advanced in the heart of Mosul, towards the exit door. It was the only time when you feel that your physical existence is a death certificate, you rather wish to be a worm or a fly or anything that doesn't capture human's interest.

Poem: Humans can kill a fly for fun!

A fly is hovering over the screen while I'm writing this,
As though it was trying to penetrate through my alphabet
"I am a character in this book!" exclaimed the fly
"I can take the role to become a helicopter
I can be the pigeon that carried the comforting letters,
Between the opposing banks of the river
I can fly to the last chapter of the book and bring the story of hope", requested the fly.
The fly is hovering, alighting, here and there...
Rambling on my fingers while tapping to weave the fates of
Ahmad who got confined by now
Get out of here dear fly!
Haven't you read what I just wrote:
HUMANS CAN KILL A FLY FOR FUN!
Humans can do everything if they can justify, prettify, and makeup the truth of the deed with different names
O fly, get out of here before I borrow your life
Before I send you, a forgotten fly,
jumping on the tossed corpses
spanning the road to the outside world
In wartime, people's roles are overlapped,
Moms become trenches, and dads become fences
When ISIS confiscated our cell-phones,
We hid one in the fridge
When the travel ban was imposed
We roamed the world through reading neglected books
Everything can happen but a fly cannot be a helicopter!

Ahmed Zaidan

Um Umar - still trying to escape

We continued dashing through the dark neighbourhood, from corner to corner, in the hope of finding Ahmad. It would have been suicide to shout because we expected ISIS to lurch into our fearful sight like hyenas. My heart was jumping because I was the one who had suggested the idea of concealing my son as a response to my intuition as a mother who would do everything to protect her child. For a moment I thought to myself that he might have got caught when trying to find his way to us.

Now half an hour has passed. I'd rather go back to inform the rest of the family to help us search for the missing member of the family and the operator of that plan. We couldn't trust the place, nor the time. The family rushed out in hope of finding its lost lamb. The children were silent, or they might have enjoyed being outside after months of being detained in the house. Absolutely they didn't estimate the magnitude of the disaster.

After one hour passed, we were deployed like a military squad looking for Ahmad. My older son Umar showed up and whispered that we must leave this place immediately, otherwise we won't be able to leave it forever.

I told him that I couldn't leave without Ahmad.

He said "Do you prefer losing 24 souls for the sake of one soul who might have found another route to survive, and he might be by now waiting for us outside."

I replied that Ahmad might have gotten caught by ISIS. Afterwards I realised my son, Umar, was right. In either case it would be useless to keep searching because it was out of our hands.

Ahmad - journeying on alone

Ahmad felt intimidated and his teeth gritted at what he saw and heard. Was it cold enough to make a man shiver like a spike in the wind? The normal line bordering certain feelings from another might get erased when the situation collapses, causing humans to unleash various emotions at one time!

ISIS fighters had just killed a family that tried to escape to try to reach those they called apostates and infidels; he heard them from a distance shouting "Allah Akbar!"

He glanced around, slumped behind the rubble of a blown-off house and lingered in a bid to learn details so that he might identify the massacred family, while the sound of marching feet was getting faster. ISIS fighters had apparently finished the job and might be talking about it by now. He prayed not to hear anything that could confirm the thoughts swirling in his head. His last connection with his family had been when his mother hid him and walked away to distract the two guys. They might've been setting a trap to let her go and then track her to where she was supposed to end. When they discovered the truth, they might have killed all the family.

The rain got heavier. ISIS members were clutching their rifles, walking carefully and swinging round to watch for any imminent enemy. Ahmad knew that for ISIS, everyone out there could be a potential target because the city of Mosul had turned into a battlefield and the narrow alleyways would make the fight even harder. But for ISIS, the Old Town is a friendly area. The locals made up the best shields. Modern armies dedicate huge sums creating the super soldier who would fight under any conditions, but not in an old city crammed with innocents.

Ahmad had heard that ISIS elements who barred people from different practices and habits by the name of God, were themselves breaking these taboos, secretly. Exactly as he had just seen from the hole in the wall. One of them had handed a tablet to each of the men who gathered under the opposite house. They probably couldn't keep fighting without getting high. They'd become killing machines with two types of pills: medical and ideological. The ideological pill was taken in the form of speech, called "brainwashing" by Sheiks and those called religious scientists in that world. This pill was a dream containing beautiful virgin girls waiting for the ISIS insurgents' arrival after death. That tells you what kind of life those folk had lived in the past. What kind of turbulent childhood did they experience? Explicitly, a life without love for many reasons. The way they looked, the society they lived in, contributed to sucking the sense of life from those beasts.

A bright light like a nuclear blast flashed in the neighbourhood. Ahmad kept frozen to his position so the frenzied ISIS fighters wouldn't feel that someone was next to them. They reacted in their usual way to that air-assault. They were fiercely shooting towards the heaven as though they were drawing the attention of their god. A chaotic minute passed before they scampered like intimidated rabbits to change their location. The pilot was about to respond while God was busy with thousands of the vulnerable families who were trying to find a way out of the death zone.

Ahmad jumped out of his hiding-place and ran quickly in a different direction. He didn't really have any clue where he was heading to. But he was sure that the zone would be immediately wiped out by the Air Force as a reaction to ISIS's shooting. That was the way the battle had been handled in Mosul. Both sides had their war objectives they wanted to achieve whatever the price. For the innocents trapped in Old Mosul, their elusive objective was only to sneak out of the war zone, the war they weren't involved in, in any shape or form. Their only guilt was that they were born and lived in the wrong place and time. That was like any war that happened in history; that war of the beneficiaries even if they were physically absent from the area, however, how much someone can be present somewhere doesn't necessarily relate to the physical status only, presence can also be attained by domination.

Ahmad hurried, running away from the imminent disaster that was about to happen. The blow sparked off a scene like in a war movie from Hollywood trying to depict the overall image from Iraq or Afghanistan, but the internal image is hard to be transferred to the cinema's flicker. The light of the bombardment illuminated the night. For a moment the alley seemed to have been fully devastated so that Ahmad himself, who lived there for all his life, couldn't have recognized the neighbourhood if someone showed him a photo of it.

Ahmad - trapped in the Old Town

While trying to find a way to the outside world, Ahmad had become trapped in the Old Town. He felt that at any time, he could be captured by the forces of evil or he could be wrongly targeted by Iraqi troops for his physical appearance: that a man with a long beard could be mistaken for what they were after, although ISIS had imposed on all adult men the rule to lengthen their beard in what fits their idea of Islamic costume.

He recalled his hairdresser, Samir, the man who lived in the Wadi Hajar neighbourhood; the most feared district for ISIS, because most of the Iraqi security personnel were living there before the conquest. Despite of that fact, Samir had been waiting for nearly a week hidden in the house, before he heard that the Iraqi forces have retaken the area. Out of happiness, Samir popped up to inform the liberator troops that there is a family trapped here, in need of help. And an Iraqi soldier, out of fear, pointed his M16 at him and pulled the trigger.

Ahmad thought that if any of the armed groups glanced at him alone, they might think he is their enemy. With the protagonists from both parties: acting either to kill or to get killed. On the battlefield, the stone you stumble on, could cause you to fall forever. Both parties were itching to target any moving object.

Dawn was paling the night sky. The silence would soon be broken by early morning battles. The darkness that had sheltered Ahmad for one night would soon be gone, and the light would reveal his presence. He figured out he was near his uncle's house. Staying outside was no longer an option; it was like wandering in the minefield.

He took a detour in the hope of reaching shelter for another day. He knew that his family could be taken as human shields to the depths, where the battles are fiercest and the chance to survive is almost impossible. They could also have found a route to the outside world.

Ahmad knew the lore of insurgents fighting among civilians; his gaze went to study the minaret of the Grand Mosque erected, flanked by pillars of fumes elevating to the heavens as though the city's colours were evaporating.

For how long would this monument keep resisting the blows of war? The hunchback that has always symbolised that pride of Mosul leaning on 800 years, the only landmark that could been seen from a vast distance, affirming to arrivals that you have arrived in the city of the hunchback, Mosul?

Very gingerly, he wandered around, with his senses at full stretch. The road seemed empty as if he was wandering in no man's land. Well, every part of the city turned into a frontline in this ominous war.

Doors of the houses were left open, so ISIS could take shelter anytime during the battle. By that time, people living on the western edge of the Old Town were being asked to evacuate. Those who disobeyed the instructions would face unfortunate consequences. All the houses were his to enter, but who knows, there could be some families who managed to hide in the crypts.

The howl of a flying object rose swiftly, it didn't give time to Ahmad to think where to scamper, just froze him rigid.

The flash had brightened the spectacle; things were soaring as if the earth stopped rotating for a minute and the gravity had erased. The blow had lifted him for a few centimetres up from where he stood and slumped him on the ground.

After a handful of seconds, he opened his eyes. The first thing he glimpsed was the chatter of birds swinging randomly in different directions, in the meanwhile an enormous part of the alley had been enveloped in dust.

He leant against the wall trying to creep up but felt paralyzed. As he flitted his sight down, he saw that his right thigh was eroded. He felt the tinnitus drilling into his ears, he couldn't hear or see anything as if he'd hustled into his inner self from his new scar that opened like a gate, the only thing he saw was the end.

He let out the breath he had been holding, in a bid to get fused with what was going on. He didn't have the guts to look at his injured part again. He looked up to the sky and thoughtfully reminisced all the wars he'd survived, his family must be waiting for him. He took off his shirt rapidly, trying to reach under his undershirt to bandage his thigh before he bled the remnant of life he needed to survive.

His grimaced, focusing on his wound. His breath trembled and his power shifted to his hands. He was in exceptional pain that engulfed his soul first, running back and forth in his body like a tornado of thorns ripping his flesh from within.

He was officially stranded in the middle of nowhere; a city was not even on the map. Staying there meant certain death. It was just a matter of time before they would find him.

Ahmad gathered his strength to try his first move. The best way to achieve that was to get support from the standing walls aligning the way to his uncle's house.

His thigh dangled behind him, but it allowed him to slightly lean on it with the help of the walls.

Half an hour passed before he realised: "Damn - this isn't going to work!"

After all that pain, he'd progressed only a few metres. But that wasn't the worst of it. At least he was moving his body, but then he reached the end of the alleyway. If he wanted to keep going, he had to cross the street. Open streets meant having to bear the risk of being fully exposed. Usually, people would lurk for the right moment to cross, having to escape the barrels of ISIS snipers and the helicopters hovering around.

Ahmad gave up on the idea of creeping across the street to the opposite side, so he decided to seek help in one of those houses that seemed empty. He only needed to let himself inside, he might find something to aid him to protract his fight for life.

Ahmad - seeking shelter from strangers

He duly dragged himself back, then pushed his tired body indoors, using the door handle to clutch on. As he came inside, his gaze went to the house yard, there was a square garden allowing two of the lemon trees to rise. He saw that the leaves and dirt littered the ceramic floor. That type of floor facilitated his move, permitting him to slip smoothly on the ground with his elbows to reach what seemed to be a kitchen.

As he entered, he saw a wooden basket stacked on the shelf dug into the wall in the form of an arch. He was busy trying only to stand and see what was in it, when a rifle was pointed at him. He flinched from a man who seemed static, with tufted eyebrows gazing down at him and a long beard wearing a costume that looked like an ISIS affiliate.

"What are you doing here?" The man looked ready to pull the trigger if he didn't like what he heard.

Time wasn't on Ahmad's side, and would saying the truth anyway save his ass? Well, he wasn't sure of that either. His breath was at its highest pace, and suddenly, Ahmad felt pain-free. All he was thinking of was what to say to that standing beast.

"What are you doing here, don't you understand Arabic?" The man's tone revealed his rage. Staying silent wouldn't prolong Ahmad's life. It only could make it worse.

"Sir, please, I am with you, I have got nothing to hurt you. I live in the next alley, and got wounded while I was on the way to the depth of the Old Town to where the Islamic State wanted us to be."

The man gave him a sceptical gaze. He seemed ready to lower his rifle but, all of a sudden, pointed his gun at Ahmad's head saying, "What if you were one of them?"

Ahmad realised that the man himself could be a fighter. In Mosul, people were divested of any weapon. When a gun was found with someone, then the charge of treason was always there under multiple labels such as cooperating with the enemies of the Islamic State. If phones or cameras were detected, one would be in big trouble, and charges would shackle that person, yes, very hard to be exonerated and a horrible death would be waiting, such as being crammed into a car that's full of explosives and being blown up, or being confined in a metal cage slung on a crane, sliding down slowly in a swimming pool, so that the victims would feel every single moment of death, wishing for a bullet to slam in the back of their heads to cut off the ongoing horror they're plunged in. Throat-slitting appeared to be a merciful way of death in comparison to what was inflicted on those convicted with treason.

People were forced to watch what ISIS had been implementing. While those who happened to be at the site of the atrocity, had to watch the execution of the death penalty. Ahmad witnessed some of that death ritual when he was at the marketplace, wandering.

"Hey, Muslim brothers and sisters, now you will see with your naked eyes the Islamic State implementing Sharia, one's of God's rules enacted in the favour of humans, I swear that that law that seemed tough to your heart, but it is full to me of mercy, because God is more merciful than moms to their kids."

Ahmad imagined an eight-storey tower where everyone was gathering in a large circle to see what was going to happen. A man with white beard in his 70s would be handed the microphone in preparation to recite the judgement of God. "You will be witnessing the decimation of those perverts who were caught practising what God and his prophets have forbidden, they didn't only commit adultery, they went to what Lot's folks had been doing, homosexuality."

To avoid taking in the scene, he had distracted himself from the current moment. It was one of the tactics he used to do when seeing something like that.

He heard young men begging and screaming before they slammed down on the ground and the voice went off, in the meanwhile the crowds chanted loudly out of fear, "Allah Akbar."

Ahmad was brought back to the present by the gun-barrel tapping against his head. "Reply to my question, or you will be killed, and tossed outside for dogs! "

"I am not one of them."

The man's gaze probed Ahmad, his physical appearance, his dialect. In Iraq, it's possible to identify people by their dialect, Mosul has a unique dialect that's obvious to all Iraqis.

Ahmad spoke the local Mosuli dialect with his family, however he used to address the strangers with the formal Iraqi dialect. He had lived in the neighbourhood and thrived with diversity, people from villages, and people from other Iraqi cities had been enriching each other by giving a wider perspective of life.

Ahmad had acquired his resilience from his childhood though a great part of it was sunk in the years of the siege and deprivation, however his primary school has taught him how to fight back or at least to defend himself. He knew that begging for mercy would make things worse, it could awaken the tyrant inside that man. He was helpless, devastated but he recalled what his grandfather had always said: "Bravery is an attitude."

He could still show that man who he was. "Now, can I ask you: who are you? Is this really your house? Are you from Mosul?" Ahmad's will to fight back had grown.

The man could see the fire blazing in Ahmad's eyes, so he had to retreat somehow.

Ahmad had noticed new details that empowered him more after he peeled off the layer of fear that blinded him for a while. Yes, when people feel scared, they don't often see real things, they tend to see the ghosts of their inside world wrapping the real image.

Ahmad's extended his right hand to the man, in a bid to reach the nozzle of his rifle, but the man jumped back and threatened to pull the trigger. He kept saying that.

Meanwhile Ahmad burst out laughing like a crazy person. "Hey man, I am not an ISIS fighter, I am not with those devils who were the reason for a brother to raise a plastic rifle and keep it pointed at his brother who needs help. Let's work together, what's your name?"

The man sighed but he still didn't want to lower his toy rifle, as though he couldn't believe that his plan had been just screwed by the injured stranger who, out of the unknown, popped up in the kitchen.

"Yes, but how can I trust you?" the man asked desperately. "In wartime, people have got nothing to prove their loyalty except the fight for their life. But the bad guys in this war would renounce their lives to prove their faith in the afterlife. If you were one of them, you would rather choose to accelerate your journey to meet with the virgins in paradise that are waiting for martyrs according to their belief," he said, as if to convince himself as well.

Ahmad - whether to stay or move on

Ahmad recited something out of the Quran to create a peaceful atmosphere. "Now help me out to sit and to get some water. I am a soul. whoever resurrects a soul, as though he resurrected the souls of all humans, the holy Quran says."

The man looked at Ahmad's scar and recited the rest of the verse mentioned in the Quran: "In the meanwhile, whoever killed a soul without a right, it is as though he killed all humanity." Then he offered his hand to Ahmad saying: "You can stay in my home safe until we get the chance to slip out of the war zone."

Ahmad leaned against the wall while a glass of water was handed to him followed by a loaf of crusty dry bread that Mosul families used to store in the abnormal circumstances. He thanked the man and began crunching the crispy bread after a long sip on the glass of water. "I see you still have some bread. Sounds like you are a well-prepared family for such circumstances."

The man replied, "My wife is cautious; she had learned that from her childhood. Her father used to serve in the Iraqi uniform back in the days. He went missing during the 1st Gulf war; nobody knows if he is still captive in Iran or martyred in the frontline. Her poor mom didn't get married, and she was the breadwinner of the family. My wife is the elder of two sisters. So, she learned from her mom how to be responsible and independent. Her mom is equal to 100 men! I will ask her to make you a splint." The man vanished leaving Ahmad thinking how both unlucky and lucky he was.

Then he heard the man's wife shouting, "What is wrong with you? How is it possible to let someone stay with us when we have no idea who he is? He could be a spy or something, and you know that we chose to be neutral as most of the people here, we only want to get the hell out of here without having to suffer more."

When the man returned, Ahmad asked, "Should I leave if your wife doesn't want me here, and she has a right in whatever she said?"

Before they finished talking, they heard a voice coming outside. ISIS members were calling on those who had stayed to leave their abodes, because the Iraqi forces had managed to break through the ISIS defence frontline. Liberation of the first part of the Old Town was imminent. ISIS elements were on their way to establishing a new defence-line upon renouncing the prior one.

Everyone was confused and nervous. It wasn't easy to be used as human shields once again. The errant bombs were everywhere, and the artillery was roaring in the meanwhile. Everything was occurring constantly, making the moment of silence even more frightening, just like the calm that often precedes any disaster.

Ahmad knew, if he was very lucky, he could be left to face his fate alone. Often ISIS members could break into houses of people to check if they'd really evacuated their houses, or if some family didn't follow the instructions, then the family might be displaced or killed if they refused.

Maybe the couple in whose house he was sheltering couldn't leave because their neighbour was ISIS and commissioned to keep an eye on the families who lived in the same quarter. But Ahmad was determined to keep trying to escape.

"Do you have any idea where they are going to take the civilians this time?" he asked the man.

"I think to the new defence-line, it is pretty much close,"

Ahmad suspected it would be even more difficult if he decided to abide by ISIS rules, they might even ask him about his family. His wound wasn't a big deal, since mortar rounds had been falling like rain, casualties among civilians was shocking.

The Iraqi Federal Police had published pictures on social media of them launching mortar rounds onto the Old Town, in a bid to get ISIS out of their dens. But the Old Town was inhabited with nearly a million innocent souls.

Ahmad sat on the floor trying to tighten his cast so he could walk. The wife brought Ahmad what he needed, including some tissues.

He suspected that neither husband nor wife fully trusted him. But with ISIS only a few metres away, any disturbance between them might lead to the whole family being killed.

It was time for him to leave this temporary refuge and move on.

Um Umar and the family keep trying to escape

Um Umar and her family, like dozens of other families, decided to walk out of the Old Town. All of them knew of a narrow gate that led to the frontline where ISIS snipers would target any moving objects.

Um Umar kept thinking of her son Ahmad. He was never out of her mind. She pictured him arrested by ISIS, and before they would shoot him in the head, the mental image would shift to depict an optimistic scene that empowered her somehow: Ahmad is out there waiting for us. I know he can do it. He must be standing with the security forces to welcome us after he'd socialised with the guys there and told them something interesting about himself.

She knew that her missing son had a lot of things to talk about, and to fight for. He was someone who had gone through a lot of adventures in his life. Moreover, he had friends from the southern Iraqi cities, two of them were serving in Mosul before the conquest, when ISIS had suddenly taken over the city of Mosul in June 2014, the Iraqi security forces were ordered to withdraw from the city, leaving everything behind. For the high ranked officers, the withdrawal was secure and smooth, but for soldiers, the withdrawal happened suddenly, and it didn't give them time to plan their trips back to their cities in the south. The road was plagued with death gangs patrolling along the way between Mosul and Baghdad lying in wait for the fleeing members of the Iraqi security forces.

Ahmad had concealed two of the soldiers for several days before faking new documents for them, showing that they were Sunni; he sent them back to their cities in the south with a trustworthy trucker.

Stories of altruism were happening almost every day, but no one dared to reveal them during ISIS time.

Um Umar wiped her tears and looked back at the alley and the road where her son got lost.

Ahmad's wife was busy with the child, while the others were waiting for instructions to make the first move. It was going to be an epic trek anyway.

Mortar shells were falling and it was only a matter of time before one of those randomly launched shells fell amidst the crowds. Mortar rounds can fall anywhere, they cause many innocents to die or to suffer for the rest of their lives.

The family had been hungry, they were running out of all the candies they'd saved, and the water was nearly exhausted.

Now it was time to take that risk, because staying there was also a risk. At least fleeing was a better risk because life was about two miles ahead.

One woman broke her silence. "If we stay here, we will perish anyway. What are we waiting for?"

According to the rules of ISIS, women's voices are deemed as an extension of their pudenda, something that the woman herself should be ashamed to reveal in front of alien men. At that moment, however, women were taking the lead because they were guided by their inner strength, the strength that was hidden in ordinary times, the strength that erupts when men stand paralyzed. It was the same power that provoked the mother to hide her son whatever it cost.

Thereafter, everyone would walk in what seemed to be a mass march, as though the crowds decided to trample on the code of evil.

As they approached the gate, two ISIS guards asked them to return, otherwise they would open fire. Then one of them went preaching among the crowds, hoping he could convince them to return. "You are leaving, fleeing the Islamic

State. God will ask you to account for that sin. It is not the end as you think. This is a test from God to see who will fail. Paradise costs a lot of patience."

But the guard saw they would persist even if he opened fire: the huge crowds were ready to swallow him up. He whispered to his mate what seemed to be approval. But he may have had a malignant motivation because, spanning the road (no man's land), there were ISIS snipers lurking for such a hunt.

The guards stepped aside, and the gate was left unattended. The crowds rushed through that small slot, like the Tigris bursts through Mosul Dam in April.

Now, people had to sprint. Elderly people were on the shoulders of young men, while the women carried the infants and toddlers, the bags were carried by children.

They were shot at by snipers along the way, but nobody got injured. They knew how to zigzag as they moved forward.

Once they could see the Iraqi flag looming, they slowed down. The Iraqi forces instructed the new arrivals to send children and women first, to put their hands up and advance carefully.

Um Umar was the first one to walk out of the group. Having taken off the white Hijab veiling her hair, she waved it to show they were civilians. Meanwhile some children were holding her dress and walking slowly. The officer asked her to stand at a distance from the military vehicles.

In many cases, ISIS would send suicide bombers; women or men dressed in women's clothes to blow up the military check point. The Iraqi Forces had been so careful in dealing with any human coming from the arena of fighting.

Um Umar was scanned carefully. Kids were kept aside. Meanwhile, Um Umar asked her family to walk slowly towards the check-points. She knew from people who were waiting there that men would be separated to be checked carefully. She asked the security personnel about her son

Ahmad. They asked her to wait while they went to check his name on the laptop.

Everyone had left, while Um Umar and Ahmad's wife waited. Several times, security personnel intercepted them, asking them to join the group. But Um Umar explained they were waiting for important information regarding her son.

One of the guards told her that it was better for her to go because at any time ISIS could send a bomb-car to target the security checkpoint. The enemy was just out of the sight of the Iraqi troops who were receiving the batches of evacuee civilians.

Then a man asked Um Umar to approach him, stripped of any belongings. Um Umar felt that the guards found something crucial regarding her son.

"Ahmad Hussein Fahmi, is that your son's full name?" the soldier asked, keeping his gaze on Um Umar's face.

"Yes, that's my son's name," she snapped.

The man nodded to his colleague in what seemed to be an affirmation of something they'd talked about before.

"Are there other men in your family still inside?" The other soldier asked more calmly.

"No, one of my sons had already been liberated months ago, because he lived with his wife in Eastern Mosul, "the left side", during the battles that took place there. They got trapped in a house alongside his wife's family. For days we didn't hear from them. We lost connection with all our relatives living on the other side of the river. But thanks be to God, we managed to comfort ourselves by SMS that they are fine, although the front part of the house they were trapped in had collapsed when a bomb-car blew up. Most of the men who were separated in the front room died or were critically injured, while women and children were crammed in the rear rooms of the house."

"Was your son sitting with the women and children in the rear part of the house?" The soldier asked. He was trying to believe her story but curious because he knew the rules:

when several families gathered in one house, men shouldn't stay with women in one room. Often the house would be divided by gender into two parts, because women could only breastfeed their infants and take the hijab off when they were unattended by men.

"My son wasn't in the house when the blast took place!"

Then soldiers had asked Um Umar to escort them to what appeared to be a distinct zone where ISIS families were seized.

Um Umar thoughtfully looked around and saw that most of the women kept there didn't look like they were from Mosul, not even close, most of the women were veiled, but she could still hear their speech. One of the women shouted, "The Islamic State is ongoing, and this is just a small stumble on the way of righteousness, we have to be patient and god will reward us!"

Um Umar realised that there might have been some mistake in her being put where ISIS families were. Then she saw a man hiding his face with a cloth pointing at her. She knew he could be an informant.

Um Umar - recalling her neighbour's son, Mahir

Um Umar's neighbour's son, Mahir, was 12 years old when the city of Mosul was conquered and she cherished him like a grandson. She was reminded of the summer of 2014, when ISIS members set out to tame people, earning the trust of some of the young people who lost their future in the time their city was gone, no schools, no hobbies, no TVs, no connection to the outside world. A totally abducted city with more than two million of its inhabitants left to encounter their fate.

One day in July 2014, Mahir got brainwashed by the Imam of the mosque who facilitated the way for teenagers to join ISIS. Mahir came back home threatening his mother that he would be a "Cub" in the Islamic State. His mother couldn't stop him, he just left. ISIS was punishing those families who prevented their children from joining the criminal group.

ISIS did not force people directly to join them, but they knew how to ease the path for desperate people to get recruited, by brainwashing and describing the advantages acquired when joining the Islamic State had become a reality on the ground. For many years, the Islamic State had been confined within folded books on the shelves of history. But the seed of the idea was summoned from the distant past, especially when Western powers began strengthening the Islamic armed groups who then fought and managed to expel the Soviet troops from Afghanistan. That was an optimal environment for extremists to migrate to for the sake of God, a proxy war that resulted in creating monsters; the terrorists that fled from their countries of origin to struggle in favour of attaining the dream of the Islamic State, that one day would bite the hand that fed it and try to raze the ones who started that fire.

Now this fire is gutting the city of Mosul, Um Umar thought, as she reminisced about Mahir attempting to join ISIS in 2014. Yes, he was just a kid then but she knew that kids who join ISIS can grow into monsters in no time. Better to go after him whatever it might cost. She knew that ISIS wasn't the norm, and one day, the city was going to be relieved, and those who slid into ISIS anyhow, would have to face the rage of people and the legal consequences. One member could destroy the whole family.

So that summer, Mahir's mother and Um Umar went after him to the so-called "palaces zone", built by Saddam, which had become a military barracks for US troops post 2003 and, later, a den for ISIS members. Together, they managed to bring the 12-year-old back, retrieving him from the jaws of the crocodile. They threatened him that if he didn't go back with them, they would tell ISIS that he used to curse God on every occasion and his mother would come to testify against him. He was frightened ISIS could cut off his tongue for cursing God. It was Um Umar who had come up with this idea. Otherwise, the boy would have been recruited by ISIS. He could have blown up his entire family.

Um Umar - queuing at the security checkpoint

Um Umar peered at the queue of civilians at the checkpoint heading towards the shore of safety, as though they were chased by lava. Her thoughts drifted.

ISIS had claimed that they basically came to save the people of Mosul from the sectarian army that had arrested men and women randomly for fabricated charges of terrorism related. For the people of Mosul at that time, anyone who would promise to attain justice and to restore their lost dignity, would be an option. At first, ISIS wasn't identified explicitly as we know it today, ISIS members appeared to be tolerant. They asked security members from Mosul who'd worked with the Iraqi government to hand over their weapons and to sign a document called "repentance" then they pledged that by only doing so, they would live peacefully in the Islamic State. Many of those uniformed men would rush to concede their remorse, standing in long queues to declare their remorse and renounce their career upon earning their lives and making the safety of their families. Those who didn't have a gun were obliged to pay cash which was equal to the price of the gun that they'd supposedly had.

She thought how the city of Mosul had witnessed a demonstration that started post the US withdrawal at the end of 2011. Families of detainees flooded what was once the Friday Market in Mosul, turned over in the past, to be "The Square of Dignity". Yes, it was the influence of the "Arab Spring" that overthrew three of the capable dictators in the Arab world. So why not in Iraq; since 2003, and the country hasn't stopped bleeding. Invasion, looting, corrupt governments, civil war, discrimination, and killing and kidnapping, so people in four major Iraqi cities saw it as a great chance to change the regime or at least to conduct a reform.

However, the government met blood with fire, and responded to their protesting flesh with bullets. Um Umar thought of the atrocity that happened in Kirkuk, when the security forces opened fire on the peaceful protesters, leaving a shower of blood behind.

In Al Ramadi City in the west of the country, the people who had once co-operated with the Americans to defeat the first form of the Islamic State in Iraq "Al Qaeda", saw themselves that they had only been exploited and once "Al Qaeda" was defeated, they were dumped.

The Americans knew how to create armed groups for proxy wars. As a result of the rise of Al Qaeda in Iraq, Paul Bremer the US leader of the coalition provisional authority in Iraq who accepted that impossible mission of leading a country like Iraq full of disputes and war traumas. The man who'd disbanded the Iraqi former army, would later contribute to make the first cell of the Iraqi Government post Saddam and De-Baa'athification Policy that would be misused by political rivals to retaliate upon the members of the prior ruling party Al Baath Party. Many teachers, directors and employed people would lose their jobs for belonging to the party which was in fact, something like an obligation in Saddam's time.

This law was used as a trap against the Sunni Community in Iraq. Here we can say that by dissolving the Iraqi Army and De-Baa'athification policy, the two potholes were made to get the wagon of citizenship bogged down in the course of new Iraq. Here where the Sunni Community felt that something should be done to save their own faces, they were estranged on their land. Through the shortcomings of the new system, the radical groups found in the Sunni Community an optimal environment to infiltrate and build the first armed groups that claimed they were the only Sunni's advocates in the New Iraq. Violence would escalate and innocent blood would be shed. Sunni Cities would turn to be just death zones.

In 2006, the leaders of the tribes in Al Ramadi and other Sunni cities created an armed group called "Al Sahwah" meaning "The Awakening" to confront the escalating terrorism in the Sunni Iraqi Provinces. Some of the leaders of the Awakening movement that once sat with Americans and the Iraqi government at the same table, became the heads of the demonstrations.

Nuri Al Maliki described the demonstration as a nasty bubble that should be terminated by force.

The rage that engulfed the "squares of dignity" in Iraq was unprecedented, resulting in protracting the demonstrations from 2011 to 2014, when finally dangerous inmates broke out of Abu Ghraib Prison in a dangerous development of events. The Iraqi government claimed that the terrorist fugitives had found their way to penetrate the demonstration in cooperating with a foreign agenda to dismantle the system.

Well, Iraq was teeming with militias and sectarianism! The concept of the system hadn't been there at all. The situation was chaotic. By claiming so, the Iraqi government acquired more legitimacy to crackdown on the demonstrations at that time.

In Mosul, the image was no different from the other cities engulfed by the movement that dreamed about change. Mosul had been a city mainly inhabited by Iraqi citizens whose prime representatives were not the tribes or religious leaders, but they were exclusively represented by the state. And when the state became fragile, the people of Mosul were disturbed.

This explains a significant fact: why most of the Iraqi Army officers who contributed to founding the first brick of the Iraqi Army in the past century, came from Mosul.

The Iraqi Army had relied on Commanders from Mosul because of the absence of the tribal trend at first place in their city. This made it easier for the army officers to be loyal to the state that the uniform entailed, not to their tribes.

Um Umar - everyone's fear of secret informants

Um Umar thought about secret informants who often gave false information to the security forces. In some cases, entire families were ruined and souls were lost in the crypts of the authorities. But why would a human inflict tremendous harm on other humans this way?

Near Mosul railway station, a family of five adult men were living with their mothers and wives. Three of them were married. Four of them were policemen. In that time 2007, being a policeman or anything relating to the Iraqi security forces was a deed of suicide. Every day, policemen were being killed by the terrorist groups roaming the city. They could bomb their cars or simply assassinate them with a silencer while they were on duty or off.

Muhannad was in his twenties when his ex-girlfriend vowed to ruin his life forever. He just ignored her threats and didn't think the woman could harm him. Muhannad's ex found a new boyfriend who was working as a secret informant. Simply because she gave Muhannad's address to her new boyfriend, she claimed that Muhannad was her relative who didn't pay her father back a debt. The new boyfriend, who was an informant working for the security forces in the town, fabricated a charge to screw up the family of Muhannad, claiming that that family had been working with Al Qaeda.

The door was blown off, Muhannad's brothers took their guns out of holsters, thinking that they got attacked by the terrorists who broke into their house to kill them, something that was happening in Mosul at any time. But when the US soldiers encountered the armed guys who stood up out of self-defence, the soldiers opened fire, thinking that the house they came to search belonged to one of the terrorist groups. Muhannad was already upstairs, on the roof of the house talking on the phone with his new girlfriend, he managed to escape, climbing across the roofs until he made it out of the danger zone.

Five members of the family were killed. The rest were gravely injured. News of that massacre spread all over the city.

Um Umar - worrying about Ahmad

Um Umar imagined her son could be one of the victims. There were a lot of ways she could prove his innocence but that would be a long and complex process.

Then she saw Ahmad's wife crossing the same area accompanied by a soldier.

"Here I am," she cried, waving to show Ahmad's wife that she was amid the crowds.

Ahmad's wife, Suhad, seemed ashen and disappointed.

How can someone believe that after all this suffering and battling for life, they would end up that way, and get seized with ISIS families, the folks that killed and raped, the monsters that worked day and night to oppress the underdogs, Um Umar and her family were just about to lose their lives to get rid of ISIS control?

Anything could happen in Iraq.

However, Um Umar believed that it was just a matter of time before they would be cleared of all the charges. All she needed to prove her son's innocence was a short phone call. But her phone had been confiscated by the checkpoint.

"I think you should call Ali or Karrar." Suhad was suggesting her mother-in-law should contact two men in the Iraqi security forces' deployment in Mosul before the conquest in 2014. Ahmad's family members had risked their lives when they sheltered them for nearly a week before sending them back safely to their families in the south. Their mothers had called Um Umar to thank her for being like a mom to their children, and for saving them from a certain death. They'd been in touch with each other until ISIS prohibited the phone's usage.

Um Umar asked one of the guards if she could have her phone back for making just one call. The guard asked her to retreat from the razor-wire because that was the order. He wasn't authorised to talk to any of those suspect women. Meanwhile, the rumble of shellfire went on.

Um Umar - reunited with her son

Ahmad was liberated about a week later. He, along with other families who had remained in the neighbourhood, decided to sneak out despite the major risks. They had endured hunger and witnessed their neighbours being bombed. Ahmad was provided with crutches and managed to make his way out. After an extensive security check, he was taken to a field hospital, which had probably been set up by humanitarian organisations, to receive proper treatment.

During the liberation of the right side of Mosul, or the western part where the old town is located, liberated families were transported to the town of Hammam al-Alil, about 27 km south of Mosul. A large displacement camp had been erected there to shelter the liberated families. From this point onward, people were finally able to walk freely.

Um Umar's family crossed over the floating bridge to the eastern side of Mosul, which had already been cleared of ISIS. She went to her other son's house. Desperately, they tried to find out what had happened to Ahmad - asking newly liberated people, showing his picture to humanitarian organisations and security forces.

A week later, Ahmad managed to contact his brother from the field hospital. He later said that one of the houses they had used as a shelter was bombed. Luckily, only the upper floor was damaged. The first thing they did when they arrived was block the windows using sacks filled with rubble and sand. No one was hurt, but the experience was terrifying.

The Author's Close Family

The Author's Uncle

Recently, before I finished writing this book, my uncle told me what had happened just days before the battles started. I believe that was in March of 2017, just after the full liberation of the Eastern part of Mosul, on the other side of Tigris River. This is what my uncle remembers:

We were eagerly waiting for the announcement that the battles would finally get started to retake the Western part of Mosul, where the Old Town is. It was a relief to see the Iraqi Flag over the hill soaring in the sky of the Eastern part, just a river between life and death, certainty and unknown. We badly wanted to be liberated though we knew the price of it, we knew it was going to be even harder than the battles of the Eastern part, because all ISIS members had stationed themselves well in the Old Town using inhabitants as human shields. For them, they had to fight to the end, because they had nowhere else to go.

I asked my uncle how ISIS responded to their loss in the Eastern Part of Mosul, especially when they saw how people of Mosul were crying out of happiness to see the Iraqi soldiers taking over their alleys while ISIS fighters would retreat. I had seen on social media that people were cooking Mosuli Kebbi (filled dumplings similar to Polish Pierogi, made of bulgur and stuffed with meat, onions, almonds and flavoured with only black pepper) and Dolma (vine leaves stuffed with meat, rice and other ingredients); and giving them to the Iraqi troops, expressing their gratitude upon starting a new era of trust between Iraqi armed forces and people of Mosul. I asked him if it might have annoyed ISIS seeing such spectacles on TV.

Yes indeed, in the very last days, when they knew that the battles were imminent, they became more frenzied going around the streets keeping an eye on people's activities. One morning, we heard ISIS spokesman calling through the mosque microphone: "All males should head to the closest school immediately."

I thought they might want us to fight for them or simply be killed for fear of us engaging in the Iraqi army when approaching the neighbourhood that had been a stronghold of former policemen. It wasn't wise to stay at home because I knew that death punishment could be the substitute. They had no mercy; they were commissioned to kill people for any reason.

I went to the school, and the moment I entered, I saw all the men in my alley had been crammed in the school yard. Meanwhile, ISIS members had their faces veiled and they were fully equipped, just ready to kill as usual.

I heard the warplanes hovering in the sky. I wished for an airstrike to target us, so things would get messed up and even to be dead by a friendly bomb was easier than living the fear of being recruited or killed by ISIS.

An ISIS member stood up saying: we have a basic checkup. Anyone who hears his name, has to come here for a checkup.

When I heard my name, I went to the desks where they had their laptops. "What do you do in life?" they asked.

"I am just a teacher at school."

"Go there and wait!"

I saw some of the unlucky ones who were taken away. They were the brothers of the fleeing Policemen and soldiers.

The Author's Father

My uncle asked me to talk to my father, because my father also had a story to tell. Right away,
I called my father who was relaxing at home in the evening,
"Hello Dad!"

"How was your day?" he replied. "I just had dinner outside and now I'm chilling at home and watching the social media reels."

"Oh Dad, you became a social media guy after all."

"Not really, just killing some time before going to bed."

"So, Father, can I interrupt your peaceful time with my weird question? You know I have made a book about Mosul and I am about to finish it. I learned from my uncle that you have a story to reveal to the world. This will be a confidential interview, only me and my readers will get to read your story."

"No way, I don't mind telling my story if it will serve your book."

"Yes! So, could you tell me please why ISIS wanted to detain you when men of the neighbourhood were asked to attend ISIS final checkup? (Sorry for bringing up bad memories and having to interrupt your reels on social media)."

This is what my father remembers:

We heard ISIS through the adjacent mosque's speakers asking every man to come to the school, I went and saw your uncle and other neighbours were crammed in the school yard. When I heard them calling my name, I advanced, they asked for my ID like everybody else, I gave my ID.

After a while, the man who was on the computer whispered to his mate, then asked me: "Have you been an officer in the former Iraqi army" (The army that was dissolved upon the US Invasion in 2003)

I answered that I was retired a long time ago in the early 90s for a political issue.

"Yes, we know that but you were willing to return to service after 2003, to the army formed by the US," the ISIS man said.

"Not true, because I wasn't interested in returning to any army."

The man made a phone-call, then said. "We saw that your name on the list of those who made an application to return to the Iraqi army." Clearly, ISIS wanted to screw me.

"I did not," I insisted.

Then they allowed me to go free.

"Oh my god, Dad, that was a close shave."
"Yes, son. I was determined to survive all wars, ISIS and then lately Covid19."

The Author's Close Family is Liberated

My family was finally liberated in February 2017 after a harrowing battle for survival. Despite orders from the enemy to evacuate and move deeper into the city, my family chose to stay and fight for their lives. They refused to be used as human shields by ISIS, a fate suffered by many families in Mosul. Those who were lucky enough to survive hid in one room, avoiding any movement or sound. Sadly, many families were unable to evade detection and met a tragic end.

From Finland, I watched their situation carefully, holding onto a slim glimmer of hope that I may see them again. However, the stream of bad news didn't cease: I heard that an entire family was mistakenly killed by an airstrike targeted at an ISIS sniper who was stationed in one of the houses. Many locals from western Mosul lost their lives while attempting to escape to safety.

The devastating news slowly crept into my neighbourhood and I began to hear about people and families that I knew personally. On social media, I saw pictures of old friends who didn't make it, posted by their relatives who were living outside of Mosul. The constant barrage of bad news was suffocating me, and at that point, I had already lost contact with my family. All I knew was that the battle for liberation had turned my neighbourhood, once known as the valley of stones, into a true valley of destruction. It was in this neighbourhood that the famous picture of a man carrying his daughter and shouting in tears was taken. The cars that had been thrown onto the rooftops of buildings and other savage scenes were reminiscent of a war movie.

I could only connect with my relatives who lived outside Mosul, and we all gazed at the city, yearning for our loved ones to break through the wall of silence and declare their liberation.

News of the battle gradually trickled in, and I learned that several houses in my alley had been bombed, just metres away from where my family was hiding. I couldn't bear the thought that after all these years, their story might end with the last words they said before the battle began: "The battle is closer now, we can hear the dense clashes. We will ditch our phones, and if God wills it, you will hear from us when we have been liberated. Take care and don't worry."

The first night of the battle, I couldn't sleep. I stayed awake, glued to my phone, scouring secret social media pages for news - good or bad - about my family. But there was nothing. All I saw were pictures of my destroyed alley, a sight more horrifying than anything I could have imagined. On the second night, I felt like a castaway, stranded in a desert, desperate to survive. For the first time, I felt lonely, powerless, and desperate.

I turned to social media to share my feelings, hoping to break through the barrier of silence that enveloped my world: "Today, the battle rages on in my neighbourhood, something I have always avoided thinking about. It's the day of truth, the day of confrontation, and I can't bring myself to watch the world news or care about anything beyond Mosul, my neighbourhood, and my family. Despite not being a believer, I find myself wishing and praying, using the old tricks of ancient religions to convince myself in a very primitive way. I think positively to fool reality and mislead the truth, hoping that the shells will fall anywhere except on my family's house.

It's a game we have played secretly for a long time, putting ourselves before difficult options and choosing the best for ourselves, despite the difficulties. It's easier for us to sacrifice ourselves rather than the ones we love, at least in the moment. Maybe it's a kind of disability or defect, a way of shortening our own suffering.

The battle is thousands of miles away, but it feels like fire and bombardment inside myself. While they suffer from the loud voices, I suffer from the scary silence. Silence is an elegant modern death, a content murderer that slides like a snake from the straws to disturb the cattle and disappears after it has stabbed one of them. It's a way of suicide, but a very advanced suicide. Because I live in an advanced country, everything shall happen calmly and end calmly, even the ruthless wars.

In Mosul, they are all crammed in one room, far away from the lights and windows, warming each other against the butchering machines. Here, I feel like a fly stuck in a windowpane or a moth approaching the light and being tossed away. Yes, nature is beautiful beyond the window glass, and life thrives with the upcoming spring out there. But I am still trapped beyond the four seasons, waiting for the gate that will eventually be opened, leading to my awaiting season.

My mother's faith is strong, believing that God will never let them down, at least for the sake of the kids. And my father, the retired officer, is probably now representing all his knowledge about safety he once earned in the army. He knows the boundaries of life, the odour of danger, and the resilience of life. To what extent life could be stretched, but not any further when the house is turned into a trench. He is probably giving instructions to three families crammed in the house, and my mother would obey him without a comment, following what seemed to her an old military speech.

The battle is nearby, missiles passing over the houses, and ISIS fighters knocking and kicking doors, driving families out to use them as human shields when Iraqi forces score an advance to the heart of the city. I am thrilled and afraid, standing on the divided line between things, between happiness and sadness, willingness and unwillingness. It's like a crucial football match, but for me, one ball in the net will end the match forever. The match that never happens twice."

I obtained a photo of my alley from an unknown source, most likely to be linked to ISIS publications during the battles. It shows an ISIS member engaging in clashes with the Iraqi armed troops.

Until that moment, I hadn't realised the power of solidarity. When people began to interact with my post and offer words of support, I felt a sense of comfort and strength that allowed me to keep fighting. One Finnish friend invited me to her home for dinner, drinks, and even a sleepover, providing me with a much-needed respite. These gestures deepened my faith in togetherness and reminded me of the importance of human connection, even when we think we can manage on our own.

On the fifth day, I received word from a relative that my family was still alive, but the situation was growing more dire. The battle was literally taking place in the alleyways of our neighbourhood, and some of our neighbours had been killed, whether by friendly fire or enemy fire. The thought of losing a loved one in the confusion of battle was too much to bear, and I felt grief for those who had been lost.

Seeing pictures of my old neighbourhood on international media was jarring. It was as if the forgotten place had suddenly said "Hello" to the world, illuminated by the flares of war. The images felt surreal, like seeing a teacher at the bazaar instead of in the classroom, or a grandfather in the schoolyard. It was an unusual and disorienting experience.

On Feb 24, 2017, while I was stranded at home, I received messages from my Finnish friends who were gathering to celebrate a winter party held by Katariina – my first female friend in Finland. She was the person who, during my second year in Finland, took my hand and walked me through the Finnish forest. She asked me to repeat the names of early Finnish flowers after her, and later took me to a Finnish sauna to wash off the dust of deserts and tar of wars and be born again in that warm, safe little world.

Katariina didn't know anything about the hell that was razing my soul. She asked me if I would join them and bring my beers.

By that time, good news was flooding in, I heard that the Iraqi army was just several metres away, their vehicles were stationed in the next street. I saw that on social media pictures. I expected my family to contact me any time. I knew it was just a matter of time before someone would bring the announcement of this momentous new phase of my life; the liberation of my family.

My mind was trying to cheer me up by just seeing the positive parts of the story. I behaved as if my family had already been liberated, walking out of the dangerous zone. I thought to myself that this is how human beings would survive the bad; at a certain level of torment, the mind would just take the leadership and activate the autopilot.

I already replied to Katariina, informing her that I would attend her party. After a week of uncertainty, suffering and bitter loneliness, my brain decided to save me from myself. I was powerless to resist or even think reasonably. I stood before the mirror staring at my pale face and withered eyes, my random beard had occupied half of my facial features as a parasitic weed, I went back to my computer and put on the weekend's songs and increased the volume.

The greater part of me was watching the cell-phone awaiting the news. I'd already commenced to shave my beard when the phone buzzed and I just left everything and scooted to see the good news.

Amid the joy of the weekend, and the sudden shower of hope that watered my arid soul, the truth jumped out of my phone to erect as a monster that would dismiss my newborn hopes, smash my tinder dream, and scatter my big wish! That was the hurricane that engulfed me and stripped my day off from the illusions.

"ISIS members broke into the house and now we know nothing about what happened to the family."

I read that phone message and tried to call my cousin who sent it. But he was busy, probably trying to secure a connection with the family. I knew that ISIS members would kill those who didn't obey their orders; the orders of evacuating the houses and marching far from the approaching Iraqi troops.

At that moment I didn't know what to do. Part of me was still clinging onto Katariina's party where I had just intended to go as the happiest man on earth, but a great shadow part of me perched on my chest like the rubble of a devastated city.

Finally, I managed to call my cousin, living in Turkey at that time. He was extremely shocked. He barely said: "They are doomed, they are doomed, all of them!"

In fact, my mind that was trying to assist me couldn't have deceived me more than at that moment. I realised my mind was also giving up. I felt as though a giant black hole had been formed in my soul, swallowing all types of lights and happiness, it was swallowing me, leaving me speechless and paralyzed floating on the nothingness.

The white shaving gel on my chin reminded me of the sparkling foam of the black sea breaking over the shoreline of despair when the waves wash up bodies of drowned migrants who tried to escape from their earthly death, but they didn't know or they didn't want to believe they were heading to a marine death.

Meanwhile, I received a message from Katariina that the party had already started and I should bring some chips with me. I just replied, "Yes, I will."

Perhaps I didn't want to believe that that was the end, I was glad that the black hole of myself couldn't absorb the glimmer of hope that refused to burn off despite all the storms gusting from all directions.

Believe it or not, despite the fact that disaster had been confirmed, and that I was helpless, I still had faith that something good would have to take place.

I wrote to a person I knew from college who knew officers in the liberating troops. I contacted him and told him the story of my family who refused to leave the house, and stayed hidden for a week in waiting for the Iraqi armed troops. He told me that it was a wise decision in the face of so many risks. Yes, he told me I just needed to wait until the Iraqi forces could go and clear their corpses if they were perished or save them if, by a miracle, they were alive.

I really began to wish they'd been killed by an airstrike on the first day, rather than passing through all that suffering that would end up in dismal fate. It was just I felt that it wasn't fair to go through all these frightful nights of waiting and then on the edge of freedom they would perish. Like a sprinter who exerts great effort to overtake the others, then fails just before the finishing line.

However, I thought that with such an honourable attempt, there would be no room to regret. They tried and almost succeeded to reach the shores of freedom but, in war, nothing can be taken for granted. When so many innocent people are falling everywhere and every day, what would make my family exempt from becoming the victims?

They were vulnerable and exposed. I believed that in such a moment one would have nothing except their faith. At that moment, I understood the importance of belief. I realised that faith is the last rope of hope after all ropes had been clipped. In the moment of deep sorrow and despair, I understood from where our religions had begun, I rowed back to the early nations who were exposed in the wilderness countering the elements of nature alone. I could see them escaping a flood or any other disaster, believing that there must be a mighty power that could cease the tragedies from happening. I felt as though I was on a ship wrestling the high waves in the middle of nowhere, no one would hear the passengers while crying for help, except the furious sky. My only comfort was my grandmother who was praying all the time for the safety of the family. My heart started to hear her mumblings that cast peace in the warzone.

Half an hour of fear and deep grief passed before I received another astonishing call from my cousin. He informed me the family was still alive and they had been liberated and transported to the shore of safety.

I couldn't take it in, I had no clue what he was talking about; just a true miracle governed by contradiction happening to me to mock my sorrow and make my demons fade away, just the roller-coaster of life, an acute one.

I learned later that my family was liberated on that evening but not before reaching the summit of fear and despair when members of ISIS broke into the house to have it searched.

My grandmother Mariam told me, "We were all crammed in one room in the depths of the house, doing our best to keep silent and avoid any noise that might turn the attention of the monsters fighting outdoors. They expected all houses in the alley to be empty, so that they would take shelter at any of the houses. We had children, sometimes they would cry, and we would do everything to calm them down. We never let the sewage water leak from the house, we had prepared many barrels and containers to store water and to keep the sewage there."

That evening, ISIS members wanted to take shelter in the house, thinking that my family had left the house a week earlier. They tried to open the door, the members of the family felt that that was their end if they didn't react swiftly.

My two brothers Ali and Taha, were the ones that ISIS would have killed immediately because young people had been the target of ISIS. They might feel pity if they saw only women and children, but not young men who could be recruited by their enemies to strike them from within, in the heart of their proclaimed state and what was once de facto-capital of the Islamic State - Mosul, their pride that they were about to lose with the Iraqi forces attaining significant advances, retaking the city of Mosul, street by street.

There is a small hole dug in the wall that connects my grandfather's house to my father's house. Since we were neighbours that gate had been a nice shortcut between two alleys. The idea of digging such a hole came after we moved to our new house which was joined to my grand-family house. Simply to facilitate our moving to and from smoothly without having to go outdoors, especially on the dangerous evenings, we had a lot of those in Iraq after 2003.

In the time of war, that hole was the enchanted gate that would save my family from evil. Luckily, the gate was dug in the cellar, so it was hard for anyone to guess that cellar was just the end that led to a new beginning.

My family members hurried to that small gate and closed the cellar door.

My grandfather couldn't make it through that hole, because he couldn't bend his back like the others, he is sick and aged, so he took a shelter in the closet, the room in the house was so dark, because before battle, all windows were covered, not only with curtains but with blankets to dim any light and to cut off their contact to the outside world. Probably the contrast between the dark and light clouded the vision of those who came from outside, so they couldn't see small details.

ISIS members doubted that nobody was in the house, so they started to search and yell.

My family could hear them, rampaging through the grandparents' house. They were in horrible fear. My mother had smuggled my two brothers out of the house. She risked her life and went out to stash her sons in the ruins of one of the bombed houses adjoining our abode.

She had successfully accomplished that mission, but on the way back to the family, she saw an ISIS member roaming in the alley. She had to hide until he left, but once she entered the house, she realised that ISIS members could take shelter in the ruins too: what if they saw her two sons there?

Meanwhile, they heard someone yelling and shooting. That was the moment everyone thought that my grandfather had just been killed. They cried and sobbed silently while looking at each other. It was a disaster that struck not only my family, but everyone in Mosul.

At that moment, my mother thought about going out in a bid to reach her sons who were still concealed in the rubble. She realised that that alley was still under the control of ISIS, unlike the alley of my grandfather's house, where glimmers of hope began to show upon the engine's roar of the military vehicles of the Iraqi armed troops.

Probably, that was the reason ISIS broke into the house, just to escape the fire of their opponents.

My uncle had a secret phone, he sent a message while they were trapped in the other house, but he didn't say that my grandfather got killed.

Half an hour later, the spectacle was wrapped in calm, nothing was heard except the suppressed sobbing and the pouring tears.

They knew that the evil had left, then my grandfather's voice pierced the silence: "Come here, they have left!"

More tears welled up, but this time from happiness or just the tears of mixed feelings. Tears are the final window through which the oppressed behold the world of justice and mightiness. It is a realm where abstract and concrete worlds intersect, where invisible sorrows take shape and become visible, emerging in the eyes like clouds that transform into rain to revive desperate pastures.

My grandfather had made it!

Amidst the sudden crescendo of happiness that resurrected the dying hope of surviving that turmoil alive and together, my mother brought her sons back. They had heard ISIS members telling each other that the apostates, in a reference to the Iraqi armed troops, were in the next street.

When my mother looked through the blanket and curtains, she saw Iraqi flags affixed to the military vehicles that were stationed just 100 metres away from where the family was confined.

They decided to go out and make it to the liberator troops. They used my grandmother's white scarf as a banner and walked out, waving the white scarf. It was hard for the Iraqi forces to believe that there were ordinary people still in the neighbourhood.

They ordered them to advance children and women first and then the men, just cautiously and smoothly.

They had them checked and verified and then they transported them to the western edge of the neighbourhood, far from the front-line.

They proceeded to the house of my grandmother's friend, where they received generous hospitality.

Finally, I felt relieved. A great part of my soul was retrieved upon hearing that my family had made it to the Iraqi forces without casualties. I would wrap up an entire week of intense suffering by having my beard erased followed by a warm shower in which I dislodged the dust of worries. I went to Katariina's party and celebrated with my friend my new birthday that was conditioned by the survival of my family.

Interwoven Stories

In the previous chapter, I shared eyewitness accounts of the Liberation. But there were some people living through that perilous time whom I couldn't interview; and others whose story I know but cannot name for reasons of their safety.

This chapter relates the story of Sahar and Taha that treads a delicate line between reality and fiction, weaving together personal narratives with collective memory. Though rooted in real events, the details have been reshaped to protect identities, allowing the work to transcend individual accounts and speak to something larger - something universal.

Sahar and Taha are composite characters - a fusion of people I've known, memories I've carried, cultural echoes, and passing encounters gathered in interviews. Like many families in Mosul who couldn't escape the old city, they remained trapped in a place that had become a sprawling prison - voices of the silenced crying behind the bars of oblivion. They are like a cinematic reel, flickering with images captured from reality. As it rolls forward, new scenes unfold and true stories are revealed.

Sahar and Taha

One family still living in the Old Town on the eve of its liberation were Taha, his wife Sahar and their three children. Earlier in his life, Taha had worked as a primary school teacher of Arabic. He used to write poetry but when the city was occupied by ISIS, he immediately stopped writing anything. His 28-year-old wife, Sahar, didn't like poetry. She always asked him to write something in Arabic, despite the fact that Taha was writing in standard Arabic, but she understood none of his vague texts. In the beginning, she pretended that she loved poetry and Arabic language because it's the language of the holy Quran, she used to say.

Sahar was a widow of a policeman and the mother of two kids. Her late husband got killed in 2009. She had decided to remain single but then she met a teacher of Arabic language at her son's school. He was single, he wrote all his poems for a woman who didn't exist, he didn't even dare to go against the typhoon of his society and try some of the MP3 relationships before marriage. The truth was he didn't know how to handle the fight in bed, because he had never had any adventures, he had always lived within the same social circle, inside the bubble of his dreams. Taha took revenge on all his dreams. His deprivation and lack of self-esteem to appear like the bold man in his poetry – even that part of him was phoney, it was the ghost of Nizar Qabbani who is the poet of woman and freedom in the Arab World who was born and died in the past century.

In June 2014, when ISIS took over the city of Mosul, Taha had lacked the courage to go out and see them roaming the streets. He knew poetry was forbidden, and he also knew that he was the poet of women as his friends used to describe him. If ISIS saw any of his nudity texts, he would be in big trouble. Taha sheltered himself at home most of the time during ISIS control, but gradually, he adapted to the new reality. He started to spend more of his time outside and witnessed most of the carnage that ISIS was doing.

Meanwhile, Sahar bore all the domestic responsibility, and she was secretly working as a tailor from home to keep bread on the table. Whereas Taha had his phone that nobody knew about, using it to get him connected to the outside world. He had always believed that he was born in the wrong country, the country that couldn't have permitted him to live in parallel to the one he used to be on paper. He believed that his wife was too much for him, too practical and outgoing, and more importantly, she couldn't sniff the breezes of civilization blowing from his poems. This is what the situation seemed to be.

He had seen his friends escaping from Mosul one by one. ISIS had strictly prohibited people of Mosul from departing the de-facto Capital of Islamic State. He'd often thought to take the gamble and abscond from that haunted city, but he would evidently think of his friends who were caught, some of them were sent back to Mosul to get what they deserved of punishment, whereas others had been instantly killed at the place. The computer would have the last word: who was going to live and who would be sent to death! By having people's data checked, it would show who was working with the infidel government, and who wasn't. Taha recalled one of the teachers who wanted to flee to Turkey via Syria, but he was sent back as a corpse to his family.

In 2015, Sahar was pregnant. She felt incredibly happy, but Taha did not. All he thought was: the burden grows heavier, and his plan of migration got bogged down. Sahar could have easily believed Taha was a dead stone, a man without feeling, without interaction with reality. The new-born baby didn't change the situation for the better. Taha just became more withdrawn, in denial, because that wasn't the life he'd been dreaming of. Society wanted him to live as a married man.

Sahar - hearing of the start of the liberation Oct 16 2016

"Did you know that we heard on the radio?" Sahar's sister, Manar, asked. "The operations of recapturing the city of Mosul have been declared last night."

"A major military operation to recapture the northern Iraqi city of Mosul was announced by the Prime Minister Haider al-Abadi, a city whose capture by the Islamic State for two years, left the country on the brink of collapse"

"The hour of victory has arrived, the operation to liberate Mosul has begun"

People in Mosul were eagerly waiting for this moment, however they coded it as "The Crescent" in reference to

"The Crescent of Eid" when people would wait until the Crescent of Eid has been observed, so they could celebrate according to the Islamic lunar calendar.

Mosul was completely blocked. It made aid difficult to reach to the locals who had already turned the alarm off. Survival mode had been in place, most of the time, especially in a country like Iraq, plagued with wars, international embargo, and tyrant regimes.

As Sahar stealthily listened to the radio, she couldn't help crying. It could also be a rumour. In a besieged city that had been waiting for hope, for any glimmer of light, misleading news could be part of the situation. People tend to improvise hope, the story that makes them feel good, even though they knew it could be fake, but this is what their ears want to hear.

She and her sister turned on the radio. In what sounded like a whisper, the broadcast leaked out from the BBC Arabic Service: *"Artillery began firing on the city early on Monday, in a long-awaited assault from Kurdish peshmerga, Iraqi government and allied forces. Tanks are now moving towards the city, which has been held by ISIS since 2014. The UN has expressed "extreme concern" for the safety of up to 1.5 million people in the area. The BBC's Orla Guerin, who is with Kurdish forces east of Mosul, says tanks are advancing on the city, throwing up clouds of dust. As the operation began, one Kurdish general told our correspondent: "If I am killed today, I will die happy because I have done something for my people."*

She guessed Taha might have known the news in advance. That could be the reason he was absent since early morning. Perhaps he strolled around the city to gather information to be sent to international news agencies. It was his time to depict what the situation looked like inside Mosul.

In the evening, Sahar turned the radio on again: *The US-led coalition fighting ISIS is backing the assault with air strikes*. "The hour of victory has come," the Iraqi PM, Mr Abadi said. "God willing, we will meet in Mosul to celebrate the liberation and your salvation from Isis (IS) so we can live together once again, all religions united and together we shall defeat Daesh to rebuild this dear city of Mosul," **Quoted from the BBC Arabic Service**

Sahar - discovering husband's secret journalism

Several days before the US-led attack on ISIS, Sahar had been cleaning. She decided to pack the important items in case they needed to leave the house. As she was arranging old books and papers that belonged to Taha, she made an astonishing discovery. Now she knew the reason for her husband being a person who couldn't stay in reality. Her new discovery made her think that Taha wasn't truly the one she'd thought him to be, he had been living a double life. She knew the reason why he was getting up at night…

Her husband wasn't as innocent as he pretended to be. He was the most dangerous man she had ever known, or he could have been just an idiot. Taha had a special phone connected to the internet, he was the eye of the world in Mosul; the witness on whatever was going on. He'd been exposing his life and his family's lives to risk.

Post-2014, ISIS had prohibited cellphones and internet usage in their bid to isolate the city from the outside world. Any connection with those living outside the city of Mosul was taboo and the punishment for those who disobeyed the rule was the death penalty. They had been executing those who were just suspected, ruthlessly.

Sahar had a flashback of the unfortunate moments they had passed through under ISIS. She imagined what could have happened to her family because of her reckless husband. Her new discovery led her to think Taha had been setting up everything from the very moment he pretended he couldn't flee Mosul for fear of getting captured and killed. She thought of the first time, when borders were open, and most endangered people had stampeded to Turkey across Syria. Taha did his best to convince Sahar the situation would be better under the Islamic State, and pretended that he knew from a friend who worked with ISIS that ISIS didn't come to stay, they came to liberate the people of the Sunni cities from the authority of army that had been oppressing and discriminating people based on sectarian reasons.

He did his best to convince her. But still, that didn't stop him being weird, vague, and freakish. He dreamed of living in one of the Western countries.

Sahar trembled while reading what was on his page that he ran from inside Mosul. She saw that he was in touch with the International News Agency. She couldn't read all the inbox on his Facebook page, but one message captured her attention: "We will reach you even if it would be the last day of your life. "We know who you are, and where you live, we know every small detail in your life. The Islamic State has decided to let you work until further notice, then you and your family will be killed, but we will need your services before your death"

Sahar felt horribly intimidated and cast down by seeing that. She went back to the inbox, and it was even more shocking. Oh God, she thought, that was exactly the story I told him about my cousin. He sent it to a publisher in Germany.

She found another astonishing detail – a group of Mosul poets called Free Mosul – was there. Taha had been networking between Mosul artists who were still practising their art secretly. A writer who sent his novel to the publisher last month using a nickname. (At seven in the time of Saturn) short story collection written by Mohammed Talal, a journalist who couldn't leave the city of Mosul. That resulted in him reading all the time and then he came up with a book that went to publication while he was still under siege. He wrote what seemed to be his farewell words to his friends: *The book is now ready. In case I am captured by ISIS, I authorise you to publish that book. I want the world to read my testimony.*

Sahar scrolled through the pages, and found herself falling down a slope of an inspiring story. Its writer, Talal, had authorised her husband to get his book published in case something had happened to him.

Months later, the Eastern part of Mosul was liberated. Probably the writers from the eastern part had stopped contacting her husband. They didn't do a lot due to the bombardment that targeted the five bridges linking the two parts of the city.

Sahar didn't know anything about her relatives and friends, if they were still alive, she couldn't have asked about them even. ISIS members got frenzied, knowing that the battle of their existence was concluded in favour of the liberators.

In the eastern part of Mosul, ISIS relied heavily on explosive cars that were blown up inside residential areas, causing a lot of casualties among civilians.

She crept over to her husband's duffel, hauling it from underneath the clothes, hoping to learn about the situation on the other side of the city. Now the old dark face of the city is the western part, the Old Town, heart of the city, where most people were still trapped. They were just the human shields that ISIS would use to protect itself.

She clicked the screen and inserted the SIM inside the phone. She went to check the inbox, and started to learn more about the situation in Eastern Mosul. She felt intimidated by the news, by the stories being sent to her husband.

Her husband can't have felt his top secret was no longer as hidden as he'd thought over the past months. Sahar had often tried to make him confess. She was stumbling on the topic of people who were sending information and stories from inside Mosul, but he would just change the topic and dismiss what Sahar was trying to extract from him. She was certain that he wouldn't admit it. He would just keep doing what he was doing, thinking no one would even dare to think Taha was that kind of person.

Sahar read stories of how people got liberated, stories already spread on social media. She wondered why they would send the stories to the confined part of the city; these stories of the liberated part.

She didn't wonder for long; the answer came in one of the emails. Taha had the contacts and he was the one who translated everything into English. He was one of the confidential sources in Mosul for international outlets.

She saw a video bearing English subtitles posted on his social media page; she couldn't believe her husband was behind all this. She clicked on the video that went on the play.

Sahar - watching video of Mosul under ISIS

A woman lying on a hospital bed, appeals to the camera:

We are from Al Falah neighbourhood Eastern Mosul. ISIS fighters came to our house, asking us to evacuate the house. We refused to leave our house; we refused to be used as human shields while they were retreating.

Next time, they violated our house and they broke into the kitchen and yelled that we ought to empty the house, otherwise they would have to open fire.

My husband asked them: "What do you want from us! It is our home that we are unwilling to leave."

"The infidel troops are nearing you. They have arrived in this neighbourhood already. The infidel troops are going commit atrocities and rape your daughters", the ISIS members told my husband, trying to change his mind.

My husband said "That is okay with me even if they come."

The ISIS element got furious and said: "I will shoot you if you stay in this house. You understand now?" Then they left.

Afterwards, we locked the doors and we stayed for four days in one room. We couldn't turn the lights on. We couldn't find anything to eat or drink. I fed my children only cookies, four days in a row. However, we were given a big shock by one of ISIS fighters breaking into our house once again, shooting the door to break the locks.

But my husband rushed to see and informed him that we are still in the house.

He said my husband is one of the infidels because he didn't depart from the house. He also accused my husband of collaborating with the Iraqi troops, supplying them with information via mobile phone.

"You are an informant working for them, and we must behead you", he threatened.

I sprinted towards them, begging them not to kill my husband. I told him that we are a peaceful family in this house, and not only my husband over here. "Please come in and you can see! There are only my daughters. We are hiding ourselves here because we have no place to go."

The ISIS fighter said, "If you don't leave the house, I am going to set the house on fire right now."

"Where to go, then?" I responded.

"Go to the adjoining neighbourhood."

Then we went to the other alley and saw many families were detained there. There were four to five families crammed in every house.

On Tuesday, the Iraqi troops finally retook the area. We felt happy and we went out to greet them. They told us that we should stay inside and get the doors locked. Ten minutes later, all the houses started to collapse over us. All the houses in the alley have been devastated. There are still many families under the rubble. No one was able to save them.

I cleared my daughters from the rubble. My sister and her son were both killed.

The woman starts to sob.

The owner of the house who gave us shelter, I saw his head was cut open. And his son was killed too. My husband and I tried to help them, but in vain. The girls were killed.

The Iraqi soldiers came in to save us. They were trying to evacuate us from the house. The facade of the house got razed by the fire. They opened a channel from the rear part of the house for us to get out. I carried my sisters in the hope of saving them. But there were two other corpses still there.

The woman cries intensely and turns to confront the camera lens.

I deliver this message to the families in my neighbourhood: Go to my house, there are our important documents and our money in a red bag. Please keep them safe. For those who can go to my old house, I beg them to take our belongings as a deposit until we return. Even though that house was devastated.

I appeal to the fine people. Close the doors if our neighbourhood has been liberated. Get all the doors locked. Because we left our houses with opened doors. ISIS asked us not to close any doors before leaving the houses. Otherwise, they were going to open fire.

I want to address my brother and sister who live in the area which is still under the control of ISIS. I tell you via this channel that my daughters and I got injured. Don't worry! We are still alive, at least. Our sister Wafah and her son passed away

The woman wipes her tears.

May god be merciful to them! May god be with us here! Let me send a message to those families who are still controlled by ISIS. I advise you to take the back of the house. Stay as far as you can from the facade of the house! Because ISIS blows up a car at any time on the street. ISIS doesn't care for civilians. I convey this message to every family in Mosul whose neighbourhoods are still in the grip of ISIS. I assert that it is important for everybody to stay at home.

If you want to greet the Iraqi troops, just do it quickly. Then you should return to the rear room of the house, far away from the street. Don't make the same mistake we did. We stayed in the middle of the house, close to the street and windows.

Oh, locals of Mosul, try to avoid being close to the outside, then your chance of survival is better in case a car bomb goes off in the street.

May God bless you! People of Mosul, you are going to see hard days, as never before. May God bless you! The Iraqi forces have helped us a lot (*Iraqi Special Operations Forces*). The soldier was carrying my daughter. He told me, "Don't be afraid, you are like my sister."

He even tried to save my sister before her death. They aided the boy but it didn't work out.

The armed forces have gotten a number of casualties, I feel sorry for them because of the car bomb. But they kept on assisting their victims and the civilians alike. May god bless the Iraqi army Inshallah!

The woman appeals to the TV camera.

I just ask you to do me a favour. My two daughters were gravely wounded and they are in a serious state. Shahid and Zahraa are in danger; their injuries are so serious. I appeal to you to find a way to take them to good healthcare because they are in danger.

Despite having injuries in my legs and head, I still have the strength to take care of my husband and daughters. God is giving me power for the sake of my family. Just I beg you to save my daughters' lives.

The woman's appeal is interrupted by a wave of crying)

There is a private hospital here that would be good for them. I heard from people. Here in this hospital the staff is doing what it can do and I am grateful to them but still I need to find a way to save my two daughters' lives.

Even the doctors here said that the private hospital could be better because this hospital is very crowded. The money that I have might have gotten burnt. I seek the chance to find a way to pay the fees of a private hospital in case we go there."

The woman starts to lament again.)

Sahar - implications of Taha's secret journalism

Watching this video, Sahar's eyes were drowning in tears. Her heart was full of sorrow, her soul haunted by fears of the upcoming battle. She knew it was imminent, just a matter of time before the Iraqi armed forces declared the second round of the fighting, to retake the other half of the city that ISIS had been centralised in.

Why not? It is the Old Town where the first mosque was built, with the old churches and vibrant heart of the town. Sahar thought to herself that people in the Old Town were running out of food. They couldn't last for long. People in the Western part of the city were envious of those who got liberated beyond the River Tigris. But they had no idea what price they paid for their freedom. No doubt, they paid from their blood, their properties and their souls that a great part of it was still trapped under rubble. Yes, people get out of wars, they think the battles have ended. Indeed, the inner battles need a long while to end. Those battles are the consuming ones, while serenity is the fuel. It is like a fight between the past and the present, between the elements of nature over the mountains. Sahar thought that when someone cut off the river, the water would need time to wash out, however, the river would find another stream into the fragile soil. This is how we are impacted by outside events, even after their actual end, they keep flowing inside us, through the most vulnerable part of us.

She was trying to go through other stories, but there was a knock at the door. She put everything in order, ejected the SIM and crammed the duffel underneath the clothes. It was their neighbour Buthaina who came in. She couldn't tell anything to anyone, not even to her family. What she knew could lead them to a disastrous end.

In the evening Taha came, asking if she knew something about Buthaina's life. He thought that Buthaina's story was worthy and needed to be told to the world. But he couldn't say that explicitly to his wife. He thought his wife was separate from what he was doing. He didn't know that she knew everything about him.

Sahar wanted Buthaina to tell her story, but she didn't want to ask her directly. She thought that one day, when the situation permits, Buthaina would release her grief. Human beings need to share, when the magnitude of the sorrow becomes larger than their hearts.

The next day Sahar waited eagerly for her husband to leave, because she'd caught sight the story of the writer, Muhammad Talal, the full version of the story he had sent to Taha.

Muhammad Talal - a writer secretly in touch with Taha

My name is Muhammad Talal, I am 30 years old. I was working at the radio station when Mosul was occupied by ISIS in 2014, I couldn't have left the city, I just sought to stay at home. At first, ISIS didn't intercept me, they probably hadn't gotten the information that I was working at the radio station. I witnessed them arresting my colleagues who had stayed in Mosul. I couldn't have left the alley. I stayed at home all the time, sometimes I would dwell at my friend's place living in the same neighbourhood.

Once, while I was hanging out with my friend at his place, there was a knock at the door at 2 am. My friend went to see who was knocking on the door. One of the neighbours was there saying: "If Mohammad is here, tell him not to go back home tonight because the Islamic State broke into his home, asking for him, and they are now waiting there."

They had been waiting for me to return home for more than an hour. That night I just couldn't go back home; I stayed at my friend's place. Next day, we staged a story in case they came again, claiming that I was not in Mosul that time. My brother told them that I wasn't there.

"Where is Muhammad?" asked one of the ISIS Security members belonging to Security Squad, the most feared division of ISIS in Mosul that time.

Next day they waited at my house to debrief me. My brother informed them that I was escorting my aunt to Baghdad. My aunt went to work out her retirement salary there.

"Why didn't you tell us about it yesterday?" another ISIS member barked.

My mother's voice rose, from behind her veil: "Mustafa was afraid to tell you about it yesterday because he thought it could've enraged you even more."

One the third occasion, they showed up asking to talk with my father. "Do you have an idea where your son has been working?"

"Yes, I pretty much know he had been working in the Municipality of Mosul." My father pretended he didn't know about my job at the radio station.

I truly had to resign from radio and the TV just a few months before the conquest due to the deterioration of the security circumstances that preceded the ominous day.

"We knew that he had worked in the Municipality of Mosul", one of them said.

"What about his prior job?" Another member asked, watching my father's face.

"I have no idea what he did", my father replied.

"How is it possible for you as a father that you don't know what your son has been doing!" the ISIS member responded while his face went sober.

"Your son had been working in a radio station TV affiliated to the local government in Mosul", one of them said.

"Now, what do you want from him?" my father asked.

"We just need to ask him for simple things," the ISIS members asked, trying to lure my father to reveal where I was.

"He is not here, he has accompanied his aunt to Baghdad, he obtained a legal permission from the Islamic State to leave the city."

I went to my grandmother's house in a different neighbourhood called Al-Sukkar. I kept myself distant from any eyes. Only once, when I had to leave the house for the dentist, I was laid on the cushion, hiding myself as much as I could. Luckily the journey in the car was short. I had to have four teeth filled in just one day. I couldn't leave the house again, so I made the most of the time being outside. My aunt sat in the front seat; in the meantime, I was lying on the rear cushion.

That was the only time I was outside. From then on, I kept myself stored inside, confined like vintage wine in the jar of time. My ideas ripened, my thoughts grew, and I had to grow in accordance with my experience.

The rumour had been disseminated in the neighbourhood that Muhammad Talal had fled to Turkey. That was a good one!

One month after my disappearance, ISIS members violated my house in a barbaric way, shouting and cursing. My mother repelled them. Their tantrum increased after hearing my mother say, "We have told you that he is not here, we couldn't have controlled his mobility."

"We have checked on him", they said. "He didn't obtain any legal permission to leave the city of Mosul."

In December 2014, ISIS had issued a resolution barring the locals from departing from the city of Mosul without having a legal excuse issued by the Islamic Court for a period not exceeding 10 days with the existence of a sponsor that guarantees the return of the traveller.

My mother broke her silence and began yelling out of the depths of her rage and indignation.

Meanwhile, I started to download books, novels, philosophy, social studies, and various fields. Luckily, I had done that before the internet went offline. I had a musical stringed instrument called an Oud. I asked my family to bring it when they come to visit me.

Muhammad Talal - ISIS persecuting musicians

ISIS went after musicians, forcing them to refrain from what ISIS called "Satan's Flutes." In the summer of 2014, ISIS had posted a video on their platform showing a bonfire encircled with locals, while an ISIS Sheikh "preacher" would deliver a sermon regarding "Satan's Flutes that rot the souls and thicken the hearts, far from God.".

ISIS members would toss musical instruments into that fire. All musicians were asked to conduct a repentance, pledging not to do that sin again.

Since 2003, it hadn't been easy to carry a musical instrument in its explicit form for fear of the growing number of the extremist armed groups in the city. But people didn't surrender. Musical lessons were given secretly and instruments were carried, wrapped with a big bag, making it look like everything but a musical instrument.

In Al-Dawassa neighbourhood, adjoining the governmental council of Nineveh, the musical shops were few in number compared to before 2003. Most of the shops had abandoned the career for fear of being targeted by the extremists.

Al-Dawassa neighbourhood was the safest area for police members and those what the extremists call the perverts. Guess what? Despite the multiple times "Ibin Tuubia" liquor store was targeted. It never closed its small window set in the armoured wall, which nourished a crucial part of life on that gloomy taboo-filled era.

Some of the police members who felt desperate, whose lives were on the verge of being snuffed out, a large number of them, needed to visit "Ibin Tuubia" when their duty was called off, heading home, or to a safe spot adjacent to one police station by the Tigris under what is called the "Fifth bridge". The lack of Music and liquor in the city indicated that Mosul was at its lowest level of freedom. In June 2014, when the new authority materialised as the Islamic State took control of the city, "Ibin Tuubia" vanished, and the remnants of the musical shops were shut down.

So, during ISIS time, it was a big sin to carry a musical instrument in the capital of the so-called Islamic State. My family bided their time for the right chance to smuggle my instrument to the other neighbourhood where I lived isolated from the outside world.

My solitude had given me plenty of time to ponder and to dive into the depths of myself and extract the pearl of creativity. I began to transform my fear, thoughts, and wishes into a book.

I wasn't sure if I would be able to make it until the city was liberated. I wrote a letter to one friend who handed over the letter to another friend stating: "This is my book, if something happened to me, I would entitle you to publicise the book."

My friend keeps that letter; it makes him cry every time he unfolds it.

Back then, my life was boring, full of bleak despair. When I woke up in the morning, I faced the same folks, my grandmother and my aunt with her spouse who didn't have children.

I couldn't go outside. I had nothing to do except read.

I would have my breakfast in the morning and thereafter I would open my iPad and tap the screen and swipe the pages of the books I'd downloaded.

I had been reading all types of books throughout my waking hours, until I had what felt to be like a saturation of reading.

Then I started to write, I had already had a story-collection I used to post on social media before the time of ISIS. I reverted to those stories, developing them, inserting new characters and I added new stories based on what I'd been passing through.

I wrote a book, I chose a title and prologue, I got it ready. I entitled the book "Seven O'clock Saturn's Time." *"During regular wars, we'd been living a luxurious life; at least we could hear the siren and get ready before the raid, our senses would get ready to fear, during ISIS we'd lost such bliss of getting ready before the raid."* (A quote from the book.)

The green graveyard in the US "Arlington National Cemetery" had inspired me to bring out a sarcastic aspect of the cemeteries in Iraq that look frightening and dismal, full of thorns and dunes.

The protagonist of that story is a person who lived next to the cemetery in Mosul who used to hang out with his friends there, once while he sat among the dudes there, he eyed the arid perimeter and exclaimed: *"In Turkey, the graveyards are green, as if they were national parks, one would feel comfortable to die there. Unlike our cemeteries that are bleak and miserable!"*

Then the war of liberation would escalate, and the death rate would peak, a mortar round would slam him dead. Due to the dense bombings, his family couldn't have buried him in that cemetery adjoining his abode, they would have to bury him in the green garden of the house.

His dream came true! The man had been wishing to be buried somewhere covered with lawn and green. That was the first story of the book.

When I wrote that book, I wasn't limited by time, one of the stories took me only one hour. On the other hand, some of the stories would take several days. I still have some of the unfinished stories unpublished till now.

No one knew I had been writing that book, except that one friend who received my letter, he'd been the only human who knew of my writing activism at that time. I had been awry; I didn't want to burden other people with my secrets.

Before I became wanted by ISIS, I had the chance to wander in the city, watching carefully what was going on. I was able to depict those mental images through my writings.

When ISIS took control over the city in 2014, they couldn't have discovered that I was working in TV and Radio. I walked free in the city for more than a year. However, I was careful, because I witnessed ISIS's brutal way in dealing with locals. I saw how ISIS gradually started to get stricter after they'd dominated everything. I knew that at any moment one could be captured for any reason. I knew that if ISIS had checked on me earlier, they would've learned that I was wanted, it was just a matter of time.

Once, while I was in a taxi, out of nowhere an ISIS checkpoint was erected on the road, intercepting locals, probing their identities. At the time, I was on the way to visit my aunt.

An ISIS member stared at my beard. "Brother, you know that trimming of the beard is forbidden?"

"I am sorry, I won't do that again." I replied, hoping he'd let me go. If he asked for my ID, and typed my name into the computer, I would've been in big trouble.

"Get out of the car and go to that group of guys who are in the van," the taxi driver told me. Then the taxi roared off, vanishing along the highway.

I knew they would take me to one of their stations with all those guys who were seized in the van. There, I would be checked carefully. The luckiest ones would be just lashed 70 times and released, while people like me would never go back home.

I had no way out, only to trudge to the van, I thought to myself that I am dead already, just a matter of time before they reach their destination and check our names, history, and connections.

I looked around, I saw that ISIS members were busy checking on other folks, I thought oh man, this is your chance! ISIS members knew that no one would have the courage to disobey their rules. They knew that even if they didn't watch the van, none of those vulnerable guys had the guts to jump out of the van and flee. However, they forgot the desperate ones like me who had no other options left, would take advantage of any slim chance. I smoothly jumped out of the van, and walked away, denying myself and the situation. I walked normally, as though nothing had happened. I strolled as if I was another person until I was far from the checkpoints. I took a taxi and resumed my journey.

If I had gone with them, I knew I would not show up again. First thing they would do, they would check my name on the computer, they had inherited all the necessary information and data from the government who fled in June 2014.

Muhammad Talal - ISIS targeting journalists

From 2003 until 2014, the city of Mosul had lost more than 60 journalists and those who worked in the media. The so-called "Islamic State" that had been strangling the city of Mosul killed Iraqi Security personnel, artists, journalists, and the informants who worked for the US or the Iraqi Forces. Journalists were targeted intensely; the number of journalists killed in Mosul was the highest in the world.

"Islamic State" or according to the locals "the guys, the group, the state" referred to the hidden enemy that appeared in the city in the form of car bombs, side-road bombs, suicide attackers, and assassin operations.

Maher Al Mulla, was a 19-year-old, who lived in one of the hotspots of the city: eastern Mosul, a neighbourhood known to be full of the hidden enemy. He started his new job as a cleaner in one of the local TV channels in Mosul. He was studying and hoping to be a cameraman in the future, he escorted the reporters twice to see how they worked on the ground. A week later he was killed in his neighbourhood, leaving his diary: *"A month ago, I started as a cleaner. Today I had the chance to accompany the reporters, tomorrow I will hold the camera, never give up!"*

That was in the sad diary left neglected on the table near his bed. He had been staying in one of the caravans that was placed in a well-guarded area that seemed, from outside, like a military barracks, where the transmitter was gushing from, the main building of the TV in Mosul.

Reporters and TV presenters and most of those who worked behind the razor-wires and the thick walls of concrete, usually stayed for months confined in their workplace, they might sneak to see their families on arranged rides preceded by high security precautions. Despite them being careful not to be seen outside, on many unfortunate occasions one of the Islamic State's snitches heard from someone that their target was off duty.

In 2010, a new reporter who was also a new face on TV commenced work as a presenter. His show revolved around the history of the mosques in Mosul, something that had nothing to do with the government and entertainment. He was a father of five daughters, who loved his career and found it a humble source of income to provide for his family.

In the past, the family had owned an old store of spices and perfumes at the historical covered-market of "Bab-Al-Sarai" where the professions are often inherited from father to son. Whereas after the father passed away, his sons couldn't have steered that career as before, a simple dispute led them eventually to decide they should sell the shop.

"The ship will sink when there is more than one captain" the reporter used to say, justifying abandoning the career from which the family earned their fame "The family of perfumier." It was as though renouncing the career of the ancestors was a sin under the ceiling of the traditional market in Mosul.

Soon, his sin would cost him a lot, and this new ship would rampage, ramming into the storm in the form of one man who knocked on his door in the evening. "Is your dad here, I am his friend from work?" the stranger said. The reporter gazed into the alleged friend's face, but no friendship seeped out of his image. The stranger asked him to advance a few steps, away his daughter who was still watching from behind the door. Then, as two men passed by, a bullet slammed into the reporter's head. Only the scent of his memory has stayed to narrate his story with such a wistful end.

Between 2009-2014, being a journalist was even more dangerous than being a policeman.

In 2010, Mazen Al-Baghdadi the youngest TV presenter and podcaster left his guitar silent and lonely after a group of men, pretending they were from Military Intelligence, wanted to ask him about a few things. Having penetrated his house, they killed him in front of his father, mother and siblings, leaving him rigid while his blood kept blooming fluffily like his beautiful dreams. He was killed in a neighbourhood bordered from the north by the military base of the second division that allegedly described themselves "the wall of the city" They couldn't even make a wall to protect one national living less than two km from their base.

In 2011, Ghazwan Anas, the well-known TV presenter of entertainment's shows, was killed in Ramadan at his house, in front of his parents and wife who rushed to stand before her husband, to prevent his death. She was wounded, while her husband, the man of the brilliant smile, fell dead. His two-year daughter burst into a horrible cry, then silence wrapped the scene forever. The security checkpoint of the Iraqi Security wasn't far from the spectacle of homicide.

In 2013, Nawras, the significant female journalist, who had been one of the youngest and the earliest media female faces operating in Mosul, had her house violated by armed men who killed the sole daughter who lived only with her mom, the father being a martyr in the war. As always, the Iraqi Security Forces would claim that they had apprehended the perpetrators, but in fact, most of the locals knew that those who would appear in TV capture were only ordinary people brought forcibly to bear the crime.

The hidden enemy was exerting pressure on the city, while the Iraqi Forces stood paralyzed to repel the killing-machines rampaging on the streets, markets, even what was supposed to be inviolate: places such as universities and sites of worship.

Everything in me changed. I became another person, my interests, thoughts and perspective on life changed. If I were to reveal my new interests, you would be surprised: I started to care about animals more than humans. The other interest could sound weird, but it has been a pleasure for me since I started to learn about "astronomy." It contributed to creating a new perception of the way I look at the world; I began forming a more distant view. Imagine, I paid two thousand dollars for a telescope to watch the stars.

Poem: Looking for interstellar home

If they encircled my city,
I still have the river and the forest
If they strangled the river and burnt the forest,
I still have the house garden quartering me.
If they bombed the house,
I will sit on the rubble to watch the night sky
There must be a magnanimous home resembling me
There must be a home in which the Oud's Strings extend
instead of the razor-wires
There must be a home in which they practise sliding the bows
on the necks of instruments,
instead of sliding the knives on the throats of musicians.
There must be home in one of those brilliant bubbles
where rain is made of water, nothing else,
where shower is made of water, not of blood
where streams sing for hope while they flow
Where lovers cannot be hurled by bricks
They are flung by the chamomile
There must be a crevice in the wall of the siege
There must be a safe corridor amidst the bombs and rounds:
a short path leading to distant homes slung in the sky.

Ahmed Zaidan

Muhammad Talal - whether to leave Mosul

I became increasingly apathetic and hard-hearted somehow. I transformed into a different person when I began to dive into astronomy, observing planets and stars. I've formed a new perspective on life. I feel I am just coexisting with the actual world, but I don't think that I belong to it.

I always had hope. Amidst the crisis, I felt that one day this would come to an end. I contacted ICORN – an independent organisation of cities and regions offering shelter to writers and artists at risk, advancing freedom of expression, defending democratic values and promoting international solidarity – they were ready to hear me, I posed my problems, they responded very well, opening the space of conducting a dialogue with them discussing my situation, until I received a letter from them informing me that I was accepted as a writer guest and the city was also selected.

I received that letter right away after liberation; the situation was still hectic and nothing was guaranteed, the city was totally devastated.

Should I leave the country; my family, and save myself? That was a hard question to which I couldn't find a suitable answer until now.

I was concerned about how to start from the beginning in a foreign country, to learn another language and having to struggle with the obstacles that strangers have to counter.

In Mosul, I've built something, it is not easy to renounce it. On the other hand, the deterioration of security, and violation of human rights were one of the most distinctive characteristics I used to see almost every day.

In crisis and fear, emotions die, you know that

The area where I lived was teeming with houses lived in by ISIS families. That neighbourhood was adjacent to the university, during the time of ISIS, many of the university personnel had to leave the city, after the university was shut down. ISIS members were seizing the empty houses. They let their families live in them.

So that area was under dense bombardment. I was psychologically devastated, especially when witnessing the pillars of smoke escalating from my neighbourhood. We lost connection with everybody; we didn't have a clue what was going on. There were nights I couldn't sleep from wondering all the time: what if my family's house or one of the beloved ones' houses got bombed.

My family sometimes had the chance to visit me secretly, they wouldn't be able to take the usual route to the neighbourhood where I had been living for fear of getting traced by ISIS. They would visit multiple neighbourhoods before finding the way to my cell. They used to visit me once a week approximately.

I decided to go back to my family's house, whatever happened, or that they should come to live at my grandmother's house. They finally concluded that they must move to live at my grandmother's house. The neighbour asked their daughter to live at our house after the evacuation. ISIS members were confiscating empty houses.

Having my family living with me at the same house helped me a lot. My psychological state improved in a remarkable way.

But that didn't mean there was no risk anymore. I let my beard grow longer, and I shaved my head, just as precautionary techniques in case they searched the houses of the neighbourhood, just to avoid any kind of problems in case they saw my beard trimmed.

I collected all my documents, visual and audio materials, memory cards and everything that could denote who I was, wrapped them well and buried them in the garden of the house.

I had lost my musical instruments; the violin and oud. They were destroyed because I'd hidden them in a damp room at my grandmother's house.

I concealed everything in a bid to minimise the danger behind the door. I knew that if they had to search the house, they would know who I was, without having to check any documents. ISIS had very strong intelligence, it was frightening. They reminded me of the intelligence services of the previous regime of Saddam.

For example, in my neighbourhood there was someone who was selling cigarettes secretly, all of a sudden, they popped up and arrested him.

Sahar - discovering more of Taha's secrets

Next, Sahar went through some of the emails, she noticed that her husband had sent emails in English language, that thing that she didn't know about him, she thought that he couldn't speak English, like many teachers of Arabic language.

She started to understand. When Taha used to spend time away from bed, claiming that he was in the toilet, he was writing there, he was practising his role being a hero again, but this time, a hero from a distance behind the screen, he identified himself as the "The Eye."

What Sahar had already read made her nervous. Would she face her husband with her new discovery? She just left everything and started to ponder that her husband was deceiving her or he had been too cautious, he didn't want her being an accomplice in the crime if ISIS had arrested him. Just he wanted to keep her away from his world, the world that could have cost her to lose her world, family, dreams of living a life without ISIS. She could have ended up in the hole of the abyss "Kassfah" where ISIS used to dump their victims.

In August 2015, ISIS killed 2070 of its detainees on charges linked to them having been working with the Iraqi government before the conquest, and then the victims were dumped into the hole of the abyss located south of the city. The families of the victims flooded the hospitals searching for the corpses but they received none of their bodies. The victims were listed in a paper affixed to the door of the morgue. Yes, that was a disastrous tragedy. Despite the fact ISIS had promised safety to those who had worked with the Iraqi government, on condition they submitted a formal repentance, most of the prior employees swarmed the mosques, filling the forms that ISIS handed to them. Former security members were required to give back their weapons or an equal sum in case the gun was lost.

Sahar pictured the spectacle in her mind's eye. Those poor ex-police officers who hadn't had the chance to flee, they just believed that ISIS would leave them living peacefully as it had claimed the first days after its takeover of the city of Mosul.

Sahar thought of her cousin who had been a police officer, and the other cousin who's "working" with the bad guys; how the ISIS cousin had lured his family members who'd run to Erbil the day of conquest. The ISIS man went to tell his aunt her son would be safe if he chose to return to Mosul. After his return, ISIS arrested him to conduct a basic inquiry, but he never came back.

Sahar was certain more than ever that ISIS elements would be loyal to their Islamic State because it was more than a state for them, it was a dream incarnated in the power being imposed on millions of people. The loyalty to the Islamic State paralleled the loyalty to God, and God is something closer than the vein according to the Islamic teachings, but ISIS elements were keen on slitting the throats of Muslims. Often, it was impossible for ISIS members to cheat, because it was not only God who was watching, their colleagues were watching as well; their state had been their last vessel. They knew whether to die together or to live in fear together. They knew that beyond the borders of their alleged state, death penalties and avenge were waiting for them. Even inside the state, they knew that it was a matter of time before the Iraqi forces would wage a large-scale offensive to retake the city of Mosul, they knew that families of the victims would not let this go in the air, no one would get away with it. They had caused pain to so many people, and the day of judgement would come sooner or later, but it would come, on which they would be condemned, badly.

ISIS men from the Wadi Hajar neighbourhood had informed on all those who seemed to have abhorred the Islamic State, furthermore, even the police that had submitted a formal repentance were arrested, all in what seemed to be a large-scale campaign, the detainees were thought to have been killed and dumped into the hole of death in southern Mosul.

Sahar thought to herself that her husband had also been doing a heroic action, he'd been fully engaged in what was going on, although that didn't happen on a domestic level, that happened on a global level.

Everything here is a death certificate. More dangerous than all the missiles that had been launched on ISIS. After 2014, the first batch to be captured and killed was the batch of journalists and liberal publishers; everyone had to deal with the media in any form.

Between 2003 and 2014, more than 60 journalists were killed in the city of Mosul.

That was the most dangerous spot in the world.

Sahar read and watched a poetry film that was made just months ago and sent to her husband Taha, material that seemed ready to get published right away after liberation.

Sahar - watching a secret poetry film

The poet was trying to get out of the city; ISIS had chased the car he was in with his family. They had driven 60 km Western Mosul penetrating the vast desert into Syria, bidding to get to Turkey. As the car roared along the highway, an ISIS checkpoint appeared out of the blue.

"Where are you heading to?" one of the fighters asked.

"We are visiting a relative who lives at the border," the driver answered, trying to convince ISIS they were not going to slip out.

In a suspicious step, ISIS fighters allowed the car to go on. The poet didn't feel good about it, nor did the driver. It didn't seem like ISIS would make it so easy for people to pass without having them checked well.

A few kilometres past the checkpoint, the driver observed a car following them from a distance. He steered his car onto a rural road, arousing a cloud of the wild sand to obscure the car. He had to drive like crazy aiming for one of the villages where he knew someone living close by. They knew that ISIS might come and check on them. They also knew that people out of fear could collaborate with ISIS in case they knew where they were hiding. The driver decided to shelter in one of the deserted barns designated for the cattle of peoples living in the adjoining residential areas.

They had to stay three days before they were able to secure the way back to Mosul.

It wasn't easy to confide in even one's relative or friends, because at any time they could be arrested and interrogated by ISIS who would extract what the people had decided to hide, but ISIS elements knew how to extract secrets from the people, by all tools of torture.

Sahar sunk her chin into her chest and closed her eyes to catch a deep breath: Do I always have to end up with adventurous men, every time? she asked herself.

Perhaps, she was attracted to that kind of men, she was a pretty tough woman; one that endured the hardest part of life. She knew how to deal with life, to what extent life would allow someone to go, and most importantly, where the dangerous zones were situated, and where the limit, the border between death and life, sorrow, happiness lay!

People like Taha weren't experienced enough. They could go wild in no time. They wouldn't go gradually in the process of change, but might take very long leaps without being certain where to put their feet next. Their life could be a gamble.

Probably Taha had found himself in what he was doing. Eyes of the world, writers, journalists, even politicians were waiting for him to post a picture from inside a city no, it didn't cost Taha much more than seconds to station himself where he knew he would never be spotted and could snap the phone from his secret pocket in his pumped jacket, and he would finish the job in one click.

ISIS had a sophisticated visual strategy, because they knew that the atrocities that people see would always be stuck their mind, in many cases, the carnages that ISIS had implemented on its victims, such as burning them alive and tossing them from a high tower block, all these bloody footages were meant not to terrify the victims who were going to die regardless of the way, it mostly worked to deter the locals.

One of the detainees narrated the story of Jasim, who worked as a policeman before the conquest. When ISIS took over the city of Mosul in 2014, it demanded all security members from Mosul attend to submit a formal repentance and hand over their weapon.

Jasim just didn't take ISIS strict policy seriously; he didn't beg pardon for remission and a formal certificate of repentance. He also didn't have any proof that he had handed over his weapon.

After the deadline that ISIS scheduled, they aimed for his house, but he managed to escape, he had been dwelling at his uncle's house for days. When ISIS elements broke into his uncle's house, they couldn't find him. They left, but not alone, they arrested his uncle instead. ISIS knew that Jasim had been there because they obtained a classified report about Jasim and his family.

When the uncle denied that Jasim was at his place, they punched him in the face, and vowed to slaughter him like a sheep tonight if Jasim didn't show up in two hours. The man instantly conceded that Jasim was in the house; the house of the uncle, but he was hiding in a secret small room on the roof of the house. So, the uncle had been released, and then they set up a plan with him to lure his nephew to the trap.

Jasim has told this story to one of the detainees who hadn't been proven guilty, he walked out to narrate the untold story of Jasim to the world. They brought Jasim in the late afternoon, he couldn't speak, he was shivering all the time, then he started to pray.

At night, he couldn't lie in bed. "Even if you know you will die, you should take some rest," one of the other detainees tried to calm him down.

Then in the early morning, the door slid open. A guard approached him while he was leaning against the wall, he couldn't have helped himself to stand. The guard gave Jasim an energy drink hoping that it could help him to walk. Two beefy guards lifted Jasim and escorted the unlucky man to his final destination.

Jasim was gone forever. No doubt they took him to the hole of death, to be executed on its edge, and dumped into the dark depths, where the stench of death penetrates the souls of the new arrivals.

The story of Jasim came to prove the brutality of ISIS that people of Mosul knew about.

Was Taha the chief informant in Mosul, the one about whom ISIS had allocated a big reward? What she saw was telling her that yes, he was even more dangerous.

Sahar gazed into the open drawer and saw what seemed to be sophisticated recording equipment. Her trembling hands probed the audio device. "Friday Sermons" jumped out of the device, from which one could enter the impish realms, where ISIS were addressing people as though it was the Middle Ages:

"I hereby say that the Islamic State will march until conquering Rome from which we will not stop until making everyone submit to the divine law of Sharia. I see it coming closer than ever. You need to rely on God only and to work, because God has pledged to assist those who persistently keep working while relying upon Him, and we have relied. We shall not stop the struggle; we shall not fail in the exam. O Muslims, this is the Islamic State erected in Mosul, the first step and the last chance for this nation to spread with an illuminating Quran and deterring sword the religion of Allah on earth who had certified all the humans before their births that they are Muslims, so no way that their parents to strip their right of being Muslim from them."

Sahar was thoughtful, recalling when Taha suddenly decided to pray and go to the mosques on every Friday. She had kept warning him not to pray at the mosques for fear of the airstrikes that were imminent at any time. But he wouldn't stay home, telling her, instead, that praying at the mosques has double the rewards of praying at home.

Sahar couldn't have prevented him from going every Friday to the mosque. But also, one thing in particular had caught her attention. After the Friday Sermon, Taha would ask Sahar to give him some privacy. He'd been telling her that he needed "Spiritual Isolation" to get fused with himself, connected to the different worlds, so he would become a better human, free of anxiety.

Now she realised that Taha hadn't been pretending - he had wanted to be connected to multiple worlds, to be himself, the self that rekindled the wick of the life he had been dreaming of.

Saha heard her husband's footsteps in the yard. She had to stop searching through what was on his device. Swiftly, she slipped the duffle into the drawer underneath Tala's tunics and pretended that she was lying on the bed.

Sahar - confronting Taha about his secrets

In the evening Taha showed up. "Where have you been the whole day?" she asked him, hoping that he would finally reveal his hidden self to his second half, the loving wife.

"Have you heard what is happening now in the Eastern part of the city?"

But he wasn't ready to reveal the truth to his wife. She started to worry her husband's madness could cast a shadow not only over him, but over every member of the family.

"Taha, for the last time, I will ask you about what you are hiding from me? I am your wife, did you forget? We have gone through everything together.

"I have stood against everyone just for your sake. I have been patient the whole time, waiting for the chance or the right time you may share with me your unseen part, if there will be a right time ever. I think now we are aligned with the same shared destiny; whether to live together or to die together. Think about the kids, our family please. You cannot pretend that you are alone. Your prior life no longer exists. The things you are doing are dangerous. I know you will just keep telling me different stories, yes, and you expect me to believe you again and again, but not anymore, Taha. I'm fed up, I need to hear it from you for God's sake."

Taha's eyes widened, and his facial features went sober, as though his hidden self was awakened by his wife's words. He thought that he was confronted by the truth, no way to prolong the lie, no way to keep telling fake stories.

The struggle between his outside world and his inside world had reached a climax. He felt driven to tell the truth, but he just couldn't. It was something stronger than him. He was programmed not to trust anyone over those things, not even next of kin. He knew the consequences if Sahar told her family, because she was on good terms with her mother. She couldn't hide anything from her. Sahar used to visit her mother almost every day.

Taha spoke calmly and reasonably, trying to explain his idea to convince his wife. "You are assuming that I am doing something secretly and dangerous? What could it be? Passing information to the Iraqi forces, for example, or telling the world that we are living in a giant prison called Mosul, or it is indeed a mass grave, soon when the battle will approach the town, we will all perish and be buried in the rubble of our houses. Or if we got to survive by a miracle, then we will get arrested and seized in the displacement zones, humiliated and stigmatised for being silent.

"ISIS has devoted itself to portraying the city of Mosul as a paradise, they bring handful of vulnerable folks and ask them to repeat ISIS slogans. Then, what they do is film and edit everything. But what about the great majority, me and you, and the other people who live in Mosul, who are eagerly waiting for the moment of liberation. They are under the rug, silent, otherwise, they get killed.

Then Taha grew eloquent, his restraint shattered, and his emotions poured out in words. "What do you think I am doing? Ok, I am telling the world that we are not happy being under the authority of ISIS, I am the hidden part of the story, I am the truth, I am what those devils are looking for, because I am more dangerous than bombs, I am the deadly stab in their back.

After catching his breath, he spoke, gesturing outward with his hands, as if trying to capture the whole scene, as though attempting to flank the spectacle with his gestures. "Whatever they have built, is nothing. Whatever they tell the world will vanish when I leak out the real story, the world is waiting for me. Not only the world, but the armed forces, some of the soldiers are saturated with that one ridiculous story: People of Mosul have welcomed ISIS. I am demolishing that stereotype. I am building bridges of communications between the civilians and the armed forces who are marching towards the city. Who knows, they might be more merciful to the civilians when they realise that people of Mosul are taken as hostages and human shields."

Sahar seemed emotionally moved by what Taha had said. However, her concern for the family didn't go away. She desperately wanted him to assure her that they were safe.

"Are we safe, Taha? Do your contacts in Mosul and outside Mosul know who you are and where you live?"

Taha smiled wryly and raised his right hand in fluffy motion saying: "Even God doesn't want to know who I am."

His wife pondered and concluded that activists in Mosul wouldn't be willing to reveal their identities to each other, the work was preferable from behind the veil. What really mattered at that time wasn't who was doing what. The stories were the core of everything. She knew that her husband was smart enough and cautious not to reveal anything which could lead to him.

Wars and natural disasters are an extension of life. They expand the world, opening a new area that allows particular people to walk in, and to shine, new heroes are being born, those who couldn't find themselves in the ordinary world, who couldn't have shone so brightly amidst ordinary daylight.

In the same way, some cities, despite their history and beauty, however deep they lay in darkness, the light of war and the flare of falling missiles brightens the sky, illuminating the monuments and the faces of people, so they appear to the world as vulnerable humans after the media had depicted them as freakish monsters.

Sahar - thinking about the risks Taha ran

Just a week before, ISIS had captured someone from the Wadi Hajar neighbourhood who was calling a radio show securely and anonymously, vowing that when Iraqi Forces recaptured the city, ISIS would have to flee like rats. The man added that the Iraqi Forces should bring with them washing liquid, because ISIS members are so dirty.

Days later, his house was violated by ISIS, he thought they came to kill him, so he hurried into the bathroom and locked the door, when ISIS searched the house, one of them went to the bathroom, but he found the victim pushing against the door, he had a fight with them, but finally, they managed to capture him. A few days later, the 25-year-old man appeared in a death suit, admitting his crime and apologising to the Islamic State, sending a warning message in the film that the Islamic State knows everything and they could reach everyone if they want. Another clip showed the man being submerged in a container full of burning acid, while he was screaming and asking for god's sake that they might shoot him in the head rather than let him die gradually in the acid. She knew Taha would not allow himself to be caught that way.

Sahar herself had to stay in survival mode.

From that day on, Sahar believed that at any moment, ISIS could break into their home in search of the most wanted man in Mosul, the secret informant. She couldn't fully trust the situation, nor her husband's judgment in estimating the consequences of his adventurous deeds.

We've just delved into the lives of Sahar and Taha, and how events unfolded from the beginning of the conquest in June 2014. Now, it is the winter of 2017, and the old town of Mosul has begun to shake under deadly battles. ISIS, taking shelter in densely populated neighborhoods, forced civilians to march and remain where the fighting was most intense.

There was a knock at the front door. It slid open and a woman in black clothes entered. She was shouting that she was their neighbour, Buthaina, the ex-wife of Abu-Hamza (one of the distinctive leaders of the Islamic State between 2007-2010.) Buthaina was ready to confide in Sahar all the details of her past.

Sahar - hearing of how Buthaina met Abu-Hamza

One day, Buthaina was doing laundry, kneading a bundle of clothes with her soft hands. As she squatted, her knees were exposed allowing the lower part of her thighs to loom under the loose dress.

At that time, Abu-Hamza was called by his original name, Ali. Back then he was 25 years old, while the girl he desired was 17 years old. He couldn't stop himself staring at her body, even while talking with her brother, his friend. Her brother became angry with Ali for staring at his sister during the conversation. He could see the flare of lust blazing in Ali's eyes and couldn't stop himself pushing Ali to the ground. He would have strangled Ali if his mother hadn't interfered, mediating between the two fighting males.

As he left the house, Buthaina's brother, paused, standing like a monster in preparation for another assault against that vulnerable girl. She left the laundry and went to seek refuge in her mother's arms.

"What has been going on between you and that traitor?" her brother roared.

Buthaina swore that none of what was in his head had happened.

That night, Ali's mother went to ask for Buthaina's hand from her family.

Her brother rejected the idea that his sister would get married to that traitor. He thought that perhaps something had happened between them, and that was the reason Ali wanted to marry her. This would be bad especially because of one of their cousins who wanted Buthaina badly. He worked in estates and owned multiple rental houses. Her brother Fawzi hoped if he endowed his cousin with his pretty sister, his chance of getting a job would be greatly increased, or at least one of those rental houses.

Buthaina had always refused to be the second wife of her cousin who was 43 years old, while she was only 17, despite her mom and sisters advising her to be rational with her choice regarding her future husband. For a moment, she would want to say yes, especially when she thought of every promise, he pledged that he would make Buthaina live as a queen, he would reward her with an apartment in Erbil, and she wouldn't have to quit her studies. Their honeymoon would be spent in Turkey.

But what about his first wife? Would she accept someone else crowding her with her man?

The other wife had no word on that since she was nearly 40 years old. She suffered from overweight because she kept thinking her husband had just dumped her after having 6 children. She had worn herself out for him! She knew that she had no other option - just to accept that her husband had become rich by chance, to deal with his new self, the self that became greedy and couldn't fit in one home, and one bed.

Buthaina had seen that poor wife, she thought of her as an aunt. However, when she started to think of her as a rival, she tried herself to think about her differently, but she couldn't eradicate the previous impression.

Ali knew everything. Buthaina had been telling him that if they didn't get married, her cousin would not leave her alone.

Ali was a trusted man among his people. He read a certain group of religious and spiritual books, something that would have made a person superior if he chose to engage in conversation, especially in a country like Iraq where most people talk about either religion or politics. He knew how to quote from the books he read, how to pose different opinions of the most reliable Islamic scholars without having to endanger himself by pushing his own thoughts. He knew how to convey his opinion via condensing authentic quotes and verses from Quran to advocate his inner idea. This was how he got to win most of the debates.

He was close to the insurgent group that started to rush into the country after 2003 bearing the name of "Jihad", the struggle against the foreign enemy that unfairly invaded the country, causing its regime to fall and the army to be dissolved. Ali thought that resisting the Americans was a sacred task upon his shoulders, especially after the US troops identified themselves as invaders. Ali cultivated his thoughts. They claimed that they were liberators, advocates of democracy then, all of a sudden, we woke up to see them declaring themselves as invaders! Is that a clear declaration of war, to provoke people, to drag more armed groups into fight?

He had consulted people close to him whether he should join one of the earliest armed groups in Mosul called the "Movement of the Al-Jihad and Al-Tuohid", an Islamic movement that promised to liberate the country from the Americans and their "tails." That was the first form of the Islamic State that would control the city in June 2014. Ali had lost some of his closely aligned friends because they had advised him to keep away from armed action. Civilians could be killed as a result of the assaults.

Although that movement had claimed in the beginning that they were only after the Americans and their snitches, later they started to kill members of the Iraqi Police and other members of the national security forces.

Finally, Ali had joined the insurgent group. That enabled him to threaten his rival, the cousin of Buthaina, in an attempt to make him refrain from tempting Buthaina and her brother, otherwise he would slit his throat. He felt that wasn't part of the true Jihad, but he justified that it was his reward for the job he'd endowed himself for. In 2006, he married the woman he loved. Unlike the traditional wedding parties, it was adequate for him to conduct a feast only for men, inviting his commanders and friends.

When he married the girl he'd slept with several times before marriage, seeing her naked wasn't a big reward for him or her, since he'd been constantly sleeping with her around dawn. Usually when her family had been asleep, her father would wake up to go to the mosque to pray. Ali used to position himself behind the bushes, waiting when the door would get unlocked, then he would utilise that time to see his sweetheart. Buthaina would wake up waiting for Ali to find his way to her room. All Buthaina needed to do was just to lock the door of her room after verifying that everyone was asleep.

After marriage, Ali couldn't stay living in the same district where he'd lived all his life. Many of the police officers were living there, the guys that had been chasing the armed groups in Iraq. Ali was given the nickname Abu Hamza; he earned the respect of his leaders in the group. Usually, uneducated young people would join such fighting groups, people that could be easily brainwashed. Also, the first cells of the militants in Iraq provided jobs for those who had no significant thing to do; but not Ali or Abu Hamza. He'd willingly joined to implement what he thought to be a religious and patriotic duty. He knew how to bring more people to join.

In 2008, Abu Hamza became a significant leader in what was called the Islamic State after allying with the well-known terrorist organisation "Al Qaida". Many of the police members were killed in broad daylight. People who collaborated with the Iraqi uniforms or with any official army were considered snitches. Abu Hamza, whose idea of joining the militants was to combat the invaders, found himself giving orders to teenagers to assassinate Iraqi policemen, interpreters, taxi drivers who'd given rides to the Iraqi soldiers.

One day, he gave orders to kill a poor taxi driver. The man had a kiosk from which he had been living, members of the Iraqi army stopped by, and bought Pepsi from him, the man couldn't have said no. As the vehicle roared off, leaving the place, Abu Hamza heard about him from his agents who were prevalent almost everywhere in the town; he personally gave an order to the men to finish him instantly.

Neighbourhoods at the edges of Mosul presented a real challenge for the Iraqi security forces to impose full control. The Iraqi forces were only in control of the central part and the area adjoining the airport; Ali never showed up in his old neighbourhood where his mother and siblings were living. He would send a special car to bring his mother to spend a short time with him in one of the villas in Eastern Mosul, they would sit at the grove, having a luxurious meal, while the younger guys were guarding the perimeter. He used to submerge her in his lavish lifestyle as a bid to earn her approval by bribery. His mother's eyes welled with tears every time she said goodbye to him. She felt that her son, who had changed so much in this short time, would have to pay for all this, with his blood if not from his pocket. It was only a matter of time.

His mother was right. Ali was convicted by the Islamic State itself, despite being arrested two times by one of the official powers in Mosul and walking free the next day, nobody knew how. That time the Islamic State charged him with embezzlement of their treasury, which came originally from blackmailing businessmen and companies that had to pay commissions to the Islamic State if they wanted to resume their work safely.

When Ali heard about that, he left everything behind and returned to his old neighbourhood to hide. He knew it was the most secure place, just spent several days at his brother's house. Later he knew that they could reach him wherever he was. He decided to attend the court. He knew that he might not be able to make it back to his family, he knew how brutal the folks he used to work with were and that mercy was not in their dictionary.

His family received a call from the local police to come to the morgue at Mosul hospital in the evening to receive their son Ali who was found dead a few metres from the hospital.

Buthaina - after Abu Hamza was killed

Buthaina went crazy with grief. She spent nights crying but she knew that she would have to survive. Her family didn't want her to live with them again for security reasons. Their daughter Buthaina had been playing with fire. She was now the widow of one of the most distinctive leaders of the Islamic State of Mosul. After the Islamic State confiscated their property, Buthaina had some money left. She had managed to hide a huge sum of money that would enable her to buy a house in a safe area.

She was living at her husband's family's house, assisting her mother-in-law, and raising her three children. In 2012, Her mother-in-law passed away. She moved to one of her cousin's rental-houses because he was the one that she could trust as a member of her larger family. She didn't want other relatives or acquaintances to know where she was living.

From time to time, he would call her and check if she needed anything. Her brothers had been visiting her from time to time. That cousin had proposed to her on different occasions; however, she asked him to stop doing that. By then, he already had his second wife.

Buthaina had intended to stay single but then she fell in love with a young man, younger than her by eight years: Muthanna. She started a secret relationship with him. What she did was revolutionary: She broke the shackles of society, she was empowered by her prior experience with her ex-husband, a courageous woman who would do everything to live her life, the natural part of life. It was proof of her being a human, a vivid human. As a female, she had been buried underneath the rubble of wars, and the cultural dust. Buthaina rose from the coffin of religion, walking to the source of the light that mostly had come from her heart to show her the way to the larger world.

In Iraq, love cannot be blind, it must be a courageous action, and lovers are rebels. For people like Buthaina, nothing seemed to be enough. She had lived years on the run and couldn't have been sure where she was heading to. She was economically independent; she bought her own house a few years after her husband's death. No one dared to intervene into her affairs, her family members were hoping that their wealthy daughter would support them financially. Against the odds, she had been generous with her brother Fawzi, buying him a car that he could work as a taxi-driver. Buthaina was an example of a Middle Eastern woman becoming independent, powerful, and resilient. If she had a thicker wallet and bravery, none of her family members could decide on her behalf.

Buthaina and Muthanna - sharing a wish for revenge

Buthaina married Muthanna in secret. When ISIS took over the city of Mosul in 2014, he started to work with ISIS as a supporter on social media, promoting how life was optimal under the Islamic State. Muthanna wasn't originally from Mosul, he came from Samarra 110 km northwest of Baghdad.

He got into Mosul University in 2007. His two brothers got killed in his city because of the civil war that engulfed the country. He met Buthaina on social media in 2011. They shared a lot of thoughts in common, perspective of life, and more importantly the sense of revenge. Buthaina had always hated those guys who deprived her from her husband, while Muthanna was waiting for the right chance to achieve justice from those who'd killed his two brothers. He couldn't have said that to anyone, not even to Buthaina. However, they were on the same page, although the wish for revenge might not have targeted the same enemy.

Muthanna hated the Iraqi security forces. He believed that they were responsible for his brothers' deaths, in the form of pro-Iran militias that swarmed over the country post-2003. In 2012, Buthaina's brother was arrested by the Iraqi Federal police that were controlling the West part of Mosul. Simply, the man started to do business. The Iraqi Federal Police was one of the most corrupt powers in Mosul that were commissioned by the former Iraqi Prime Minister Nuri Al Maliki to crack down on the people of Mosul.

In 2010, Nuri Al Maliki didn't win the election, most of the people in Mosul voted for one of the most secular figures in the country that time, Ayad Allawi, by that time, Al Maliki had frozen all the Shia militants. Al Maliki had stayed in power by creating a bigger political bloc that was what appeared in the media. Under the rug there had been another narrative, the true one.

Years later, Ayad Allawi would mention in a TV Interview that he was barred from getting into office as the next Iraqi Prime Minister due to the Islamic Republic of Iran that explicitly didn't agree on him becoming the head of the government in Iraq.

2011 was the year of the US military withdrawal. In that year, the Arab spring blew into the country, prompting the people of major Iraqi Sunni cities to flood the streets demanding reform, justice, the release of innocent detainees like those taken instead of their husbands, brothers or sons on terror-related charges, and giving fair chances in the Iraqi security forces that had been mostly led by Shia commanders who basically were loyal to the Prime Minister and his religious party "Al D'wa" supported by Iran.

The Iraqi government used force to suppress the demonstration, whereas Nuri Al Maliki described the demonstration as a nasty bubble, vowing to use power to stop it. Demonstrations lasted until June 2014, the year when ISIS had taken 40 percent of the Iraqi territory.

Meanwhile, families of detainees used to visit what was called the "Dignity Squares" in the hope of getting their voices heard by the world, which might put some pressure on the Iraqi government to respond to their demands.

Buthaina used to go there almost every day. Her younger brother Othman was innocent; she knew it very well. Everyone who knew Othman would say so. He didn't care about a lot of what was happening throughout the country, he only thought of football matches. All that filled his mind were the English, Spanish or Italian Leagues. He didn't have any political tendencies. If you asked him for his opinion on what was going on in the country, he would simply say: Very complicated for my small brain to understand.

All he did was to start a business, and that's what lured them to approach him. He was arrested by the Elite Forces in 2009. His family couldn't find any trace where he had been imprisoned, until Human Rights Watch revealed a report that there had been a secret underground facility called "Muthanna Jail" in northern Baghdad controlled by the Iraqi Prime Minister. Its detainees were facing all sort of torture on daily basis.

Othman was one of the innocent detainees that were plagued by their names that referred to a sectarian belonging that those who were in power didn't like. Othman had been released in 2011, but he was arrested again despite the fact that the judge had cleared him from all the alleged charges.

In Iraq, when someone was known to the authorities, that person would become an easy target on every occasion. They accused him of financing terrorist groups in Mosul.

Buthaina knew that her brother was innocent, so she marched every day to flood the demonstrations with her calls mixed with tears, appealing in front of the cameras that her brother was innocent and everyone in the neighbourhood was ready to exonerate him.

In the meanwhile, she agreed fully with her boyfriend who had been on bad terms with the Iraqi Government. They commenced to share not only love but hate against one enemy.

Ironically, Muthanna bears the same name as the facility that turned Buthaina into thinking that the Iraqi Government was the reason everything had happened to her. The terrorist groups were only the result of a fragile, corrupt government that had been unfair to its nationals.

Muthanna succeeded in convincing her that terror is a normal symptom of an unhealthy system. He told her that terrorism is like fungus and bacteria that swarm over the scar if left untreated.

In 2013, Othman walked free, but for how long? The security forces were next to him on every occasion.

In 2014, the situation in Mosul had reached boiling point. Social deterioration was at its peak, violence escalated, and people were being killed randomly. A group of the most dangerous detainees who were able to break out of the well-guarded "Abo Qarainb Jail" found their way to what was once a peaceful demonstration. Lawyers, journalists, and celebrities were the first to pay the bill; they were being killed sporadically.

Emad Al Najmawi was a lawyer who'd refused to defend detainees belonging to the Islamic State. His family got a phone call from a stranger asking him to check how Mr. Emad was doing. His wife called his brothers, and they went to his office. His office was closed. They tried to reach him on the phone, but it was in vain. They broke into his office to see that honourable, brave lawyer covered with blood, tossed on the ground as a corpse, while two cups of coffee were still on the table. The crime had happened in a district that teemed with security personnel.

Wathiq Al Qathannfari, the most famous figure in Mosul, a well-known face to all people of Mosul "The guard of the Mosuli memory" who presented a TV show that revolved around the features of the city from different aspects, promoting the history of Mosul as never before. The man got killed, the military checkpoint was so close to the site of the crime, however they couldn't prevent the homicide from happening.

June 2014 was the final strike that stripped the country from the last governmental presence, whether in the form of security forces or civil officials. According to eyewitnesses who fought alongside the Iraqi local police that were the weakest among the fighting groups in Mosul: "We were commissioned to form the first front-line spanning the march of ISIS from the West. They came from Syria and the Western desert. We couldn't have lasted longer with our humble weaponry and ammo shortage. Most of our members were from the city of Mosul. They had no other way, only to fight, otherwise, ISIS would capture them if the city fell."

Muthanna and Buthaina lived a stable life in Mosul after ISIS took control of the city. But one day, Muthanna came back home confused, ashen and helpless.

Buthaina - Muthanna's memories of sectarian violence

Muthanna had seen an ISIS member from his hometown, Samarra, where Shia militias had killed and kidnapped locals as a type of the sectarian expansion in North Baghdad. It was the Sunni city in which "Al-Askari Shrine", one of the most significant Shia shrines in the world, was bombed by the extremists in 2006 causing a widespread anger among Shia.

After that incident, the Iraqi Civil War between Shia and Sunni erupted, causing a regional exodus based on sectarianism. Sunnis were forced to evacuate their homes in cities inhabited by a Shia majority, while Shia students who studied in the universities in Mosul and other Iraqi Major Sunni Cities were killed, the rest had moved back to their hometowns.

Along the way from Mosul to Baghdad, a 400 kilometre road full of horror and uncertainty, at any time, a security checkpoint might be installed, asking for passengers IDs, in which the religion was fixed, but not the sect, however, being a Christian or Yazidi or Sabian was a kind of exoneration, while being a Muslim put the passenger before two possibilities; whether to get killed if the death checkpoint was from the opponent sect. Peoples' sects could be often identified by names, hometowns, and dialects. Shias would rarely give names such as Omar, Othman, Khalid, or Aiysha to their children. On the other hand, there are names not common among the Sunni community: like Mortada, Jaffar, and Baniin. The luckiest ones were those who bore common names among Shia and Sunni. Since those checkpoints had no slogans or any banners, one could not guess what their sects were.

In Tal Afar city located 63-kilometre Western Mosul, Sunnis and Shias had lived for a long time without dispute. In 2007, as a result of the civil war, the population dropped from 200,000 down to 80,000. The government troops contributed in cleansing the city of its Sunni inhabitants who then found their way to the nearest big Sunni city, Mosul.

The detainees from Mosul were transferred to sectarian jails to face torture and agony based on fabricated charges. One of them narrated: "I had a stall at the market-square of Mosul, where I sold women's clothes amidst the bustling crowds. I lived my life like anybody else at the age of 19. One night, I was awakened by the nozzle of a weapon. I heard them cursing, they got more frenzied when they knew my name was Omar. They captured me, veiled my sight, pushed me outside, then I was flung into the military vehicle. I felt that there must've been others crammed in the same trunk.

I heard one of them barking: "What is your name?"

I was so scared to repeat my name, but then another one struck me with what felt to be a baton. "My name is Omar."

Then I got punched in the face, and humiliated. We reached the place where detainees were crammed in a narrow space, having to stay standing to fit in. The broken figures dumped on the floor were those who returned from the interrogation sessions. They would go there walking and return on the stretcher, and then were tossed in severely by the guards, if there was any space left.

I stayed awake for several days. They tied me outside on the pillar. It was cold, every time I was drowning in a slumber, they would splash cold water on me. They buried me in the yard that night, they decided to plunge me into a hole that looked like a grave, only my head appeared.

I felt that staying alive had become a burden, I yelled that they could shoot me and save me from that torment. Then they left, and I fell asleep in the grave!"

Muthanna knew many such stories. He had met an ISIS member who was one of those detainees. They took him for committing no sin. While in the jail, he found his network to seek revenge once he was out of prison.

Buthaina - hears Yazidi girls are being marketed by ISIS

The ISIS member whom Muthanna had seen reminisced: "Your brothers got killed by the Shia militants. Now it is your time to bring back the glory of your brothers, otherwise, you will stay stuck in the grime of shame."

Muthanna decided to join ISIS. Buthaina could do nothing to stop him. She saw him in his ISIS uniform coming home, saying that tomorrow he would bring her one of the Yazidi servants to help her with her domestic works. She didn't like the idea; she knew he would want her for other reasons. Buthaina saw on her husband's phone a recent video that spread on social media. When she started to realise the truth, her stomach was churning.

She clicked to play the video: "Today is the market of Sabaya, girls taken by force from their Yazidi Communities, mostly from families who weren't able to flee to the mountain of Sinjar adjoining their towns and village. Today you get to choose one of them, they are all halal, whoever wants to get one extra, have to pay extra money." The man was filming inside a marble hall, where ISIS fighters were sitting on the couches beside their rifles. He started to interview the ISIS fighters:

"My servant girl has bad teeth; I should get another one for free," one of them said.

Another babyface fighter who seemed to be an underage boy raised his hand, asking for a girl.

"Are you capable of managing one of those cunts?" The filmmaker asked him.

The boy nodded with a shy smile, as though his nature was preventing him from taking the role of monster.

"Oh you, Mulla," they said to a man who seemed to have ascetic features, "do you want one, it is our property."

The man lowered his head, as if he was asking the camera to pass him swiftly. It seemed he wasn't fully convinced of what was going on.

Buthaina started to see these men weren't as they had claimed themselves to be. They were leaking such videos from time to time, to lure those sick-minded guys who mainly had suffered from deprivation under an extreme social burden, making women look like a far-fetched lottery prize.

Buthaina realised her husband had joined the terrorist group leaning on all phoney justifications that someone could come up with, but that was not the real incentive, just like most of those had joined the armed groups fighting in Iraq. Muthanna wanted to practise authority over ordinary people, and to get what others couldn't obtain. He sought a higher privilege, and soon he had two Yazidi girls.

From then on, Buthaina began to abstain from sharing the bed with him. After those girls confided in her and told her their stories, Buthaina felt even more pity for them.

ISIS lyrics known by extremists who fought in Syria and Iraq

O my mate, O my mate
Never ask what has happened to me
I am captivated, thinking of her all the time
Oh, my heart, never get saddened
Never refrain from loving
Be sure that you will win her
The one who truly struggles for her,
will eventually find her.
I don't mean the mundane girl,
the girl who infiltrates the group of men like a snake,
the girl who exchanges the faith with sins
the girl that betrays the man who loves her.
I refer to those who are in the heaven of eternity;
the ones that never make you bored of them
O my friends, find me a solution!
I can't wait anymore.
The virgins of the paradise are growing on me
Please my god, endow them to me!
Keep me fighting for your religion
So that I can walk with her in the paradise
When she walks, she lurches for me
When she precedes me, she stops and turns to stare at me.
When she laughs, the lighting looms
The world shall blaze for her sake,
for that lucky man who sits or walks besides her in heaven.

Oh my god when she sings,
the branches of the trees dance together
I truly miss her when she enjoys me
And I enjoy her
Her saliva, when it drools,
all the oceans become so sweet
Her breast is tight and palpable,
stark, when she goes back and forth.

Unknown, translated by Ahmed Zaidan

Yazidi girl, Suzaan, tells Buthaina her story

In August 2014, we heard that ISIS was heading towards Sinjar, Western Mosul, in which most of the Yazidi community population lived. I was married to a man from another village. That night, I was at my parents' house. I received a call from my husband informing me that ISIS was on the way to take over our territory. In my village, many families had fled to the mountain to take shelter, in the meanwhile some of the families had stayed. We heard that ISIS had nothing to do with the civilians. It was our biggest mistake that time.

I learned that my husband had walked for 6 hours at night, to get to the mountain of Sinjar.

We thought that the Peshmerga, the military forces of the autonomous Kurdistan Region of Iraq would repel that invasion of the Islamic State. Unfortunately, we witnessed the same scenario that happened in Mosul - the Peshmerga had also withdrawn – we were left alone to face our destiny! Our men took over their guns and positioned themselves to protect their families. But you know with the lack of ammo and brutality of the enemy, the battle was concluded in favour of ISIS.

We were taken to the schools' yards. Men were separated from women. Most of those men were detained and then killed.

Women and children were distributed to the members of the terror group. I was taken to Mosul; I knew that I was endowed to one of ISIS princes."

First day in captivity, the younger girls were taken to a school in Southern Sinjar. I saw a girl with her sister, she was 19 years old. She had been the most beautiful one among us. ISIS fighters had taken her as a servant after killing 7 members of her family. They did that just a day before. The prince of the group had opted to have her for himself, he gave her a razor and shampoo, asking her to take a bath and get ready for him. One hour passed before they found her dead in the bathroom, she used the razor to kill herself."

Buthaina had realised more than ever that human blood has one colour and the tragedy of humanity is all one. She began to understand that ISIS was a pure criminal organisation that would do anything to sustain its existence. Upon the bones of vulnerable people, those men had built their house of justice.

Yazidi girls escape, helped by Buthaina

Dalia, Muthanna's Yazidi servant-girl, agreed with Buthaina that all she needed to be free was sleeping pills. Muthanna would occasionally send Dalia to assist his wife in domestic work when it was needed. After more than a year of this intermittent contact, the servant-girl confided in Buthaina. They concluded that Buthaina would supply them with the pills, in the hope they could escape slavery.

It wouldn't be easy to do so since the whole city and the surroundings were densely attended by ISIS control points.

The night came, and Dalia imagined her two paths; the one that led to the abyss and the path that ends at a gate where her husband, rest of the family and her old self must be awaiting her eagerly. Would she ever reunify with her old self again?

Buthaina helped Dalia contact her family and to pass on the news of other kidnapped girls. Her father who was residing in Erbil, the autonomous region in Iraq, managed to contact his Muslim friend in Mosul beforehand to secure Dalia's escape. Her father's contact in Mosul would have to shelter her in his house for weeks before securing the way to get her smuggled to Kurdistan, northern Mosul.

While ISIS fighters were getting ready for an enormous banquet, Dalia was preparing food in the kitchen with other Yazidi girls. They had been escorted by their kidnappers to the feast to be shown off and serve in the feast.

With steady hands, Dalia dissolved pills in the heavy dark tea. She increased the amount of sugar, she knew they liked the tea bitter and sweet at the same time.

That night, Buthaina was absent. Muthanna often sent her to her family's house when the brothers frequented his house. He fought shoulder to shoulder with those fighters. But when it came to the sensitive lyre of life, they couldn't trust each other. They were all obsessed about women's nudity and the number of virgins each one of them would have after death.

Their lusts were nourished by fantasy lyrics that were one of the primary incentives for them to get frenzied during the fight. ISIS utilised every possible way to get these desperate people to fight for the unseen reward that addresses issues of disappointment and deprivation in them. It addressed a giant failure in reality, issues that most of its members couldn't have dealt with, the dreams that were matched to the size of their pain. They live for another life that would give them what they wished for and failed to get in earthly life.

When the men fell asleep, Dalia and six other Yazidi girls sneaked out gingerly. Her father's friend and his brother were waiting, sitting at one of the local restaurants. He would get a ring from Dalia's secret phone. Then the two cars would head to the district to pick up the girls.

They received no further information how the man, who didn't want to be identified, would smuggle them to Erbil on one of the riskiest journeys. He said that he had endangered his life and gambled his family's future.

Muthanna went crazy after that incident. A few months later, when he learned the battle to retake the city of Mosul was imminent, he vanished from Mosul, leaving his wife Buthaina alone to bear the responsibilities of life with her three children.

Yazidi student shares her sister-in-law's story

The author's brother, Mustafa, who studies at Mosul University, provided an important contact of a Yazidi student who was ready to tell the story of her brother's wife. She requested to stay anonymous, which is understandable after all her people had gone through. The interviewee barely spoke Arabic since her mother tongue is Kurdish. The virtual interview wasn't long but full of emotions and painful memories. It revealed the tragic genocide and exodus the Yazidi community was exposed to in the summer of 2015, when the fighters of Islamic State were waging a large-scale offensive and targeting Sinjar District in Western Mosul, the home of the Yazidi Community in Iraq.

When ISIS took over the city of Mosul, I was about 14 years old. I had lived a normal life alongside my family, without any problems. I was in the 7th grade in school when my village was swiped out by ISIS. I remember everything that happened to us.

At first, we were hearing rumours that ISIS was going to conquer our regions. Mosul was conquered on the 9th of June 2014. We hadn't seen ISIS; however, we had been hearing frightening stories that when ISIS would conquer our regions, they would rape our women, kill the men and abduct the children to have them brainwashed and trained, to be suiciders in the "Cubs Squad."

On the 14th of August 2014, ISIS started to take over the areas inhabited by the Yazidi community. In the night we got a phone-call from the adjoining village that ISIS had captured that village. We just decided to leave everything behind and to leave on foot to the mountain of Sinjar. We had to leave at 5 am.

Yazidi fighters tried to repel the offensive waged by ISIS, but with the limited number of amu and primitive weaponry, they couldn't have lasted for long. So, they knew that the battle was concluded in favour of ISIS, they commenced to call the locals, informing them that they should instantly evacuate their houses and escape to the mountain to take shelter.

We started the walk at 5 am up to 10 am. We reached the mountain of Sinjar. We saw the men positioned themselves well to guard the mountain. ISIS fighters. Couldn't have infiltrated through the mountain. Our men were privileged to know the terrain very well. Some of them had spent all their life in the mountain area, this made it impossible for ISIS to approach from the mountain.

I remember that we took shelter in a house located on the groove of the mountain.

The owner of the house said: "My children have been days without food; I need to sneak out of the mountain area to the town to bring them some food."

The man promised his little daughter that he would not come back empty-handed.

I peered out the window watching him descending towards the abyss, he was walking against the storm, probably he had been the only one who went in the opposite direction, towards the fire. I kept on gazing out the window while the man had been swallowed by the giant terrain, I saw him trying to run into hiding, like an intimidated animal that wished to be unseen by a frenzied predator. Then I heard a string of shots. The man slammed to the ground, dead.

We stayed at the mountain for 11 days. It was cold at night on the mountain.

We had to survive without aid for many days, we were confined. My dad and brothers would secretly risk their lives and sneak to the town to bring us the needed food and water.

There were ISIS members on the streets, controlling the road of the mountain, but Yazidi men had been going to the suburb of Qahtaniyah, smuggled in.

I remember when we had been trapped in the mountain, there were two wounded men who got injuries in the leg and the hand. Their families were taken by ISIS; my family had to take care of those two. We gave them water and food and medical treatment. We stayed in the mountains for 11 days. We finally found a way to reach the autonomous region of Kurdistan by the assistance of fighters affiliated to PPK.

Some of the families who got captured by ISIS due to the rumour that spread that time that ISIS would have nothing to do with the families of the Yazidi community if they didn't fight them back. So, some of the family had stayed in their homes.

People also found it hard to leave everything behind and leave. Those people had paid the consequences. We went to Kurdistan, and we stayed nine days there before going to Turkey. We went to Turkey by smuggling, we again had to walk to Turkey.

This is the story of my brother's wife who was among the survivors of those taken. It is not easy for her to recall her story when she was kidnapped by ISIS and taken as a servant woman. My brother's wife went to visit her family's house in another village, and on that night, ISIS waged an offensive on our regions. Kuju is the name of the village. Her family decided not to leave the house. When ISIS invaded their village, she was taken away as a female servant.

We hadn't heard anything from her for more than a year. Later, we learned that ISIS had transferred her to the city of Mosul, the stronghold of ISIS that time.

She was 16 years old when ISIS had taken her. Suddenly, one year after her departure, she contacted my father. My father was so happy to know that she was alive. We saw there was a hope to get her liberated from ISIS. She informed my father that ISIS had forcibly converted her to Islam. She didn't like that she had to pretend that she was a devout Muslim who would pray and fast and wear Niqab imposed by ISIS on all women.

She cried on the phone and begged my father to help her to escape. "Even if I get killed while trying to flee, I won't care," she said.

She had had to stay with ISIS for three years. She managed to run away, she said. She had been seized in the city of Mosul, they were ready to run away, but their plan was revealed. ISIS members tortured them. "We got detained in a dark room; we were deprived of food for many days."

She said that regarding rape, seven ISIS men would rape one girl on one night. "The night of escape, there was only one guard keeping an eye on us. So, I gave him a sleeping pill in his tea.

When we were on the way to Kurdistan, one of the cars was targeted by an airstrike, some of the girls were killed and others injured. But luckily, our car went through, to make the journey to Kurdistan.

The city of Mosul was besieged that time, ISIS didn't let anyone go out and come into the city. The air-force saw any vehicle trying to get out of Mosul as a possible enemy.

2017–2021: Citizen Heroes

This chapter features eye-witness accounts by people whom I interviewed in the summer of 2021, who were willing to have their stories written explicitly. At first, I was thinking of combining their stories with imagery, however, every time I revised their stories, I felt that they were inspirational the way they are, so I simply transcribed and translated them into English before rewriting them in their final format.

There are many stories from the Old Town depicting these tragedies that the city of Mosul had witnessed. An old man from Mosul described that war as the most ruthless he had seen in the 8 decades he had lived. However, when you have war, you have heroes, and our heroes here are women and artists, our heroes are ordinary people who found themselves combating the most brutal enemy.

Maha - leading her family's escape

When ISIS took over Mosul, Maha was studying at University of Mosul. By 2021, Maha had become a civil activist. She sought to tell her story as a way to release her burden of sorrow. I could see in her eyes a gateway that led to the alleyways of the Old Town of Mosul; to my childhood while roaming with friends the alleys of the Clock Church alley and Farug; when we knocked on the doors and scampered off like a herd of deer, running and heading nowhere, until we vanished into the Bab Jadid, the remarkable marketplace, disappearing into the crowds and smells of the barbecue that made the distinct atmosphere of that area. Maha lived not far from that marketplace that I thought of as the last valiant candle when all other candles had surrendered to the despair engulfing Mosul after 2003. The triangle of life that started from Bab Jadid, Dawassa and Wadi Hajar in which we somehow made most of our memories.

Maha's words take us back to the dark era, to the time we know how mainstream media depicted it. Defying the stereotypical image often cast upon Middle Eastern women, Maha sails against the prevailing narratives, reaching back to her own Big Bang - the beginning of a story where suffering forged the strength that shaped who she is today.

This is her narrative on the military operation of the liberation of Mosul from the grip of the Islamic State that had ruled the city for nearly two years:

Maha - planning the escape from Old Town

We are from the Old Town, at the time of ISIS, we had been suffering from extraordinary conditions, as though the situation seemed like a fantasy.

That time, I thought to myself that we had to escape from the Old Town, and we should cross to the safe shore, which was behind the 5th bridge in Mosul, where Al-Shifa and Al-Rifai neighbourhoods were erected. My father had been always rejecting to depart from the house, he sought that we should just stay at home, he thought if we'd evacuated the house, ISIS would confiscate it, because usually ISIS was taking the uninhibited houses. There was a series of bombardments in the neighbourhood, the house was shaking, in the meantime, the alley had been destroyed. We were forced to evade that situation and slip out. We didn't have time to put on shoes and wear our veils. We stayed on the street exposed to the elements of death. Our house was almost falling down. We ran through the Old Town barefoot, in a bid to reach the house of my uncle in the Al-Mashahda neighbourhood.

We got there safely, we had to stay at my uncle's house for 25 days, we couldn't stay any longer, so we decided to go back to the central part of the Old Town. We found a house close to the Grand Mosque of Mosul (located in the central part of the Old Town that was blown up by ISIS upon their final defeat. It is the mosque of the leaning minaret from which the Islamic State was declared in the summer of 2014). We lived there for around 2 to 3 months, and we dwelled in a crypt. During that time, we kept waiting every day for something to happen. We were under tremendous stress. The city was besieged from all directions, and seemed like a mass prison. Our sole window to the outside world was the radio, from which the news was flowing.

We listened to Al-Qad Radio (The Radio of Tomorrow). But in the meanwhile, we bore the risk of doing so, we had been hiding the phone and we were listening stealthily with a low volume, because ISIS members were roaming in the neighbourhood all the time. At that time, they could break into the house. My father was keen on staying where we were, however, my sister's house was located in Ras-Al-Kur alley by the Tigris River.

My father kept saying: "Either we go back to our house, or we stay here, or we go to my daughter's house in Ras-Al-Kur."

I rejected all three options, I thought that we should evade the Old Town and go to Al-Shifa neighbourhood spanning the Old Town from the north, because I had a connection with my cousin who was living in the Eastern part of Mosul (already liberated) via phone and also with my female friend who knew someone working at the Governmental Council of Ninawa (Nineveh). I was receiving instructions. People were afraid to take risks when they gave their opinions on that, because we were a big family, with elderly and children. So, if everyone wanted to escape, then it would be their own responsibility to take such a decision.

That time, the Iraqi troops were at (the 17 July district) northwest of the city, and they were heading to Al-Rifai neighbourhood, the area I wanted to take the family to. The next neighbourhood was getting ready for the upcoming battle.

There was a constant bombardment targeting the Old Town. The Iraqi forces were bombing, and ISIS members were bombing, whereas we were confined in the middle. We got bombed with all types of weaponry all the time.

That was the reason I insisted that we should slip out of the Old Town. I thought to myself that staying there was a kind of suicide, whereas trying to walk outside was also a certain death. However, I thought to myself that I shouldn't give up. I am human without any disability, I have got my full senses healthy: what would prevent me from making the right step, why should I give up and let myself be buried here?

I aimed for one elusive goal that time, I would run towards it whatever it cost. I wanted to save my sisters, my nieces, the wife of my deceased uncle with her two orphaned children. At that time, I dared to go back to our old house. On the way back, I was intercepted by one ISIS member. I had the courage to talk to him, I argued with him, "For how long shall we stay here suffering? What would be our future if we stayed?"

"Only the few luckiest folks would have the chance to get out of the Old Town alive. Our intention is to destroy the town, we have agreed with the other party that is fighting against us, we have agreed to demolish the Old Town." he answered.

Yes, he really said – the party that is liberating you – that we both have nothing to do with you, we have agreed to dig the Old Town to the ground! The ones who would rise from the rubble, are the luckiest ones, it means that God has endowed them with a new life. He said that apathetically.

I asked him about his own family, and he answered that his family was evacuated to the liberated eastern part of the city; the families of ISIS, most of them got to cross to the eastern part safely, according to him.

I asked him: "What would happen to us, we are the vulnerable folks who got trapped here, you have confined us to a battlefield, you haven't been merciful to us, you never cut us slack to escape from the town?"

After a thoughtful pause, he said: "Because you have been a good neighbour in the alley, I would advise you – we were 3 families in the alley – today you have a time if you would want to go to Al-Zanjelli neighbourhood, otherwise if you chose to stay, you would be beaten up, lashed and killed if any of you try to escape the blazing old town, today is your chance to leave without having to face all these consequences. We are going to intentionally confine you in the Old Town that would be your mass grave."

Then I went to my stubborn father who'd decided not to leave at all. We all know the old folks when they have already made up their mind. He decided not to abandon his house saying: "My house! I will never get out of it until I die!"

He thought that God would save us, and the army was going to liberate us soon.

I told him: "O Dad, this is a ruthless and deadly war! The army won't throw roses on ISIS. There will be death and sacrifices, there must be a blood-shower and pillars of smoke carrying the souls of the inhabitants to God; will they narrate their stories to Him, so He would feel pity and stop this ominous war!" I went back home. I had tried to make him give up on his decision but he stubbornly refused to leave.

We had had a lot of arguments among the family members. Then we decided that we would cross to the opposing side of the river to the eastern part of the city, my sister, my brother and I, we would take a boat, we agreed with the neighbour of my sister who lived by the river, that the man would come to take us with his sister and her children who would be on the boat, while we would be tied to the boat with a rope, floating on rubbers, and hauled by that boat until we got to the other side of the river of death, the river that once gave life to the city of Mosul over the years but during that war it turned out to be the river of death that carried the corpses of the escapees that would be targeted by both sides, why not if it was the river that bordered between the plagued part and the healthy part of Mosul, as though we lived in a locked down city where a deadly pandemic was rampant.

At sunset, my mother and my aunt said goodbye to us – while we were heading towards the river, mortar rounds started to fall everywhere, we were leaning against the wall to avoid the shrapnel, and then we would dart along swiftly, utilising the time in between falling shells.

We kept walking in that way until we arrived at my sister's, then I thought to myself: how could I leave my sister and her children alone? I was the only courageous woman in the family, in the sense of making decisions and fighting for life. I just thought of my father and I realised that he didn't want to make any decision because as a head of family, he thought about us, he didn't want to risk making a wrong decision, he didn't want us girls to get hurt because of his decision to leave the house. It was the reason he preferred to stay where we were, to avoid any remorse. He thought in that limited way, my mother had thought the same way.

Maha - heading for the Al-Refai neighbourhood

People who drag a heavy burden of life experiences are the ones who don't move swiftly until they have secured every aspect, to evade the risk of disappointments. Disappointments over years can work like nails that pin people to one place.

Experiences are good but sometimes too many of them make people stuck to where they are, however one should have the capacity to decide the right time to summon or dismiss various types of their life experiences, and also to borrow the experiences of others within the same context.

Maha had the advantage of being younger with less weight of experience. It would enable her to hurtle towards the horizons of freedom with no gravity exerting on her any type of authority; she would pull her family members with their burdens to move more swiftly, exceeding the traps and evading all platoons of death.

She was about to make an epic journey to the north-western part of Mosul, to a neighbourhood located on the verge of the Old Town from outside. That would mean crossing one of the most dangerous zones that made the defensive-line of ISIS adjacent to the 5th bridge. Not only that, the main danger is nearby what was once Mosul Hotel entrance, from which ISIS fought fiercely in June 2014 and got all the Iraqi forces' defensive-lines to collapse. Maha made a brave move by accepting the responsibility of her decision. But would they make it safely to the Iraqi armed forces?

My brother and I had decided to cross the river. But I heard that crossing the Tigris River in such circumstances wasn't as easy as it might sound. I have aquaphobia, I fear water, I thought shit! I can't do it. I had to retreat, but I knew once I went back, I would never fold my hands and see death approaching us. Things would not be the same. I decided to take my family to the Al-Rifai neighbourhood. I told our neighbours with whom we had decided to flee that the plan had changed. "Let's go to the Al-Refai neighbourhood tomorrow!"

My neighbour asked me to take the responsibility of such a decision. I accepted the responsibility for my action. Whatever happened, I would have never surrender.

When I went back home, my mother was in shock, she was already crying because she didn't know what kind of future was ahead of us. I told her that we must leave immediately. I got to communicate with one of the officials in Mosul, who had been a member of the Governmental Council, his name is Husam Al-Abbar, he is our relative.

I punched in his number making a phone-call. "Please, Uncle Husam, we are in the Old Town."

"Look, dear Maha, tell the family that they should try to get out of the Old Town whatever the price. Try to reach the 5th bridge in any form as soon as you can!" my uncle replied.

I asked him where to go? He replied that we should go to his family's house in the Al-Rifai Neighbourhood.

Then I asked my mother to get ready. In the meanwhile, my father was staying at that house we had dwelled in, adjoining the Grand Mosque of the leaning minaret, he was there with my sister."

The Grand Mosque was blown up by ISIS in a last desperate act, inflicting great damage to the diameter of the mosque. It was the same mosque from which the Islamic State had been declared to the world, the leaning minaret of the Grand Mosque called Al-Hadba (hunchback); it had been the pride of Mosul for nine centuries. Nowadays the mosque is under reconstruction in a step to revive the spirit of Mosul by UNESCO, financed by the UAE. Maha's decision to flee that neighbourhood was crucial and saved their lives, as the battle approached the heart of Mosul, more damage took place, when ISIS members were fighting to the last man because they knew that escape wasn't possible at that time.

Maha - a new escape plan

Next day my father went back to our old house because he heard that ISIS members were robbing uninhabited houses. My mother was exhausted. So I came up with the "escape plan" for my younger sister Ziina and I, alongside my niece.

At first, I took my niece. My mother had a bag full of medicine obtained from the doctor Alaa Jennat who deposited that bag with my mother, because she is a pharmacist. The doctor asked us to keep that bag until we were liberated. Then we would give it back to her, because medicine was so expensive and rare at that time. ISIS had been looting her pharmacy from time to time.

I told my mother that she and my other two sisters should take the bag of medicine to camouflage them at ISIS checkpoints. If ISIS members asked where they were going, my mother would say that she was heading to the hospital, located close to Al-Rifai neighbourhood - our destination – because she wanted to donate this bag to the hospital.

That would enable her to reach my friend's house in Al-Shefah neighbourhood as the first stage before slipping out of the danger zone.

We would follow and meet at my friend's house. We couldn't go in one group as an entire family. If we did so, they would kill us, because they would conclude we wanted to flee.

The plan was if ISIS questioned any of us, we would say that we were going to the hospital.

Before going out, we distributed nine gallons of drinkable water and other well-water. We donated everything to the locals who stayed in the alley. We had some potatoes, some wheat. We gave our stored food to our neighbours who didn't have the courage to make the journey of death that we were about to.

My mother was saying we should give all what we have to charity, so God would help us on our journey to escape from death. Even if we failed, God would find a solution for us.

While we packed our bags, we were crying out of either happiness or grief or probably fear. We had decided to head into the unknown. We were psychologically devastated, defeated from the inside. But the will to live was growing in strength with every step we made.

I escorted my younger sister Ziina to our old house in the Al-Faruq neighbourhood, to inform my father. "Dad, that's it, we must exodus!"

He said that he did not support my plan.

"Dad, I will run away. Even if I get killed, at least I would be killed while trying to escape, rather than staying at home and getting killed here, just waiting for death!"

Then I put on a lot of clothes, and concealed all the SIM cards and cell-phones. I decided to take the risk of doing so because I was the pilot of that voyage. My father had a credential of a certain party affiliated to the Iraqi state. ISIS would kill anyone carrying such a credential.

I told my family: I want to carry all the dangerous things. If I am searched and debriefed by ISIS members on the way, please say that you had no idea what I was carrying with me, in case they find out the truth. You could also say that our daughter deceived us by keeping those documents and stuff undamaged. We asked her to burn them but she stored them for a reason we don't know. I would rather only one member of the family perished. I had the honour of being the scapegoat on the road of salvation.

(Maha's note: My reason for taking the documents and the other stuff, which were something of an ISIS taboo, was that I wanted to feel victorious by passing through ISIS checkpoints carrying what ISIS members were after. They would kill everyone carrying a voting card, or anything related to the Iraqi Government, as well as the memory-chips and the sim cards, while cell's phones were something so dangerous to possess in that time when they are found with sim cards. I felt that I was victorious by being able to hide those things for a long time. I admit that I was naïve. Our way of thinking had been so simple, but significant)."

Poem: We dealt with life that was stripped of accessories

We were in contact with the core of the things that had been solid and rigid
We are the children of wars, we saw the importance of small details
Everything was meaningful,
amidst the path of death,
we inhaled the brisk breeze of life,
we glimpsed the chamomile flowers cracking through the grime and rubble,
sending the smell of hope mingled with the stench of death.
We had to leave the alley that was ruthlessly bombed;
the home of our childhood.

The gateway under which we lingered when it was raining,
the gateway was entwined like two lovers' hands to protect the school children.
The corners that never revealed us when we played hide and seek
WE DON'T WANT TO BE ACCENTUATED ANYMORE!
WE DON'T WANT TO BE!
The city of Mosul is rattling on this side
The Old Town, the heart of the city is bleeding, but we still cling to our dignity.
Has the alleyway forgotten who we are?
The windows were dumb, and the doors were open like jaws of a hungry wolf
"Never slam the door!"
ISIS shouted.
"We might need to be quartered when air-raid howls, when missiles roar"
ISIS contemplated, as loud as the blast that took place in the adjacent alley.

Ahmed Zaidan

Maha - more preparations for the escape

Our neighbours – the two guys who'd told us we should flee – showed up and asked if we would escape?

"Yes, we will escape whatever happens." I talked to them. I was wearing the Islamic costume that was imposed on women.

They said: "We will also flee after you have fled."

We had agreed with many families to run away, but we needed to adjust our escape into smaller groups. I went back to the house where we lived to take both my sisters.

We informed my mother that my father had refused to go with us. "You are now my responsibility, but keep in mind if something happens to me or to any of my sisters, it is God's will. One going is better than all of us."

Based on that, my mother had brought my other sisters who threw away their iPads because they couldn't carry them. They only had to put their clothes on. My mother carried the bag of medicine with extra clothes and towels, so ISIS members would believe that my family were really going to the hospital to donate the medicines.

I explained my thoughts to my mother. "If ISIS members tried to follow you to check you were really going to the hospital, you could take the way to the hospital, even if you have to stay there for a night." That was the plan.

Meanwhile, I took my little sister Ziina in a bid to reach my married sister's house by the river. I arrived there at 8:30 in the morning, and they were having breakfast. They were shocked to see me standing in their house yard.

I asked her husband to get ready now, because we didn't want to die trapped at the house. Without exaggeration, I spent an entire hour trying to convince my sister to escape, alongside her husband and kids, and my uncle's wife who were displaced to their house. Finally, I managed to convince them to go. I convinced them not to carry anything other than their personal documents, money, and the gold they had.

I asked my uncle's wife (my aunt) to say, if she got intercepted by ISIS, that she was a widow, and the Islamic State had taken her house to make it a repel-point by the river. She was to tell them she was left homeless, stranded without anyone, and needed to go to her sister's house located in the Al-Shifa neighbourhood.

I told her, "You can go there, if anything happens, I will come to take you later."

There were a lot of fears, stress and negative thoughts stirring around.

My married sister had taken my younger sister Ziina, and my cousin, because, if they were caught, then they were a small group.

I accompanied my brother-in-law and his son.

Her husband was afraid to go out. Despite the fact that ISIS didn't care much about men because they knew that men couldn't run away without taking their families with them. ISIS watched women carefully, because they realised women can go alone and the men can find a way to follow them later.

Meanwhile, my brother-in-law was talking outside at the front door in their neighbourhood that was full of Russian Insurgents (People of Mosul attributed the white insurgents to "Russians" who originally came from Russia and its neighbours of the Islamic countries such as Chechnya).

A man from the neighbourhood rushed towards us saying: "Maha, either stay here, or run away instantly. The informant knew you would go out, and he has informed the Russian insurgents. You must escape now."

That left me only ten minutes to run away. I sent my aunt out first and counted from 1 to 10 while she was running. I pushed my sister out and counted from 1 to 10. Then I started to run. There was enough distance between us to see each other. My little sister was the youngest, so she ran faster than my aunt. She overtook her.

I stayed behind, to watch everybody. We decided to go to the 5th bridge until reaching the Al-shifa neighbourhood where my friend's house was located.

While running, we reached Barqa alley by the river. There was an ISIS station standing there. I heard my brother calling me loudly. I was stressed and confused, and there was a possibility of losing any of the dearest ones at any time. I thought that certainly my family had been struck by one of those mortar rounds that were falling all the time like rain. I lay on the ground thinking that something bad had happened to my family.

He approached me and I asked what had happened. He said that our neighbour who was working with ISIS, had warned him not to go out at that very moment; that he'd better to stay home because ISIS had ordered its members to arrest any woman they saw. The neighbour also passed information to my brother that we should slip out in the afternoon.

I didn't know what to do. Then I sprinted to reach my aunt to inform her to stop running, but we found ourselves surrounded by an ISIS car that was following us. Two of the men jumped out of the car to ask us: "Hey sister, where are you going?"

"My little sister Ziina has been sick, suffering from stomach pain, and we are taking her to the hospital" At that moment, we were shivering out of fear and cold, thinking that they would take my brother.

"What hospital! How can we believe that you are really going to the hospital?"

I watched my sister, while they were talking with us, and replied, "If you don't believe we are going to the hospital, I ask you to accompany us to the hospital, so you can be sure where we are heading."

While I was keeping an eye on my sister, I saw five ISIS members heading towards her and the children. They were carrying pistols. I knew they had been killing instantly those who were trying to flee. Meanwhile, my brother was convincing ISIS members that our little sister was sick, so we were taking her to the hospital.

There was a moment when I thought, that's it, we're done for. I felt hopeless, desperate, and broken from deep inside. It was my plan; I had endangered my family!

My sister was with her daughter and my little cousin there. Five ISIS men were walking towards her and the children. There was just a metre separating her from the armed monsters heading towards them. Then something unexpected had happened. It changed the course of the story.

It was like a miracle took place before our eyes. While they were pointing their pistols at my sister and the kids, just as they were approaching them, all of a sudden, a mortar shell fell among the five ISIS men, killing them instantly.

My sister fell on the ground. I thought that she and the kids might have been wounded by shrapnel from the exploded mortar round.

I looked at the three ISIS members who were investigating and questioning us. They left us instantly and rushed to aid the ones that had been killed or injured.

As I got closer, I saw three women had been killed and one teenage boy lying on the ground. He had just been killed by the ISIS members who patrolled that road. The wounds were still fresh, and blood was still warm.

I reached my sister, and another miracle took place: not a single piece of shrapnel had touched them. They were completely fine. I thought to myself that that must be impossible because she was so close to the ISIS members who perished.

The other ISIS members were confused, busy with their injured or the dead ones. They had just lost five members.

I told ISIS that our house was in the Al-Shifa neighbourhood. Now we seemed like a grand family, they couldn't figure it out. They asked us: do you live in Al-Shifa neighbourhood; what have you been doing in the Old Town?

We replied that we went to the funeral of one of our relatives. We had fabricated a story while they were questioning us.

They immediately let us go towards the Al-Shifa neighbourhood. When we arrived at my friend's house, my sister fainted. We tried to awaken her. We gave her a check-up. Her body was clear of any shrapnel, thank God. We reached our destination safely. In the meanwhile, we were worried about my mother, my two sisters (1999 and 2001 their years of birth) and my brother. His year of birth is 1997 and he was supposed to bring the cart of food, with my dad and my brother-in-law and his son.

There were six members of the family waiting for them. After half an hour, there was a knock at the door. We saw my mother alongside my two sisters. My mother collapsed when she saw us. We asked them what had happened to them, they replied: we got to run away, while ISIS members had been busy talking with each other. An ISIS member told her: "Go back, this is not the time to go and donate the medicine to the brothers right now. Go back now and come in the afternoon, because now, we will kill anyone who tries to cross."

There was one ISIS member sitting on the 5th bridge. His pistol fell down from the bridge, the other ISIS member who was talking with my mother, rushed to pick up his friend's pistol.

At that moment, my mother sprinted, running away towards Al-Shifa neighbourhood. She said that it was as though God had assisted us and blinded ISIS members.

They arrived at my friend's house. After 10 minutes, my father and my niece also showed up. So, the only missing members of the family were my brother and my niece.

We were there at noon, so they offered us lunch, which was cooked wheat.

After lunch, my father suggested we go back to our house in the Old Town. I told him: "If you want, you can go back alone."

After all that, he wanted to go back to the Old Town.

We had nearly got killed on the way, bidding to escape the Old Town, and now he wanted to go back. I told him that it was impossible to go back.

The plan was to resume the way to the Al-Rifai neighbourhood. If ISIS kicked us back, we would come to the friends' place again. But we had to try to get to that neighbourhood. They said that there was a battle going on in the Al-Rifai neighbourhood. I thought to myself, they will say that all the time, and we would have to wait for a long time, and nothing will happen. Let's rely on God and go out.

We started the trek to that neighbourhood, walking and walking. We encountered ISIS members along the escape route, they were staring at us, we heard them saying to each other: "Look at this family who are going to the infidels."

It was as though we were in a fiction or horror movie, we were walking and seeing dead bodies along the way. We were blocking ourselves from seeing all that, we pretended that we didn't see anything. We were deceiving ourselves, while the fear, stress and confusion had permeated the air, I can't even describe the situation. At any moment we could be targeted by an air-strike or mortar shell, or a drone could've dropped a bomb on us, ISIS could've arrested or killed us. The way was teeming with road-bombs and the mined-bars attached to explosive barrels.

The street was destroyed; the pavement had been dug up; it seemed like the apocalypse was taking place in that city.

We arrived at the Al-Zennjelli neighbourhood, we saw my father's friend who lived there, he offered to let us stay at his place. We refused to stop. We thanked him and said: "We need to get to Al-Rifai neighbourhood, and if ISIS members intercept us, we will come back to your place."

We rested at his place and drank water, then started off again. We arrived at the so-called Pepsi Street. Later on, that street earned new fame as The Street of Death. due to the number of families that got killed there. My father's friend escorted us to Pepsi Street, saying that if any of you fall to the ground, any one of the family members; dad or mom or one of the siblings, the rest of you must run fast, because that street is full of ISIS snipers.

My sister got more scared, she was worried about her children, but I encouraged her. Then we relied on God, and decided to cross that street.

The first group had to run, and then the second group. I was the last one watching everybody cross.

I kept in mind that if one of them would fall, I would be there to help. However, I kept repeating: "Never stop running, even if one of us is targeted, you just keep running and never turn back whatever happens!"

I decided to be the last one to cross. I had been trying to make sure that everyone would be safe, I thought to myself I could help if someone got shot.

My aunt was carrying a bag in which she hid the money and her important belongings, so I carried her bag and we both were the last ones to cross Pepsi Street. Not even a bullet broke out.

We reached the Al-Rifai neighbourhood, and as we arrived, we got to see our neighbour who had moved to that area. They hosted us at their house, they begged us to stay over, but we refused. "We are aiming to reach the house of Hussam Al-Abbar. Would you show us the safest routes in this neighbourhood?"

They recommended that we should sneak through the narrow alleys.

The last part of the journey started; we walked through the alleys. For 10 years, we hadn't been to that house, so we didn't know where exactly the house was located. We crept through the complex alleys. I felt something was wrong. I told my father that we should get out of the narrow alleys and find the open area where the street was.

Meanwhile, ISIS fighters were positioned on the roofs of the houses saying: "Are you escaping to the Shia Popular

Mobilisation Troop?" (The Shia Militia, founded in 2014 to repel ISIS from reaching the Shia districts)

We pretended as though we didn't hear anything, just kept progressing until we reached a house where ISIS members were storing mustard gas capsules. It was a big risk to be there. At any time, that house could be targeted by an air-strike, and then we would perish from the mustard gas.

We took a detour to the other alley. We saw that the road had trenches dug in it. There was a big hole, about 10 metres long, down the middle of the street. ISIS members were on the ground surveying, and the ammo bar was sliding while one of them steered a shooting weapon, targeting the Iraqi Forces ahead.

Then, for the first time, we managed to see the Iraqi military vehicle from a distance looming beyond the front-line.

The ISIS fighter who had been shooting towards the Iraqi troops, ISOF (Iraqi Special Operations Forces) ceased firing and turned to us. He looked shocked; children and women and an old man, an entire family:

"How come you were able to reach this zone?" he exclaimed.

I caught the attention of a huge ISIS guy with beefy shoulders, equipped with all sorts of weaponry. I couldn't understand how he was able to do so. He even carried mortars, ammo bars, everything...

One of the ISIS group was Iraqi. He was the one who saved us! Despite the fact that he was ISIS himself, he saved our lives somehow.

The huge one, I couldn't even tell where he was from, told us: "You deserve the death penalty because you are trying to reach Popular Mobilization Troops."

At that moment, I was whispering into my father's ear: "Dad, don't tell them that we are from the Old Town! Tell them that you are from the Al-Uraibi neighbourhood that was taken by the Iraqi forces, and we were forced to come here; to the Islamic State!

"I will not tell lies!" My father replied.

"Dad, please tell lies, only for this time!" I tried to convince him.

Meanwhile, they were yelling, ordering us to come closer. They couldn't have seen I was whispering to my father, because my face was veiled with Al Burka.

My father was so hesitant because he hadn't been in such a situation.

"Where did you come from? From which area?" they asked him.

A moment of silence preceded his answer. I was about to reply instead.

Then my father said something astonishing, "We came from the Old Town."

The ISIS member was furious and said: "Now you deserve the death penalty with your family. All of you will be killed now."

My father begged them not to kill the family, for the sake of the women and the children.

"Where are the men of the family?"

The only good thing was that my brother and brother-in-law were behind us and hadn't arrived yet.

"I am the only man in this family," he said.

"You are such a villainous man; you are taking your woman and daughters to the Popular Mobilisation," the ISIS fighter barked.

They decided to execute my dad. My mom took the children away, so they wouldn't see their grandfather getting killed before their eyes.

"Down on your knees, now," he shouted at my father, preparing to shoot him dead.

My sisters and aunt, all of them, turned away in tears, sobbing severely. My sister Ziina and I were the ones who stayed, standing close to my dad.

"Say Al Shahada before your death! Or don't say it, because you are not deemed a Muslim, you were caught while you were trying to reach the apostates, you are an apostate now," he told my father.

"You will kill me now, but promise me that my family will be safe thereafter," my father said,

My little sister started to cry saying "Please, Uncle, don't kill my dad, please don't kill my dad, please, I beg for your mercy, my father hasn't done anything wrong that entails him to be killed."

He pointed the gun towards my father's head, and we heard the slide of the gun click open.

I was speechless, I couldn't have said anything, my tongue got stuck. And then, I hardly muttered those words.

"Please, Uncle, my father didn't lie when he said we came from the Old Town, but our house was taken by three of the Islamic State families, it has been seven months since they took our house, we were forced to move to Al-Ureibi neighbourhood that was occupied by the Popular Mobilization troops, So we had no place to go, we were forced to come here."

At that, the Iraqi ISIS lowered his gun.

That idea, or that fine lie, came out of me unconsciously, I didn't know how...

Then they asked my father to stand up and take his family to the Old Town.

We turned back, and I was screaming and yelling on the street, while my father was in a rage arguing with me. I told him that it's impossible to go back to the Old Town, even if they killed me now.

Those ISIS members who were on the road started to mock us: "Poor family, they were going to run away to the Popular Mobilisation forces, but they couldn't have made it. The brothers had kicked them back." They sneered.

ISIS members had been letting their families go to the Iraqi Troops. But we were not allowed.

While we were walking, I persuaded my sister to knock on the door of a house we saw ahead of us. "Please go and tell them that we need to be sheltered in your house for a while," I told her.

My sister rushed to that house, pushing the door, but what she saw was shocking.

The house-yard was full of ammunition and weaponry. It seemed that it was an ISIS affiliate house. My sister got intimidated saying: "We have been trying to avoid ISIS, but now we have run into their house."

"Hey, please knock on the door of the kitchen!" I said.

When she knocked on the door, a man showed up, gazing at us trying to study our features. I didn't know what to say, because I wasn't sure if he was a civilian or an ISIS fighter.

"O Uncle, are you one of the brothers (in a reference to ISIS members) or you are one of the ordinary people?"

"I am one of the ordinary people,"

"Please Uncle, please, save our souls! ISIS is going to kill us," I said, bidding to earn his sympathy so he would quarter us at his home for a short while.

He kept staring suspiciously.

"Either you give us a refuge in your house or we'll die outside."

But when my father saw him, they knew each other, he apologised to my father that he wouldn't be able to hide us. But we begged him until he agreed to let us stay in the kitchen for a short while only.

ISIS members could've killed him and his family if they knew he had concealed us.

"I am sorry, you cannot stay here for long," he told my father while we all crammed into the kitchen. His house was teeming with many families of his relatives.

My mother said: "I would like to go to check on my relative's house nearby." My mother, my father, my sister, my aunt, and the children were in one group who left before us. I stayed with my other three sisters and my two nieces.

After they left, we were waiting, five minutes passed, I didn't know if my father was still alive or had been killed. Those five minutes felt like 50 years. My heart was on the boil, getting ripped from within. I couldn't have cried or done anything.

And then my father showed up saying: "The ISIS member whom we saw, Abu-Omar, knows that house we are going to (Hussam Al-Abbar family). ISIS has confiscated their house, because of Hussam who works as a representative in the Provincial Council. ISIS had decided that the family of Hussam Al-Abbar was obligated to provide for the families of ISIS who were living there."

So when we told them that the family of Hussam Al-Abbar were our relatives, they started to treat us differently. They gave shelter to the first group of my family, then my father returned to take us to join the rest of the family.

We were going to go to the narrow alley. "Don't go there," the ISIS member shouted. "You will be spotted by planes hovering around, but you can enter this house."

"I am sorry, I can't trust you,' I said. 'I am afraid that you will kill us."

"What happened to you? You are like my sister," he interrupted.

"I am not like your sister; you have been killing us."

"Ok, Ok, I will evacuate the house, so you can be there without me if you can't trust me." He stepped aside, and we got to enter that house.

We were terrified, waiting in the kitchen, when there was a knock at the door. It was my father. He asked us to hurry up, he wanted to take us to the house of Hussam Al-Abbar.

He told us that while he was looking for that house in the neighbourhood, the ISIS member we had seen before intercepted him angrily, "Where are you going, we had asked you to go back to the Old Town. Are you going to the house of Um-Omar, the relative of Hussam Al-Abbar?"

"Yes," my father answered.

"Alright, I will let you go, because this family is paying for ISIS families, mandatorily because their child Hussam Al-Abbar is part of the government," the ISIS fighter said. The members of Hussam Al-Abbar's family were treated as hostages, they had been feeding the families of ISIS, and providing for them.

"You pretended that you knew that family, now I will knock on their door to see if they really know who you are." ISIS fighter, Abu-Omar, said.

"Yes, do that," my father said.

"But if you were lying, you'll instantly be executed, this time." Abu-Omar grinned.

"Yes, you can do that"

"I will also kill your family," Abu-Omar threatened. Then he knocked on the door, calling the old woman, Aunt Noofa, a conservative woman who didn't socialise very often.

She had rarely seen my father. After all those years, my father's facial features weren't the same. A man with a beard and creased face, slimmer than before, he also had grey hair.

When she opened the door Abu-Omar asked her "Do you know this man?"

She paused, gazing into my father's face.

My father exclaimed, "Hey, I was your neighbour."

"Stop!" Abu-Omar interjected. "We will kill you, if she doesn't know you."

She was able to recognize my dad's voice. "Are you Abu-Karam?"

"Yes, I am Abu-Karam, we are your relatives," my father answered.

"Is he really your cousin?" Abu-Omar asked Noofa.

"Yes, he is my cousin," she emphasised.

"Swear to God that he is your cousin!" Abu-Omar asked her to make an oath, so that if they found out they were lying she would be executed for using God in making a false oath.

"I swear to God that he is my cousin." She took the risk of making a false oath.

Meanwhile, we were waiting for him to see if he would be lucky enough to make it back to us. When he showed up, we felt extremely happy. We escorted him to that intended house. While we were on the way, Abu-Omar intercepted us saying, "Are you messing with us again?"

"I told you that I have a big family. These are my unmarried daughters," my father said.

"Ok, you can cross," he said.

Three armed ISIS fighters said "Don't cross through the door, because you will be spotted by the plane. You can cross from between the walls."

"No, I can't do that, because you may want to kill me," I said.

"Sister, I swear we won't hurt you; I know that you are escaping," one of them said.

"I can't trust you, who says you won't take me to another house and kill me there?" I said loudly.

"I will get out of here, and then you can take this route from between the rubble to get to the intended house," the fighter said.

Then we walked between rubble and walls until we reached the house of Hussam Al-Abbar. We entered that house, and stayed there. They were so generous and hospitable. We couldn't stop crying.

The family said "We thought we were about to be liberated."

I told them that ISIS had a giant arsenal out there, I thought they had the capacity to resist for one more month.

It was 4 pm, when we arrived at their house. We had started our journey at 9 in the morning, escaping from old Mosul.

We stayed at their house that day, and they cooked for us, rice, pasta, and tea with tahini.

We hadn't had food like that while we were trapped in the Old Town. We'd been eating grass, bird feed, and wheat and bread, Broccoli, cannabis or the ordinary lawn. Children were roaming in the alleys to sell it to the locals, one bag cost 5,000 dinar, like 3 dollars. Some people who had birds started to sell the bird feed to the locals. We would sift it and cook it. We had been buying oil and tomato paste but had to do that secretly.

We used to ask a mediator to bring those items to us, the man would conceal the stuff in the clothes, and then we would pay him the price in cash.

At that time, a bottle of oil cost 45,000 dinars, like 30 dollars, and the can of tomato paste cost 35,000 dinar.

Luckily, we had cash in US dollars. But we needed to exchange the currency into the Iraqi dinar, and that was a big risk. Because no one should know that we had money, otherwise that money would be confiscated by ISIS. The last time they were searching houses, when they found a bag of flour they took half of it.

We had been living such a restricted kind of life, suffering acute nutritional deficiency for more than three months.

The Eastern part of the city had been fully liberated; the government took a break for 3 months before initiating the fight in the Western part.

The battles commenced at the end of 2016; however, it took a long time until we got liberated, we were liberated in May 2017.

While we were there, everyone was crying, saddened, depressed, especially after they heard our narrative regarding ISIS members who were ready to resist longer than the time they'd anticipated. Everyone was disappointed.

I told them, "Now I need to return to find my brother and brother-in-law."

They said: "It is impossible for anyone to make it back and forth in such a circumstance."

We couldn't use the phone, because ISIS fighters were positioned on the roof of that house, they could detect the phone signals, then we would be killed for being espionage.

We stayed one night, then at 7 am, we saw Iraqi special forces popping up in the crypt where we had been hiding.

It was a great joy, fear, and sorrow, because my brother and my brother-in-law were still trapped in the Old Town. We were in shock; my mother didn't know if she had to cry out of happiness or grief.

My mother said to the soldier: "Are you the Iraqi Forces or ISIS fighters who came to check our reaction and then kill us. You think that we would be happy seeing the Iraqi Forces and then you kill us for that?"

"I swear to Hussein that we are the Iraqi Forces" (ISIS banned mentioning any of the Islamic Symbols when swearing, they swear to Allah exclusively.) "We have come to save you!"

My mother burst into tears and passed him the IDs of my brother and my brother-in-law that we were able to run away with just yesterday. She informed them that they were still inside the Old Town. The officer debriefed more information and said everything was alright.

Meanwhile, we took the military vehicle to get evacuated to the displacement-zones where camps were erected to receive countless numbers of families after they walked free from ISIS' firm hold. My father shaved off his beard and we were taken to certain buses.

Before we left Al-Rifai neighbourhood, we learned that my brother had already made it to my friend's house in the afternoon. We got to make a short phone-call. He was at my friend's house, they didn't let him go because the battles had escalated outside, he also brought them a cart full of food. I asked her to take the food for themselves because we had been liberated. My brother-in-law stayed in the Old Town.

I called my brother, asking him to escape to Al-Zanjelli where my uncle's house was. He went there, but they led him to the Al-Sahha neighbourhood. I contacted that house in the Al-Sahha neighbourhood and learned that he and my brother-in-law had arrived there safely. They had implemented my plan.

He was so embarrassed to be there, among women he didn't know. I asked him not to feel embarrassed, and to try to stay normal.

I asked him to take a tomato paste can, so if he got captured by ISIS, he could say that he brought those items from his grandfather's family to his family. Because they didn't allow us to buy food at that time, they would confiscate the food and money. We had reached that level. At that very moment, another cousin of my mother wanted to run away to the Al-Rifai neighbourhood. We knew that the army would be there soon, so I asked him to take my brother-in-law and my brother with him.

We knew it could take a week before they saw the Iraqi troops. My brother-in-law and my brother went separately to another house. They got to know someone who was a good person. He called us and we told him: "We are the relatives of Hussam Al-Abbar, I had been calling him."

Two days later, my brother called us informing us that their area got liberated.

But when I called that man again and he said: "I am sorry to inform you that your brother is laid under rubble now!"

"What happened?"

"There was a lorry that got stricken by an air-raid. Your brother was close to the blast. The house collapsed and your brother-in-law can't speak now because he is crying, traumatised, he was wounded in his arm and leg, in the meantime your brother is under rubble. We have no idea what to do now."

I was shocked, I felt that the world had ended for me. I couldn't have said anything, neither did I cry.

I collected myself to reply: "I will wait for you to exhume him from under rubble, I will wait to hear his voice when I call you next time."

I couldn't inform my family; I didn't have any clue what to say! I was waiting at the house-yard crying silently. My cousin saw me and hurried to ask me what had happened.

"My brother is under the rubble but don't tell anyone."

I kept crying. *(Sobbing)* I waited for 15 minutes full of wistful thoughts and clusters of emotions.

I dialled his number again to talk with that guy. My brother answered the call. Nothing had happened to him, despite the fact that he was under rubble, but we kept hope of seeing him again, that time we had nothing except to keep the flare of hope on.

My brother went to Umeimma's house (my friend's house), my friend who lived in Al-Shifa neighbourhood, I told her that we got liberated.

She was stunned, saying: "Yesterday you were here."

I replied that the Iraqi Special Forces had liberated us.

Suruur - Corpse Clearing and Women's Cycling

Suruur is one of those whose lives took a detour that she'd never imagined. She discovered the potential power in herself through the sacrifices she made, the new self that grew stronger rapidly; the self that would save her family and take a new course in her life; work that might sound weird for a woman to do in the eyes of the stereotype, but a woman like her would not fit in any of the ready-images. She decided to draw her own image, the new era when women are empowered by their deeds; sacrifice and strength.

Suruur was a student at the Nursing Institute alongside her husband; they had lived a normal life. Like many people who lived in the city back then, they hadn't thought one day that they would get to that level of suffering.

After she graduated, she lived in the dark ages under ISIS authority. She couldn't have anticipated what kind of future was ahead of her and all the residents of the city; in short, the future was unknown. Surrur resorted to reading; she felt that the realm of books was giving her a safe shelter of a normal world that exceeds all walls and borders of the grim reality.

Suruur had the foresight to recognise a social and public health challenge. The bombing was so intense the people of Mosul weren't able to leave their basements or shelters during the battle. When a family member passed away, the corpse would be kept in the same room until the chance was found to bury it in the garden or the yard. This posed a serious risk to residents.

Suruur - life under ISIS occupation

My name is Suruur Abdul Kareem Al Husseini, from Mosul. My year of birth is 1995. Ninawa Province, city of Mosul. I come from the right bank – the western side – the most devastated part of the city. Back then, I was living in Al Yarmouk and AL Risaalah.

When ISIS was waging the major assault to conquer the city, we were doing the final exams at the university. Several months later, when the city of Mosul was occupied by the so-called Islamic State, the universities in Mosul were shut and my study was suspended.

The Iraqi Government would have allowed the students in Mosul to resume their studies in the neighbouring cities, mainly in the autonomous region of Kurdistan, as well as in the city of Kirkuk at substituent locations of the higher educational institutions of Mosul. I thought of going to Kirkuk to perform my final exams. But several months after the conquest, Mosul was sliding towards the ditch of isolation. People of the capital of the Islamic State are prohibited to go elsewhere. ISIS used to grin after locking everyone in.

At that time, I thought I should resume my studies, but it wasn't so easy to journey beyond the borders of the proclaimed Islamic State. There were 11 of us girls crammed in that vehicle. We pretended we were going to attend the funeral of our relatives, because it was also prohibited for students to perform their exams elsewhere. It was very difficult, not only for us, but for anyone thinking of leaving the town.

Before the time of ISIS, I was holding onto the hope of being a journalist in the future, but it didn't happen. I had to study nursing because I thought that I might be assisting my sick mother. Thank God I became a nurse!

Living under the authority of those monsters who imposed their ruthless codes on us, was something unbearable. In the meantime, we had to obey without question or argument We started to feel we were inmates in a mass prison, where our lives were determined by our jailers who were keen on snatching the essence of life wherever they found it.

I was reading a lot. After a year, I had become a reading addict in order to avoid encountering ISIS members. I only left the house to visit relatives or go to the doctor.

I graduated from the substitute location of the University of Mosul in Kirkuk. However, I had to go back to Mosul because she couldn't leave her sick mother alone. I didn't have any other option, only to take the journey back to the most dangerous city."

Mosul was now passing through the dark ages under the authority of ISIS, who were gradually escalating restrictions on the locals and strangling all types of freedom; women's freedom in particular.

During ISIS, I got married after graduation. My family is very supportive, and is seen as an open-minded family compared to others in Nineveh province, however within social boundaries. My father worked as a senior non-commissioned officer in the former Iraqi army that was dissolved after the US Invasion in 2003. My family allowed their daughter to have ambitious dreams. I have two brothers and one sister.

Living under ISIS required people to have a lot of patience and reliance. But Suruur sees herself as a woman with a temper that can be provoked easily.

My husband was arrested by ISIS, because men were targeted in the first place. I couldn't barely keep my mouth shut, I was near to breaking out of my silence, which could be a deadly action. Women could be lashed by ISIS female members, if they got caught doing one of the offences. Some of the women got killed for fabricated charges.

    One day I had to go out without a male chaperone from my family. When they intercepted me, I argued with them. I knew they would arrest my husband for that. So, after graduation, I stayed home and went back to reading.

Poem: In every book there are secret gates hidden in the lines

the routes that are unseen by the oppressors
the journey of the travelling light in the universe
Here, I am the sparrows who see the lines of the book as cables,
transmitting hope to the distant and forgotten villages,
I will alight on and sing

Here, I am the prisoner who sees the lines as razor-wires
I will travel through my sights to touch the sunset
I will hold the blades of the truth! Until the blood of impossible oozes
from my palm hides secret routes, hills, oasis, rivers...
and a decommissioned broken moon who suffered from loneliness.
I hide the talks of the stars in my soul,
I will not be a stone!

I opened the book, and the old author spoke to me from beyond the yellowed centuries:
"Daughter, you are not the first and never the last,
I will keep telling the story of hope,
Hope is creating the sun
Hope is holding on to the flame
Hope is the way to liberty."

Ahmed Zaidan

Suruur – losing touch with her loved ones

Large-scale military operations began to recapture the Western part of Mosul. Meanwhile, the Iraqi troops began to progress and liberate suburbs and villages. I was living in the Al-Resalah neighbourhood (Western Mosul). And my family were living in Al Yarmuk, which is about 10 minutes from where I lived. I was keen on visiting them every day until we reached a level where we had been intercepted a lot by ISIS elements when they saw us out.

She couldn't visit them as often as before as a result of the combat that was at the doors of her neighbourhood. People had been trapped where they were, awaiting the vehicles of the Iraqi armed troops declaring their freedom. Suruur lost contact with her loved ones. Phones were prohibited; however, she was hiding the cellphones in the fridge or in the food cellar. She barely communicated to learn if her family was fine at the time.

On the first day of the liberation battle, all houses were being shelled, Suruur was able to escape from that neighbourhood alongside the family of her husband that she lived with.

It was such a hard decision to leave the house and walk to the Iraqi troops; there were snipers spanning the way, we had to tread cautiously, targeting those families who attempted to flee. We ran away collectively; many families had to gather in one place and then they had to leave at the right moment taking a trek in which any flaw could lead literally to a mass grave for the whole family.

Luckily, they were able to go against all the risks along the way to the Iraqi troops. They trekked for six hours, where it wasn't easy to retreat or linger, the sky was a fire-rain, while the inferno framed the perimeter; pillars of dense smoke escalated carrying up a blend of souls of the innocent people or the bad guys' ghosts.

The decision of exodus wasn't easy. It was my husband's idea. Because in many cases, going out of the house indicated a certain death or an extreme risk of punishment for treason.

When we were trapped inside the house, the bombardment was getting nearer while the hopes of salvation were vanishing. We felt that we were waiting for our destiny to die under the rubble.

My husband said: "If we are going to die anyway, why don't we try to survive before we die?"

Staying at home seemed like desperate death. Dying while trying to survive was still death, but it would be a death at the edge of hope. What's harder than death itself is the feeling of death, then you feel dying at every second, this is when the end becomes a rest.

There were so many families crammed into that one house, children and elderly; about 20 souls facing one destiny. We gambled with our lives, but thank God, we reached the shore of safety and we made it to the Iraqi armed forces.

Because of my career as a nurse. I was treating people during the battles. I provided them with first aid and nursed their injuries. When I was trapped at home with the family of my husband and other families, there were people in the same neighbourhood who got injured because of the air-raid and the car bombs. I looked after them. Also, I started to treat the wounded people on the way when we were heading to the Iraqi troops.

We walked non-stop for six hours to reach the army, and afterwards they took us to the displacement zones (the camps of internal refugees). We had started the journey before six in the morning. We reached the Eastern part of the town where my uncle lived at ten in the evening.

At the displacement zone, people were asked to choose between two options: Either to stay at the displacement zone or to go to a relative's place elsewhere. There was a check in the system to probe people in search for ISIS members and their families. For that reason, people could get delayed until they are exonerated.

Crossing to the Eastern part of the city wasn't easy at all. People from the Western part of Mosul needed to go all the way south and cross through a rural road where a floating bridge had been installed by Iraqi armed forces to facilitate the movement of troops and civilians alike. The battle was creeping like blazing dry grass on a farm towards the heart of old Mosul, where most of those who couldn't make it out were marched by ISIS as human shields to the narrow alleys of Mosul.

Seeing my relative in the eastern part of the city had given me a beautiful feeling. At the same time, it was worrying, because half of the family was still confined in the battle zone. I was thinking how they could slip out of the area because I experienced how hard it was to escape by risking your life.

They stayed for two days in the Eastern part. She was trying all the time to reach her trapped family in the hope of speaking with them and knowing their news. She just wanted them to stay at home because she knew that her aged mother might not be able to make it to the Iraqi troops. She kept calling them for two days in a row, but in vain, until she fell asleep while the phone stayed awake. Later the hope was flowing from her phone when she opened her eyes and it was six in the morning. She thought why not give it another try!

I punched in their number and dialled. My younger brother answered the call. Usually, it was my elder brother who answered my calls. I thought to myself that they might have been taken by ISIS who would force one of the family members to answer the phone. I wanted to know their news, what had happened to them, but I could barely hear what he said because of the bad network.

He started crying: "Our family has been bombed and they've been underneath the rubble since yesterday."

I had been trying to reach them. They had no idea that we'd managed to escape from the battle zone. They also were escaping from the neighbourhood, so they headed to my neighbourhood to take me with them from my husband's house.

But her family saw that the Surrur's house was empty. They decided to resume their trek. When they were moving on, trying to approach the Iraqi forces, an ISIS sniper pointed his rifle at them, gesturing that they must go back, otherwise he would shoot them. Surrur's house was closer to the front lines. Her family took the way back to Surrur's house where they had to wait until the chance permitted them to escape again.

There were ISIS snipers everywhere, including the rear alley, so they got assaulted by an air strike, and my sister got injured, I knew it by the phone call, when the line went off while I was talking with them, I felt, I had to go back to the war zone, to the area controlled by ISIS. My husband tried to convince me to give up on the idea of me returning to danger.

Surrur decided to save the trapped part of herself; her family of course. She couldn't have enjoyed freedom while her beloved ones were still struggling to live on a slim chance. The war in Mosul has contributed to strengthening the value of altruism among families and friends. Many people helped escapees and wanted people either to hide or to resume their escape. Also, the theme of altruism was incarnated in the female elements who appeared to be the heroes in most of the stories.

When my husband heard I was insistent on going back, he wanted to escort me. But I refused because if my husband went back, he might not be seen again. Both sides perceived men as potential enemies. He might be intercepted by ISIS or even the Iraqi Forces might capture him, thinking that he was ISIS. I decided to go back, so we went back again alone.

The way back was extremely full of challenges, more than the way of escaping. Imagine you are going back to the area where everyone escapes from. Just imagine you are hurtling back against the storm! Well, to the centre of the typhoon.

Suruur was intercepted at security checkpoints affiliated to the Iraqi forces; because it seemed insane going back to the ISIS stronghold, whatever the reason was.

They warned me, if I crossed the frontline, it would be the point of no return, I might not be able to make it back.

"Let me go! My family is confined under the rubble, they have been bombed, they are trapped now waiting for my help! Whatever the price is, I will go, it's my responsibility now. No power can prevent me from going back to my family!"

An older army officer walked slowly towards me saying: "Let her go!" He gave me his phone number; in case I was intercepted by other security personnel and needed assistance.

I was sobbing, begging everyone just to let me go, even though I knew it was inevitable death. I saw the Iraqi elite troops called Counter-Terrorism and rushed over to them asking for help: "My family is trapped under the rubble."

They commissioned an ambulance to my family. I found my family members waiting by the highway, people had helped them to get out of the rubble.

It was lucky we didn't have to go back to the house, because ISIS had retaken control of the area. My little sister aged 14 years old was martyred, and my other family members were gravely wounded. My eldest brother wasn't there because his son needed to get hospitalised, so he escorted his son to the hospital controlled by ISIS.

Actually, during the battles of liberation, cell-phone companies assisted the locals to get them connected to the network for free by disseminating the network in the areas under the process of liberation. I was in touch with them.

As part of the security procedures, it was forbidden to transport corpses from the western part (in which the battles were still ongoing) to the eastern part (liberated part of Mosul). I was begging them to let me carry the body of my sister, a 14-year-old girl. How could they leave her buried in the house-yard?

Surrur - the journey into voluntary work

Surrur's study had given her the privilege to be listened to by the security members. Being a nurse in such a critical time is definitely an indispensable career. The Iraqi armed forces would give Suruur a pass to her family on condition Suruur agreed to collaborate with them as a nurse.

The security member knew that I was a nurse, so he asked me to come and work with them as a volunteer saying, "People are in need of your help now, why don't you come to the barracks and utilise what you have studied?"

I looked back. I saw dead people, injured, laid on the ground suffering from the lack of medical support. I thought to myself that this is my chance to be who I want to be, a free woman who would take part in life-making!

However, I wanted them to allow me to collect the body of my deceased sister. "If you allow me to collect my sister's corpse, I will come back to work with you, I promise."

He grinned. "Sorry I can't believe that you will show up again. If the men of this city weren't able to fulfil their promise, how would it be possible for women to do so?"

I was provoked by him bringing up this topic and making generalisations about Mosul citizens.

People of Mosul had been accused of letting their city slip into the hands of ISIS without armed resistance. Since the US military withdrawal by end of 2011, Iraqi Security forces had swarmed the city of Mosul. Three armed military divisions whose commanders were affiliated to the Iraqi Prime

Minister Nuri Al Maliki who was electorally defeated in Mosul in 2010 and 2014. Mosuli citizens had been exposed to different types of governmental terrorism carried out by the official armed forces. Many locals were detained on fabricated terrorism related charges. The Iraqi security forces had stripped the locals from any kind of defending instrument, confiscating the sole weapon by what was called the security-cleansing over the neighbourhoods. People couldn't have defended their city when the three military divisions collapsed, withdrawing swiftly, leaving the disarmed locals to face their gloomy destiny under the authority of the new oppressor ISIS that deemed the possession of any kind of weapon as a big crime threatening the existence of the Islamic State. All the Iraqi security members from Mosul, the city of Mosul who couldn't have fled for whatever reason, were asked to hand over their guns and to sign a document of remission, vowing not to be engaged at any form in the Iraqi armed forces and to show a great regret over their prior job. A year later, the decommissioned security members were asked to attend again to verify their attendance. At that time, they were detained and collectively executed and dumped into the hole of death, Southern Mosul.

Sailing against the hurricane strengthens the boat. Suruur decided to go back.

After we'd crossed to the left part of the city, I discussed the idea of returning with Dad, who was my prime supporter. He encouraged me to fulfil my promise.

"Dear daughter, you are a nurse. It is a humanitarian career, it is your honour, you will save souls. If you stand for your decision, just do it and go back to the barracks! I couldn't be prouder of you than today."

Three days passed, during which Suruur's family got to conduct the funeral of their daughter. Afterwards, Suruur went back to the battlefield to fulfil her promise and advance assistance to those who needed it. They were shocked when they saw her entering the barrack; they treated her as a sister. At that time, she was the only female doing voluntary work in the advanced frontlines, the most dangerous zone in the world, guided by her faith.

The mobile-healthcare centre was based in a school. But then, they moved on to another location after the army had liberated a mosque that became their new site, and then a big house was owned by ISIS. They used to station themselves there while advancing to the heart of the Old Town, where the fierce fighting took place.

I heard from my family about my brother. I knew that he was exposed to another attack with his injured son. His son was taken to the neighbouring city of Erbil; the boy was suffering from brain injury.

Meanwhile, my brother was forced by ISIS to be a human shield, as was the case with many people who'd failed to slip out.

ISIS was forcing people to stay at homes during the battles so that they would be used later as human shields. This is how ISIS secured its withdrawal. They tended to burn people's IDs as a way to demolish their identity, so that it would be easier for ISIS members to hide among the civilians who got liberated by the Iraqi armed forces.

Suruur worked with the Iraqi Security Forces for 5 months, providing wounded civilians with essential medical support. Sometimes she took care of injured military members of the Iraqi armed forces.

Some of the ISIS families didn't feel ashamed or hesitated to uncover their real identities, men fought until the last breath, while women didn't easily surrender amidst the constant brainwash that depicts a world full of perverts that want to erase the radical version of Islam, they simply believed that moderate Islam is a result of culture clash and globalism, they believed that the West are crusaders who appeared in the Muslim world in the form of humanitarian organisations and malignant media that got to insert the liberal ideology into every house. They often sought to prove their claim by the military interference of the West in the Middle East.

Suruur was offering aid to civilians, regardless of their beliefs, especially when it came to women and children. One day, she encountered a wounded child and had to give him medical support swiftly.

There was a child who suffered from critical injuries, so we gave him first aid, he was bleeding. It took us nearly two hours to revive him.

Afterwards, we brought him to the ambulance, and I called on the women who were there: "Whose kid is this?"

A woman exclaimed saying: "It is my kid. And I don't want him anymore. He became impure because you're the infidels and heretics have touched him. He is no longer my child!"

There was another scene which I feel is unforgettable. I saw a man lamenting and slapping his face while crying: "I have lost all my family members. Everything I have built over the years, has gone in a second."

He was appealing to the corpses of his family: "Please, don't leave me alone! I need just one of you to stay with me!"

Some of the soldiers were crying as well.

When I saw what happened to the people, the tragedy they had to pass through, I thought how lucky I was to have lost only one family member.

During the soldiers' advance, they had collected six children whose father got killed on the street and left in that dangerous zone. The children's mother had also passed away when they were on the way to us. The eldest child was crying, begging the soldiers to go back to save his father. However, everybody knew that it was impossible to go back, and his father had died.

We gave them food, but they didn't want to eat anything. The youngest girl among them accepted the food saying, "I will take this food to my mom because she must be hungry now."

Her mom lay dead in the coffin.

She said: "I would like to feed my mom! I want to lie down beside my mom! I would like to sleep beside my mother!" They couldn't bring her dad's body because he fell down close to ISIS. They only managed to transfer those who ran.

It was so difficult, I was begging the little girl to eat, but she insisted on feeding her dead mother. The soldiers were crying once more while watching.

Suruur - becoming a volunteer

We have become more resilient; we have seen everything. We have nothing left to lose.

During the liberation operations, I noticed that people lacked a lot of knowledge regarding first aid. I don't know if they really don't know or perhaps because I am a nurse, it made them notice those things. Imagine that a dad brings his daughter who was shot in the leg, then she would bleed to death. But what if her dad had knowledge of first aid, he could have saved her life?

Her journey into voluntary work started when she went to the youth centre asking them to be a trainer, voluntarily teaching people how to do first aid. In the first lecture, she was surprised to see that a large number of people had attended her lesson online. She realised that people were interested, so she kicked off a series of online lectures. She built a team of more than 50 volunteers. When the team grew larger, she started to expand beyond the Mosul city limits to cover the suburbs as well. Her team even visited the neighbouring city Erbil. The number of trainees hit 1000 members.

During the training process, the team made a visit to the Old Town of Mosul, to gain a perspective on how to initiate the work in the most devastated city in Iraq. When they stepped onto the rubble of the Old Town, they were shocked by the horrible spectacle of corpses tossed all around the place. The number of corpses was enormous. That was in 2017. When Suruur saw the huge number of dead; she told her team:

We were lucky because we lost only one member of our family during that war. But we could lose more of them now. If this situation is not taken care of, a pandemic could be rampant because of the decomposing corpses. Another tragedy could take place in Mosul.

Suruur - the Corpse Clearing Team

The first thing the team had to do was to appeal, calling on the Iraqi Government to intervene in hope of preventing what was to happen. The Civil Defence Directorate couldn't do anything. They claimed that working with unknown corpses wasn't their business. The team learned that the Health Directorate was responsible for clearing of the corpses. When they addressed the Health Directorate of Mosul, the response was negative. The Directorate abstained from offering any help claiming that they were busy doing a more important job than taking care of dead people. The team had witnessed mass graves in the city of Mosul. They obtained a permit from the Security Forces to be escorted by a medical team to the sites of the mass graves.

We went to the Municipality who told us they were working on it though it was too difficult.

I told them: "What if my colleagues and I help you, we are six people?"

They said: "We haven't seen a woman who can help on that issue, exhuming dead bodies!"

I told them: "Yes I can do it."

Next day, we went and voluntarily worked in the Old Town, lifting dead people's bodies. They saw how we had worked well. They liked what we did. They asked us to come again.

Before beginning to work with them, the team were asked to show a formal permit, allowing them to do the job. Luckily, we were able to obtain multiple formal permits from the Provincial Cancel and from the Nineveh Operation Command and from the Police Command.

The team was asked to provide a name for the team. Suruur came up with an idea of giving her name to the team so it became The Suruur Team of Voluntary Work. Suruur means pleasure in Arabic, something that has nothing to do with clearing bodies in a disastrous town. The team didn't have any support from the official institutes. Only the Youth Centre supported the team by providing them with the needed space to conduct the training. That was the milestone of everything.

My best supporter was my father. He did encourage me to do the job of clearing the corpses. However, on the first day of the actual work, my father passed away from a heart attack. After I obtained the death certificate of my sister, he couldn't cope with the fact that his little daughter had gone forever. When my father saw the death certificate he was saddened. He slept that night and never woke up. He wasn't old, he was only 50 years old.

After his death, I just collapsed. Imagine, my biggest supporter had passed away at such a critical time! I went speechless, I stayed at home all the time, not willing to meet with people.

Then, the team came and said: "This is the campaign that your father had encouraged you to do."

So I decided to carry on, I decided to go against my emotion of sorrow. We worked for five months, and exhumed 1350 corpses during that time.

The work was full of risks and challenges. It wasn't easy to take a walk in what appeared to be a battlefield, a deserted land full of explosives and mines. Suruur remembers:

The most dangerous thing was that the corpse could be attached to explosives. We got used to that level of risk. Every day, we were losing a beloved team member.

Suruur - challenges to the Corpses Team led by a girl

It was unprecedented in the Middle East for a woman to lead a team dealing with dead bodies. It had never happened before in the region. People said it was weird that a girl was volunteering to deal with corpses. Something that had never happened before in Mosul. As a result, Suruur was highlighted by the mainstream media.

One day, she was surprised to learn that the Friday Sermon in the mosque was revolving around her and what had happened to her. The sermon was very positive, bringing into focus her will, persistence and patience. The Imam of the mosque looked at her working alongside the team, and he decided to follow her activities. Suruur's story spread widely on social media.

I started with social media. I gave my first interview to a Yalla Facebook page (civil, secular Iraqi page). Later, the mainstream media competed to bring my story to their channels, and I was also interviewed by international media.

We made a documentary movie on clearing corpses. It was very realistic because the footage was taken while we were working on the ground. Let's say it was a short film that depicted the suffering. One of the international channels was DW; the German Arabic Speaking Channel.

Jaffer, the famous TV Presenter in the German Arabic Speaking Channel asked me to give an interview to his well-known controversial show Shebab Tuk. We were filmed lifting corpses and so on… I thought to myself that what I was doing was normal. I didn't think about the consequences. He called me asking me that there could be an interview in his show about the corpses that haven't yet been lifted post-war. I agreed to attend the show; I had been to other interviews before that one. Media had given us significant visibility and it facilitated more people to come and work with us as volunteers. We began with only six people, then the number grew to 40 because of the media. People liked our team when they saw and read about it. The media has contributed to our team growing larger in a short time.

I thought that the interview would be conducted in the format of question and answer. I got myself prepared for that. When I went to the show that was being aired live from the Old Town, I was shocked to see the Governor of Nineveh (Naufel Al-aquub) sitting as a guest. This man was the first Governor to be appointed as a governor during and after ISIS, he took the office between 2015 – 2019. He has since been imprisoned on charges of corruption.

The Governor began attacking me during TV breaks, but restrained himself when we were on air again, so I would seem as though I was the offensive one. He was threatening to arrest me, claiming that we didn't have legal permits and the authorization to deal with dead bodies. And he denied the truth, claiming that there weren't any dead remains in the Old Town.

The Operation Command of Nineveh interrogated me and I was released. There was no evidence that could convict me. An allegation authorised from Baghdad had investigated me. They kept interrogating me due to the fabricated charges, then I was released, they found nothing on me.

Later, I was invited to the court (Investigative Courts) and then transferred to (Misdemeanour Court). The judge was furious when he asked me: "What happened between you and the Governor of Nineveh, Naufel Al-aquub?"

They forced me to pay a bail of 5 million dinars to buy my freedom, however, they transferred me to (Misdemeanour Court).

There was a journalistic interview in Erbil. I took the chance to get my voice heard by the public. There was a petition published all over the country ("sign for releasing the civil activist Suruur Husseini"), in one day, we were able to gather more than a thousand signatures.

So, my case became a case of public opinion. It coincided with the ferry incident.

(*The ferry sank, causing over a hundred people to drown and go missing in the spring of 2019. Over 200 people were crammed onto the ferry. The Mosul Dam Directorate claimed that it had warned the Tourist Island to which the ferry was crossing 2 days before the incident that "the gate of the dam would be opened and that would cause the river level to rise."*

Popular rage on social media accused the government of being "apathetic". Rescue teams are not prepared to handle such crises. More than 120 people died after the ferry sank, and dozens are still missing. Voluntary efforts by locals accelerated to align the river in hope of lifting corpses that have been swept away by the rapid current. Social media users expressed their condolences, and mourned the victims. Entire families are believed to be drowned, and their relatives are stacked in the hospital. Lists of the survivors have been published on social media accompanied by pictures in some cases).

For a year and two months I was on bail, during which time I often got summoned to be interrogated. My life has been like the ECG; swinging between despair and hope, life and death.

Because of everything that happened to our family – my mom witnessing her daughter and her husband dying before her eyes and the miserable situation we'd gone through; with the bombardment and all the chemicals the city was exposed to – my mother was diagnosed with cancer. However, we couldn't have detected it because of the panic we had. Currently, so many people in Nineveh Province are suffering from cancer, because of the chemicals, war remnants and fear. One of the main causes of cancer is fear.

Suruur was the first to learn her mom had cancer. At that time, the hospitals of Mosul weren't equipped enough to deal with a complex illness like cancer. Most of the patients had to buy the remedy from external sources, and it was so expensive.

When I first got to know that my mother had cancer, the doctors told me that the tumour was prevalent and her cancer was in its advanced stages, especially when someone suffers from blood pressure and diabetes alike in the age of 50s.

It was very difficult. Doctors didn't give me any hope. The disease was hitting her hard. A surgery "tumour excision" had been conducted for her. The tumour weighed 7 kilograms. The surgery had taken place in a hospital affiliated to the private sector. Although it was a private sector hospital, it was contaminated. As a result of the whole situation. So the first surgery didn't go well. She had to be operated on, again and again. She began receiving chemo.

Suruur escorted her along the way; she'd been lying in intensive care. Suruur believed that the best remedy for such cases was enhancing her mom's psychological well-being. She hid the malignant fact from her mother by telling her that the tumour wasn't dangerous, though the woman had to spend several months in the intensive care ward before going back home.

But still, how to convince a person who had a tumour and must submit to cancer treatment that that had nothing to do with cancer. Suruur told her mother that there is a precautionary dose, it is good to take it, because it can prevent future tumours.

Her mother started to notice that her hair had begun to fall. So she started to suspect she might have a malignant tumour. But Suruur told her mother the hair was falling due to the anaesthesia because of the operations she was exposed to. The mom could do nothing but believe in her nurse daughter, since she was the best to assess her medical case.

It was very good that I didn't tell her the truth. Very few people completely get rid of that illness in a country like Iraq. I had her checked last month, and the test results showed that she had been fully cleared of that disease. Until now she still doesn't know she had cancer. I don't think that anyone will tell her. She lost her husband and daughter.

Suruur - a new kind of voluntary work

Suruur started to work with charity baskets. She got backing by herself, striving for every possibility to assist those in need of help. Food baskets were on the way, organised by the mosque, bidding to access the poor of the city. Suruur's team transported aid packages and handed them over to poor people.

Life wasn't easy without a dynamic source of income to support Suruur's work in a city that suffered from all types of crises. Soon, that would be taken care of, and she would get a job that facilitated her move and made her voluntary work run smoothly.

I got appointed as a nurse after I was acquitted from the fabricated charges. During the previous voluntary work of corpses' exhumation, I didn't have that job. Although I worked with "Doctors without Borders" organisation as a nurse, that wasn't a permanent source of income.

After the time of coronavirus, I also began to do voluntary work at the city hospital, at a time when the city of Mosul had witnessed the earliest cases of Covid19. Unfortunately, the city of Mosul hasn't been cleared fully of all corpses. We had to quit because of the complications of doing such work.

The difference between Suruur before the liberation and after liberation: it seems that the whole situation of war and its consequences cast its heavy shadow on Suruur, life tossed her on an unexpected shore; a place she'd never imagined, doing things she'd never thought of.

Life has brought me where I never anticipated to be. I had never thought that someday I would be a civil activist that dedicated herself to helping people. Honestly, positively, and negatively. Sometimes, victory could give one two options, it can make the person either stronger, or weaker who is defeated from the inside. However, I needed to resist. I had to resist from within.

Suruur - the price of her victory

In life, people struggle with either losing or gaining great parts of themselves, people struggle to retrieve what they have lost of their genuine self. Such experiences have definitely erased a great part of Suruur's youth, turning her into another person. She found the voluntary work as a way to retrieve her missing self via rebuilding and resurrecting the human before anything else:

If I had lived in a normal country, I would have found a job after finishing my studies I would have resumed my life without having to go through all that tragedy, I would have become the one I dreamed to be. I would have attained whatever I had previously planned.

I have lost many things, not just one thing. For instance, fear: I have grown up a lot, I feel that my mental age is much older. There is a mental age not only a biological age. This is not a pleasant thing: I couldn't live the actual phases of my lifetime. I guess that no woman would want to see dead bodies, just deformed corpses and not feel intimidated. But for me it has been normal seeing corpses, something which itself isn't normal.

That has taken a great part of myself, it was the price to become who I am now. In addition to my family's losses and my prior dreams that had vanished.

The ambitions I want to attain in the future are dynamic; they go accordingly with the common need of my city that has always influenced my dreams and goals as well.

Our team is still there, but the need for it at the moment is less. Our work isn't like before.

Today, our voluntary work has been shifted to another level, I managed to get rid of the trauma, however, I believe many people couldn't get over it. I feel lucky to have managed to dump that burden away with less casualties in comparison to what had happened. Currently, I am assisting people to become active members in the society.

Some people are still traumatised. We want to build humans. We want to qualify humans to be part of its society. Today, the Mosuli people, they have changed after the war, they became tougher. For instance, we started to have a lot of traffic accidents in Mosul in the aftermath, it is not humane when people would just film the accidents. This is a psychological issue that we need to deal with in our society. Yes, they have seen corpses and they have lost their beloved, but we still need to retain our humanity.

The mechanism we use in raising awareness amongst people is to give lessons on Human Development. We provide people with the entailed lessons to develop themselves, thereafter classes of first aid will be given as well.

Suruur - a women's cycling team for Mosul

In a city like Mosul, which is deemed a closed city that suffered from the lack of the international presence in the form of cultural happenings, building a bridge to the outside world was the solution to get united with the civilised world. It was a step that seemed very hard to take without bringing social justice into the scene, delivering certain initiatives that would provide intense messages that the past era is terminating. The initiative that would be seen by everyone is the birth of hope, which is identical to the birth of the moon from the womb of devastation, a deadly war between elements.

In Mosul, it wasn't familiar to see women driving a vehicle! For a woman to ride a bicycle was something almost impossible. Before the time of corona, my brother brought me a bike. I started cycling for short distances in the beginning. I used to go by bicycle back and forth to my workplace from the right side to the left side of Mosul. I used to cross the bridges of the city using my bicycle and I found it so practical.

Suruur saw in her bicycle an instrument for exceeding social boundaries. In a city that had just split out of the control of the Islamic State that had been working hard to get the locals radicalised, messing with the social taboos was a risk. Suruur had thought about that carefully before taking such a crucial step. To normalise her action, she needed to cycle around and probe people's attitudes, then the next step would be taken based on that.

It was only a bicycle, and bicycles in general don't cause a lot of accidents. But regarding the criticism I got previously,

I had assumed that I would face a string of criticism. However, I didn't receive it from people, explicitly. Then after corona or at the time when the curfew was erased, I thought to myself: why was it only me, the only woman who rides a bicycle in Mosul?

I enlisted one other activist to help organise. We are originally affiliated to the Youth Centre of Nineveh. When we wanted to organise a public event for a cycling marathon for women in Mosul, we needed assistance from the International Organisations that were operating in Mosul.

The role of international organisations in reviving the city of Mosul has been significant. It has opened the space for locals to get to know the role of the international community in resurrecting their city by employing a large number of people and funding their projects.

In Mosul, you can find an activist in every family or a person who'd done voluntary work. A devastated city like Mosul, is most likely to be a vivid example of rapid international convergence that follows the long-term isolation in a country that had always countered wars and crises, and sandstorms as a result of desertification and governmental neglect!

The international organisations have brought new dimensions to the city and, in many instances, new values are being cultivated. The wages that the international organisations allocated for training and projects, was tempting, in addition to the core of the story, which was materialised in engaging more women in daily life to be part of future-making.

Suruur thought that she needed to carry on implementing her idea of getting her counterparts out of the crypts of the traditional domes. Outside, the sun would bake the bread of their life, and fresh air flitting on their faces would expel the ghosts of past eras and the dust of conflict.

The other girls were young. I think we have scored success riding bicycles in a city like Mosul as girls. We were the first 30 girls who tore off the usual image by us riding bicycles and roaming in the city of Mosul. The ones who attended, they belonged to open-minded families. However, we have had difficulties in gathering all those girls. You know that we have a connection in our Institution of Youth and Sports via which we managed to gather the girls. We have founded groups on WhatsApp and Telegram after the event to stay connected with each other.

The organisers of the event saw that the best place to conduct such a marathon was the left side of the city, a new part of Mosul. After the war, the right side of the city where the Old Town is, was regarded as a devastated part, deserted, empty of any elements of life. Rubble was blocking most of the roads, and the pavements were invisible. Suruur wanted to send a message to the world through that marathon, she knew that such an event would gain international visibility.

However, they wanted us to conduct the marathon in the left part of the city. But we rejected that idea. We decided that the best place to start the marathon was the Old Town of Mosul. We wanted to show the world that Nineveh Province has started to develop, to stand again. But on the other hand, Nineveh needs to be reconstructed.

It was like a message we sent from the heart of the Old Town that the city of Mosul still suffers from devastation. We wanted to attract the attention of the world so that they would come and work with us!

During the marathon, we didn't face any criticism, but we drew strange glares from the people. The security forces were collaborative; they did intercept our move.

Even in the Old Town, frankly, the security forces were collaborative with us even when we were exhuming corpses in the aftermath. The security forces had been accompanying us to provide protection with the corpses' exhumation process.

We only faced problems with the explosive corpses we had to deal with. I was the one who would enter first to secure the area before I would let the rest of the team come in. In that phase of trauma, one can do things without having to think: how deadly those things were, but later, when the impact of the trauma goes away, one realises: oh my god! That was really dangerous!

Nowadays, when I watch videos of me two years ago, I think to myself: oh god, how crazy I was to have done all that, I had been amidst explosive bodies, trying to diffuse the explosive. Now, after I have restored myself and realised how dangerous it could be, I wouldn't do the things I did in the past.

Suruur and her team resumed their work, despite the imminent danger and the corpses charged with explosives.

Some members of the team fell because of the rough terrain; imagine rubble of the houses and so on, even if you didn't carry a body, it wouldn't be easy to walk there. So, we started to have injuries.

Among all this, the question is: what brought a young woman to do that kind of job, putting her life at risk? Her life could have ended at any moment. What could make her choose to do that work? Was it the impact of the trauma?

First my sister and then my father passed away. That was the succession of events that traumatised me, making me stronger. I also wanted to keep others safe. I wanted to save what had remained of our people and our city. I had nothing to do, only to make it work out, ourselves, because the government stood paralyzed.

My friend Ibtihal went out of the city to do her Master's degree exam. While heading to that city to do the exam, their vehicle was exposed to an air strike. Close to Sinjar, two cars were bombed, one of them was carrying pilgrims who got killed. Her husband was also killed, and she was badly injured, losing one of her legs and one eye. They transported her to Syria. And from Syria they took her back to Iraq. After liberation, Ibtihal did a master's degree on the psychology of the disabled. She is currently a person with special needs, supervising similar people at Youth and Sport. She was a determined woman who pursued her dream despite all that had happened.

I believe we need to focus on women's freedom in Iraq. Then many issues will be solved thereafter. Nowadays in Mosul, women have gained their rights better than before.

Naqam - a Human Rights activist

Naqam worked as a clandestine activist for Human Rights Watch prior to and during the ISIS period. I encountered Naqam in Mosul, specifically at a renowned international gathering place known as "Station."

Being there, I felt a profound sense of connection to the world. As we settled in at the café and commenced our conversation, Naqam closed her laptop in preparation for the interview. Naturally, my attention was drawn to the slogans and posters promoting human rights displayed on the laptop. Everything pointed to one undeniable fact: Naqam is a part of the civilised world that transcends all borders and cultures.

My name is Naqam Muhammad from the city of Mosul, I am one of the people who have lived all their life in Mosul, even during the time when ISIS took control of the city of Mosul, I didn't depart from the city. I am 27 years old; I am a graduate of computer sciences; I work in the field of civil organisation.

Before ISIS took control of the city of Mosul. The situation in Mosul was hectic; observers described the years following the US led invasion as the worst years in Iraq's modern history. Civil wars and total disconnection with the outside world had left the country paralysed, charged with fears that nourished the malignant ideology to grow and strangle any vein of life that gushed from outside. Iraq was an optimal environment for violent radicalisation under the name of "Jihadism", the struggle towards the righteous. All kinds of freedoms were suppressed and freedom of speech topped the list of taboos. It had been rare to see a woman operating as a journalist or a civil activist, something which wasn't even easy for men to do. The so-called Islamic State: "the hidden enemy" was lurching to strike hard any attempts of connection or collaboration with the civilised world that had been peered at as the world of infidels and apostates. Naqam had to bear all that risk if she really wanted to be part of the international community that had been secretly operating in the city of Mosul.

I come from a quite open-minded family compared to the other typical families in Mosul. When I was a child, I had the chance to question things exceeding the known limits. In many cases, if a woman has a hobby or if she is talented in art such as poetry, drawing and so on, she cannot talk about it loudly. There is always a problem when women express themselves.

After 2003, the city was controlled by the terror groups like Al-Qaida Organisation and later ISIS. The city was strangled by conservative lifestyle that was tightening all types of freedoms in the society. People were forced to be closed to avoid the radical groups. Before 2014, I created for myself a religious shell, decent in my costume, I wasn't socially active, I pretended to be all that, attempting to camouflage who I really was.

I was the international eye operating in Mosul, I was secretly writing reports to some of the humanitarian organisations, I would say that I was like the observatory eye of those organisations such as Amnesty and Human Rights Watch.

I couldn't bring that to the public in any form because at that time, if anyone was convicted of doing such things, or even that person was a suspect, they would be immediately killed or in the luckiest cases, that person would be threatened and be forced to escape from the city.

I started that kind of dangerous work when I got to know a friend of my aunt, a reporter working for a certain TV station. She noticed that my linguistic skills are good in Arabic, I was a person who read a lot and I have got interests older than my real age.

She asked me: "Why don't you write? I would help you with editing and revision."

I was so thrilled by that idea. I started to write simple things, and later she took my writings and looked at them. I don't know until now: how many of those writings had been published, how many of those writings didn't get published.

That female journalist in Mosul was killed on her doorstep. I think that was in 2010. After that incident, my family got so scared, worried I could face the same consequences.

My family rejected the idea of me resuming what I had been doing. One of my relatives who was living abroad encouraged my family that I should resume the writing job but in a different way. He promised that no one would even know about that since he suggested that I work anonymously. That person asked me just to write what was going on in Mosul, just to observe what I was seeing. For example, in case I heard a story from someone regarding human rights violations or I saw something happening or someone got killed or received a threat. That man was editing what I was writing and then he was the one who sent all the materials to the organisations.

I was receiving fees via money transfer, and that person pretended that he was sending assistance to my father who is his relative. I kept working secretly until 2013, when something happened that changed the course of the story. That time, I couldn't demonstrate my financial status, I didn't want anyone to suspect that I was working. When I got into the university, my activity peaked, because the university is an open space, I met more people and eventually I got to write more. At university, I had more mobility, so people didn't pay attention to my motion. I got to know more people from different provinces who worked in the same field. My relative who lived abroad was networking with us. He lived in the US, he is originally from Mosul, he loved the city and found in me a platform to bring Mosul to the mainstream. After 2003 until 2017, the city of Mosul was blocked out, people didn't know much about what was going on inside.

When the demonstrations engulfed the Sunni cities, in what was called the Arab Spring after 2011, the situation started to be dangerous. One of the people I worked with decided to go to Anbar province who had been studying at the University of Mosul. He wanted to learn about the protest that was ongoing in Anbar, Western Iraq. There was a square where the demonstrators were gathering. My colleague had been there two times, on the third time, the Iraqi Security Forces broke into the square to forcibly terminate the demonstration, causing many of the civilians to be killed and wounded. The security forces opened up with live ammo randomly, and my colleague got killed there. It underlined what appeared to be a threatening message to all of us: "Hey, we know who you are!"

I felt the situation had become seriously dangerous. I kept on writing until the city fell in 2014. It was a turning point in my life.

By 2014, life was semi-dead in the city of Mosul, in terms of personal freedoms; you couldn't see a woman unaccompanied by a man, going out. It was forbidden somehow. All women were veiled with Hijab. Even the Christian women were wearing Hijabs. One couldn't differentiate between the Muslim woman and women of other religions.

The situation was so restricting for me as a woman. I couldn't have done or said anything at the time. I was in touch with Human Rights Watch via a mediator who preferred that my real identity stay hidden. Since he was living outside Iraq, he decided to be the one in the front. They already knew that he had a female source in the city of Mosul. He wouldn't give any explicit information regarding my identity; he was so careful.

I was distant from the spotlight, but I was the one who passed him the information on what was happening in the city of Mosul. I was doing that mission until June 2014 when the city was conquered by what was called the Islamic State.

I made photos and videos on the day of the great exodus when people in large numbers were marching on the streets bidding to escape an uncertain future.

Naqam - working as a citizen journalist

On 8th of November 2014, it was a normal day, we absorbed the reality that ISIS was controlling the city of Mosul. As women we had to wear a "Niqab" that covered our faces and, also, we had to put gloves on. In short, ISIS didn't allow any part of women's body to appear.

That day, I received a message on FB stating that we know who you are, and we know your father. They underlined all the personal information of my family and me. They even wrote my address. They said: At any moment, we can break into your house and arrest you.

I saw the flag of ISIS on that account, and I also got a notification that my Facebook account had been hijacked. They changed my wall photo into the flag of ISIS.

I realised that all my attempts to hide my real identity had failed and ISIS could reach anyone when they want to.

After receiving that message, I had to inform my family that ISIS was imminent. Right away, my family decided to send me to one of my relative's houses to hide.

One hour after my departure, the ISIS patrol had arrived. They told my father: "We know what your daughter was doing and with whom she was in contact. You have one of two options, either to hand her over to us or we will take you instead of her!"

My father said: "I will go with you instead of her."

They had managed to reach me through one of the people that I had worked with. They arrested him; he revealed our detailed information. That person was executed later.

In fact, I was working alongside other people in Mosul, one of them was a professor in the university. He had been moving between Mosul and Baghdad. He had a double life, he would seem a supporter of ISIS in public, while in secret he had been working against them. I didn't know that he was an officer in the Iraqi Intelligence.

We were his workmates, though we didn't know that he was an officer. Before ISIS, he used to say: "I am one of you guys, we write reports and observe what is going on in the city." I knew four of my workmates, we used to see each other at the University of Mosul. We spread a rumour that we were relatives to justify our meetings if someone saw us together.

After 2014, that person announced that he became a supporter of ISIS. We felt confused because we knew his thoughts and lines. Then he disappeared until he was arrested by ISIS itself because of espionage.

ISIS searched for me desperately. They became frenzied knowing that we were doing such a job in the city of Mosul.

There was one high-ranked ISIS member who decided to help my family, he was our neighbour: "I will guarantee that that girl would refrain from what she was doing, but if we find out she hasn't ceased her activities, then I assure you that I will kill her by myself."

He saved me by promising the other ISIS members that he would handle me. So, the verdict was I had to stay under house arrest. I wasn't allowed to leave the house. Each month, they would check on me by coming to my house and see if I was there.

I remained in that situation until the city got liberated in 2017.

Nobody knows about this story, I haven't told anyone, even now I don't have a clue why I am bringing it to the public.

Naqam - life after liberation

After liberation, I had no one left to contact. Everyone I knew went silent or vanished. I renewed the contact with my relative who is living in the US. He has strongly encouraged me that now is the right time to speak, to say things out loud. You can even write with your explicit name without having to hide your identity. So, I can say I have initiated work in the voluntary field in Mosul.

The city of Mosul was swept up in voluntary youth work after liberation, in almost every family there was someone who was doing voluntary work.

Mosul was almost razed to the ground after liberation. People found it crucial to start rehabilitating their city themselves, rather than waiting for governmental slow redevelopment. International Organisations made it possible to unify the effort and to get the work oriented in the right direction. Workshops were organised to enlarge the scope of the view of how voluntary work should be carried out in the most vital way in what serves the city of Mosul and its people.

Today, the city of Mosul is different. The situation has changed magnificently. Today, as a woman, I have freedom of mobility. I can stay outdoors for long. I would say that society started to accept what has been kind of unacceptable in the past years. New things, we started to witness here, a woman who goes to work and appears on TV. I don't claim that we have gained a perfect freedom, however things seem to be moving on the right track.

In the past, it was impossible to see a woman outside working freely.

Even men have attained a certain level of freedom on social media. Again, not full freedom, but I would say that now there is more freedom of expression. Day by day, things will get better.

Today, I work in one of the international organisations and I love to do journalism from time to time, I write stories and so on…

The foundation stone of empowerment is to earn the support of the family. My dad has always been proud of me and of what I have been doing, so I don't care what other people might say. Even those who try to offend and detract me, I already know that I am protected within the circle of my family and my beloved ones, I don't mean physical protection, I would say mental protection. I know that I have a family who is proud of me. That fact makes me feel alright; it strengthens me up to confront society. Yes, sometimes, I will face some of the bullies on social media, I know in advance that this kind of person exists everywhere. When someone exposes herself to the public, posting her photos online and her materials, other people might think that they have the right to say whatever they want, so some of them can enter into the zone of bullying.

I hold hopes for the future that the wind of change may blow towards the city of Mosul and uproot all the toxic values from the society. As an open-minded woman, I wish to see the city of Mosul thrive with freedom; at least no one would pay attention to what I wear and do. I wish that everyone in Mosul could live the way they want if they don't cause harm to other people, why not. It is not easy but possible.

Anfal - an artist from the heart of Mosul

My name is Anfal. I am a young woman in the fourth stage of college, studying political sciences.

Currently, I work and study at the same time. When we were liberated from ISIS, I got to complete the last grade in school and graduate. It was like a war to finalise my school study. When the war with ISIS ended, my war started; my life became full of wars that entailed me to fight on all fronts of life to survive as an independent woman.

The freedom I pursued; I had taken it in the way of war. Work had been a war, my studies, and everything in my life turned to be a war.

When I did my exams in 2017, circumstances weren't on my side.

My story stretches back to high-school before the city was conquered by ISIS. Back then, I was an ordinary girl, in the last grade of high-school. And one day, we woke up upon a city stripped of the security forces, and the only thing that filled the skyline was the black banners of ISIS that declared the start of a new fearful era that would perch over the city of Mosul.

I dreamed of studying English because my English is good. I also wanted to study law, however I truly wanted to study art because I like painting and so on. People were advising me to avoid studying art because it has no future in Iraq. I regret that I didn't study art.

When ISIS conquered the city, we stayed at home for three years. Time stopped and we lost connection to the outside world; we became prisoners or hostages. I strived for the chance of finding any link to the outside world.

Humans cannot grow without interaction with new emotions and thoughts.

I thought to myself that reading books could be the secret gate that the oppressors couldn't find. I started reading multiple books, mostly philosophy. Reading transported me into new realms; I met new versions of myself. I beheld alternative facts that tempted me to build a new understanding of life and faith. I even read atheist books; everything has changed, and I am no longer my old self; the self that I inherited from my ancestors and the environment.

The society I live in, provoked me to question many things; there must be an answer, there must be another type of values that could have prevented all this from happening! I have become a different human, I have new opinions regarding religion; I don't belong to anything now, I only see myself as a human being. I opted to study political sciences; I had never thought to go for it. I have earned my experiences from life; I am skilled at computers and languages.

My story with writing commenced when I got to know a facilitator of a writing workshop and then I managed to get to know other people who shared the same passion for writing with me.

Before then, I used to write for myself. I now started to write at a broader level. I wrote about the siege we had undergone under ISIS. The suffering we were exposed to. We got trapped in old Mosul for seven months. We ran out of food and fuel. We couldn't go outside. Several families were crammed in just one house; 25 souls shared with us the same destiny. We didn't know them, just knew that they were like us, struggling to survive, to make it out of that mass grave, the Old Town. Those families were driven out of their houses; they found themselves knocking on the doors of strangers. We welcomed them, we knew that those folks were innocent, their sin was that they were living in Mosul at the wrong time, as were the rest of the civilians.

In such a situation, people are minerals, they radiate with love to comfort each other, in a city that was stifled with hate aroused from the fight, love was the only path towards life.

We lived in the neighbourhood spanning the river Tigris, on the hill that was occupied by the old houses. The houses that survived over the past centuries, the heart of Mosul and the identity of the town.

My father was someone who used to risk his life, walking outside under the bombs raining down and the blind rounds, to bring for us some water from the well. We knew it was a damn risky task, but we had no other option.

We were the last ones to get liberated; we had witnessed all the atrocities and carnages that took place in the town. Once, we didn't eat anything for three days. With the shortage of water, we almost perished, we suffered from malnutrition and dehydration. Our bodies were ready to shut down. The battle peaked and death leaked from everywhere. My father rose, sacrificing himself to bring us water, something he used to do. We drew from him what seemed to be a farewell gaze, then he vanished beyond the door into what was once a vibrant city that remained in our memories only. Now the city was decimated, with the houses reduced to the ground.

Everyone had been waiting for the man who walked into the haze of uncertainty. We heard a motorcycle roaring outside followed by a bombing. The motorcycle had been used by ISIS members to accelerate their motion in the narrow alleyways. After a while, my mother slipped out to check what had happened. She was worried about my dad. I was shocked to hear my mother screaming. I knew at that moment that we had lost my father. Just a matter of seconds parted him from life. He coincided to arrive home when the targeted motorcycle passed by him. A small piece of shrapnel travelled through his back; it was a deadly one.

It was a massive impasse, a dead father waiting to be buried, and a family lamenting over his corpse. If we had a garden inside the house, we would have buried him in the garden, but we didn't.

We skimmed the ground and buried him, we had pots of plants inside, we took out the plants and emptied the soil over his body bidding to cover him. We brought bricks and rubble from the roof of the house that was bombed by a mortar shell. It was impossible to get out of the house, people got killed while they were on the way to flee. A helicopter had been hovering, scanning the area, and targeting any moving objects.

Both sides were randomly bombing, they didn't pay any regard to the civilians dwelling in the city. Who I am today can be attributed to that incident. My current character was shaped by the hard times I have experienced. Yes, I had a strong personality before then, but nothing compared to what I am now.

After liberation, when the battle concluded, we went to exhume his body to make a proper funeral for him, but we couldn't find the corpse, although we searched all over the place. We heard that it was picked up by organisations as an unidentified body.

There are many things that I can't even bring to the public.

In the city of Mosul, when the pace of the fierce fight peaked in the besieged old town, many people were killed as a result of targeting the elements of ISIS in the inhabited zones that ISIS purposely took advantage of: the densely populated areas, thinking that would provide them with a certain level of protection. During my visit to the city of Mosul, I was shocked by the large-scale devastation that was inflicted on the houses. I would say it had been a blazing hell for the poor innocent families who were trapped inside. One of my relatives narrated their story of liberation. As I have been told, every family in Mosul holds their own story of liberation, as the battles of recapturing the city were engulfing the city from door to door like a sacred flame to expel the evil from the haunted town, narratives of the locals vary.

My relative told me that they were forced to evacuate their village in Southern Mosul and march towards Mosul, ISIS used them as human shields. They ended up trapped in the Old Town. They stayed without basic needs for many weeks. They had a limited amount of potable water and food; they couldn't take a shower or wash. They ate soup with flour and one meal for the whole day. One night, while they were crammed in the crypt of the house that contained windows which were half opened, facing the yard, a new offensive took place, the house was shaking. An old woman started sending her prayers to God. Before she finished her prayers, some shrapnel found its way through a small opening in the armoured window and slammed into her chest, leaving her a rigid body on the bed. The family couldn't do anything, they just covered her with a blanket and waited until morning, when they buried her in the square garden in the middle of the house, under the lemon tree.

Anfal - volunteering and work life

I started civil activities in 2019, when I got to know Dr. Hana of Arabic Language. I come from a quite open family. I have only my mother and brother who are younger than me. My family wasn't against the idea. I have encountered problems coming from my other relatives. Our family members trusted each other, but the relatives didn't let us alone. You know they would speak behind my back when they saw me going out alone and sometimes, I would come back home late. So, I heard that they had something to say. But I didn't care because I knew that if I kept being guided by society's taboos, I couldn't have earned my freedom.

For females, work life in Mosul is bad in general. My journey in the labour market commenced when I was visiting the court that issued a death certificate for my deceased father. There was a shopping-mall adjoining the court in

2018, so we coincided to visit that mall. I saw two female employees working as cashiers. I thought to myself why I don't ask them for an open position.

"Hello! Do you need someone to work here?" I asked.

"You can leave your number," she replied.

I gave them my number and, three days later, they contacted me. At that time, we lived in a place where it wasn't easy to leave the house alone. I would say: They barred me from breathing where I was, so what if I go out and work. Then I thought that I should escape from that house if I wanted to insert myself into the labour life, which wasn't easy in a city like Mosul that had just brushed off the dust of the dark ages brought by ISIS.

I started my new path in labour life that eventually would lead me to attain a sort of independence. I knew that when the woman is financially independent, that is the key to loosening the shackles somehow. I ploughed my memory; the aroma of the gloomy past permeated the air – images of us being taught that women's glory is incarnated in her obedience to her guardian.

Poem: A New Morning

A new morning
With a song oozing out through
the wounds of the windows and doors,
to colour the walls of the wistful neighbourhood
to cast on the walls of the neighbourhood, the aroma of tea.
The red-cheeked faces of depression
under the warm sun of love
reveal the gemstones concealed in the mines of my soul.
A new evening:
a glass made of leaves is getting full gradually,
with the tears, we forgot why we shed them -
on that evening
my head was cracked because of the hammering of
solid memories that were rampaging inside.
Aloft, my cries escape from me
I reject being submitted
I toss my words and my silly jokes, apathetically,
then I ask myself: am I really crazy?
A new night
while walking, I stumble by the spiders' fabrics, I fall to the
ground
I stand
Then I ram into the walls
I retrieve my balance
I clear myself of the lights of lying
Then the truth would twist my arm.

Poem written by Anfal

It took me six months to rise from the debris of the society and start again. The first thing I did was to find a new apartment so my family could obtain their independence as well.

During my journey in work life, I was exposed to physical and verbal harassment by the owner of the shopping-mall I had worked at. The owner was Iraqi. I began screaming and defending myself by hitting him and rushing out of the place. He started to beg me to keep silent.

Until this moment, I still feel I am in the wrong place; I am still in search of the place that I truly deserve. However, it is not easy to find such a place because I have a commitment to my study at university. After that incident, I quit my job and started to look for another place.

At the new place, I also got harassed by the owner. I acquired a certain knowledge enabling me to detect when a man concealed the intention of harassing me. For that reason, I have worked in multiple places. Every four months, I needed to change my workplace.

I finally ended up working in the Turkish malls in Mosul. After liberation, the city of Mosul became a fertile ground for foreign investors from Turkey that commenced to open what's known to the locals as the Turkish Malls. In the Turkish Malls, I had been exploited, with low pay and long working hours. We work for ten hours for small pay.

I worked for a tourist company for one year, but was laid off because of the pandemic. I stayed unemployed for one year, then I found my new job. I have been working for a year and two months. Every day, I think of quitting this job, but I don't have any other options. I kept looking for a job, and I would be invited to the interviews. Once I got an invitation from a contractors' company – I saw weird stuff going on there. I realised that they weren't normal. The boss seemed to be creepy. I saw that the surveillance cameras had been turned to the wall. It was the first thing I noticed at any new place; I would study the position of the cameras. If they didn't make any sense, the situation was suspicious. I would leave and skip that opportunity.

For that reason, I stayed working at this mall; at least it is a public place where there are cameras fixed everywhere. I don't trust the institutions in Iraq because I have had experiences. Once there was a man whom I thought of as a friend. One evening, when I left the workplace, he popped up and started to harass me; he snatched my phone and so on. So, I had nothing to do, except to defend myself and to yell on the street. I cried for help, but no one advanced to help. I tried to find a police officer, but in vain, I hurried to the main street, I glanced at a traffic policeman, I ran to him asking for his assistance: he interacted with me in a cold way: "Where is he?"

He didn't even bother to talk to him. When the security forces arrived, I thought to myself that those guys were just showing off to attract me perhaps.

The police officer had given me his personal phone number and asked me to contact him. The offender got handcuffed and tossed on the rear seats of the car. "If you want to make an official application, we could take 6 months, otherwise he could walk free if you forgive him."

It is not easy to trust anyone. In Iraq, the system is built according to the social scheme.

The man is the only legitimate defendant of the woman, otherwise women could be left literally vulnerable. However, I have learned skills to defend myself throughout my experiences. I have got my hands, bag, purse and sometimes to defend myself, I would hide a razor in my bag, just in case.

I got off work at 12 am. Sometimes I face a situation when the car breaks down. One day, I got back at 2:30 am because of car issues. That moment, I was ready for everything. I was afraid internally but externally I looked normal; I couldn't have shown it to the men who were with me in the car. I Just grabbed my razor in case something happened. Nothing happened, luckily. But thank God they were good guys who gave me a ride to my house without any problems."

Anfal - writing as a way to explore the world

My journey with writing started from my early beginnings, back to my father's library at home. I just dragged some of his books to read from time to time. As I child, I pictured myself as a famous writer and people would swarm me asking for my signature on my books or portraits. I like to paint as well. I used to write my diary and some of what I had been going through.

In 2019, I got to enter the world of writing via a writing workshop where I met people who would listen and read with interaction and constructive criticism. I managed to enhance my writing by taking their notes and working to fix the flaws. I got to know a lot of things. I have built friendships with people who resemble me at an ideological level and so on.

Once we were discussing something, everyone had shared the same values. We deem ourselves feminist women. We share almost the same faith. Spiritually, human beings need to have faith in something, just to obtain the serenity of that faith. However, there are things, clearly to be put by humans not supernatural power, to be able to detect that, you need a certain level of knowledge.

Now, I wear the Hijab but still, and let's call it the prevailing costume. However, within the frame of these social limits, I can be rebellious, or in other words, I can break the rules of my society. I am not convinced of the necessity of wearing a Hijab. But should I choose to take it off, my family would get hurt first. The family could get exposed to various types of verbal offensives. What I wear now, I would consider a bid to break the rules within the frame of the society.

This is what a normal human would wear. We are not animals to show off by exposing our bodies. I don't see any justification for women to hide their hair. This is my style even if I take off my Hijab, I am convinced. I do what I like.

I don't deny that I have some crazy ideas, which could be expressed in my paintings. Once, I got a work offer to work as an artist – this is what I have always wished to be – when I sent them some of my paintings, they apologised saying that my paintings are scary.

Sometimes, I would write a text and then I would draw my writings. I have texts, yes.

I draw this character as a hairless person that represents myself. This is how I picture myself. I strive to develop my art in terms of using the painting's equipment and so on. But again, I haven't got enough time to do so.

I hope for the future to work in what I love such as the art I make and my writing.

I want every girl to realise that she is a human being; she is equal to men, the only difference between man and woman is biological.

The instrument to attain social justice, a great part of it lies upon the shoulders of the government, starting from daycare, kindergarten, and schools. The first brick is to erase gender discrimination by eradicating separation based on genders in the schools, having gender-neutral schools. Girls and boys should go to the same school and sit on one desk. We need to raise awareness in the schools by getting pupils sexually educated rather than avoiding discussing such issues.

I believe when obscurity is left behind us, everything should be fine.

We have had multiple shocks in our life. Those shocks could emerge in one of our texts or pictures, or even when I am emotional about something. I think we should start tracking back that emotion to the roots.

I have always relied on myself; I used to do my own things without having to ask for somebody's assistance, however I have a brother with whom I grew up. I didn't like when people said: you are a girl who shouldn't do this and that while your brother could do what he wants because he is a boy. I didn't like to hear that.

When the girl laughs, they shouldn't crack down on her laughter by asking her to stop laughing in public. These kinds of things can fracture girls from within at an early age. She becomes a burden on her society and on the man himself. She cannot go out alone to buy anything. She would even be unable to open the outside door. She is afraid to do a lot of things. Because she depends on her man entirely.

Anfal - women need to be financially independent

Personally, when I scored my financial independence, I started to steer my life the way I want, rather than waiting for someone's permission to tell me what to do and what not to do. Women should rely on themselves rather than depending on men in everything. This is a shared life. When a woman gets married, she would share common responsibilities and duties with her spouse. But here in the Middle East, the man doesn't even help his wife in the kitchen. I have seen many people where the man is always the master of the situation.

Sometimes, the woman could be the source of the problem, because she thinks that the man should be distant from the domestic duties, they are fine with the traditional idea; the man is the provider of the family. However, men would feel happier if women would share part of the responsibilities and burdens with them.

In the writing workshop, some of the female participants have faced difficulties to convince their families to let them take part in that workshop which was meant to be for girls exclusively. There was a girl with us whose brothers glanced at her while heading to the car, a strange guy was staring at her, then her brother went furious and prevented her from coming to the workshop. She was like a normal human walking to the car, the guy was staring at her, she probably didn't even know about it. However, her brothers wouldn't let her come here again.

Here in this place, which is called the station, which is indeed the most international place, international values are being promoted. This intellectual space was founded after Mosul was liberated from ISIS. I would deem this space as a bridge to the world. Sometimes I would gaze at someone by chance while thinking of something, it doesn't mean that I admire that person.

Poem: Reunifying with herself

When she eyed the sky
She dug into depths
Her thoughts were a sickle
She penetrated the space with sharp stares
The night for her was an open duffel
A girl with unruly hair sat on the crossways,
tapping on the phone, while crunching an apple
In the sophisticated cities,
when tower blocks stood tall, like spears
or like questions without answers sank in the clouds
The girl who escaped from the desert
pulled out a cigarette branded the Camel -- the straps of
smoke cannot tie her
to the tribe she fled.
The breeze of freedom tattered the beast that erected in the air
flicking more fears..
She recalled her trek to reunify with herself:
People who are barred behind the cell doors, they are perched
in the cellar,
they are sliced into two selves:
the one who's shackled in the chains of religion, society,
and a mirage called "great honour"!
While the other self,
tries to rip off what positions a girl,
distanced from her true colour:
The books I've read made crevices in the wall of prison.
She uttered the last words before hauling her pocket drink out
and sipped on it:
In wars, women are much stronger!

Ahmed Zaidan

Marwa - founding a team of volunteers

My name is Marwa Al Jubouri, my marital status is divorced. I am 29 years old, currently I am a civil activist and I have founded my own voluntary team after the liberation of the city. Today, I would say that I have been engaged in voluntary work for 5 years. Before the city was occupied by ISIS, I had been a normal human. I spent most of my time sitting at home, as a result of that I was a victim of a marriage of minors.

I was forced to get married when I was 13 years old. However, I separated after 5 years. I had to stay at my family's house. I tried to revert to my studies, but I faced so many challenges. Today, I consider myself a person who was created by tough times. Before the time of ISIS, I had a dream of becoming a writer. Honestly, that was my dream, I used to write short stories and scenarios and so on. When ISIS took control of the city, my dreams were scattered, I felt that everything was going in a hard direction.

After my separation, I drew critical looks from society as a divorced woman. When ISIS occupied the city, I felt that my tragic life had been completed. During the time of ISIS, I used to write a lot, I wrote down everything, even the simple moments that passed through. I used to write everything, especially about women. As a divorced woman, I had been one of the target groups that ISIS put into focus. ISIS thought that the divorced woman was in danger and that she should be married again as soon as possible. My family had to take extra care of me, so I had to stay at home during the time of ISIS, as though I was in a prison.

After ISIS, at the beginning of liberation, there was a need for voluntary work in Mosul such as doing first aid, working with organisations who were advancing assistance to the locals.

One day, I took part doing some voluntary work, my father had encouraged me to do such a job. I received the needed training for doing first aid. That was the beginning of my journey, the journey that I had never thought about.

Following the hard times I had gone through; I felt a need to fight back through doing voluntary work. I founded a voluntary team. At that time, the right side of the city had not yet been liberated. Battles were still going on, on the other side of the town. It was unusual seeing a woman on the street doing any kind of work. People hadn't seen a woman working with the security forces or with men in general. After living as a vulnerable woman in the past, I found myself moving swiftly to dismantle the old image of women in the country.

I founded my team and I worked in hard conditions; we were seeing death every day. I escorted the Iraqi security forces when they were advancing in the city. I don't deny that I have faced social problems regarding my family and my tribe. However, I am still at odds with my family due to my current work as a journalist and civil activist.

My father had been my best supporter; he passed away si months ago. The problem is doubled now because I am a separated woman.

I proved that I am strong. I had been escorting the liberator troops to offer aid to those trapped in the rubble during the battles of liberation. When the city was liberated, I resorted to journalistic work. Today, I am the chief of women in the journalism union. I also work at Al Nur University. I am a freelancer for a number of agencies. I still work on humanitarian issues; I have worked with orphans, thalassemia, and cancer patients. I also worked with the war injured, providing artificial limbs to them. Today I choose to work in journalism.

Marwa - Marriage of Minors in Iraq

My strength is a result of the days of vulnerability I experienced in the past. The day when my family made the decision on my behalf to have me married, which I deem a crime committed against me and my childhood. I had to quit my studies in the hope of resuming it after marriage. But things had changed, and my husband didn't allow me to continue my studies. I lived with a sterile man – sorry for such details – he also suffered from psychological issues, something that had influenced my life, my personality, in that time, I was a child. The social pressure was great, making things even worse. My ex-husband was 15 years older than me. I decided to separate.

After separation, I decided to revert to my studies as a first step to retrieve my old self, but I also had to suffer because of society. The problem of our society, in the beginning, I was a victim of the wrong decision of my family who forced me to get married, then I became the victim of my own decision of separation.

The talk that was revolving around me – a divorced woman and so on – oppressed me a lot. I had to build walls to protect myself, so I stayed indoors for many days, just to avoid being criticised and judged by my society.

I thought to myself that the only way to get over that was to create a voluntary team of guys that would be led by a woman who had been suppressed. It was my message to emphasise that women can lead in society – it is not necessary for men to be responsible for women or the leader in everything – yes, that was my second challenge that I had to overcome: A divorced woman who leads a group of men in public.

I started to encounter domestic problems from members of the family, but I have been stronger than all the social currents that tried to drift me away from my line.

Today, I see myself becoming a source of strength to my family, their pride. Unlike the ominous past in which I was broken and vulnerable, today I feel that even my tribe started accepting me the way I am. Members of my tribe sought my assistance on many occasions. In the past, they thought I was the discordant or the black sheep of the family.

Thank God, today I am stronger than everything, however honestly, I would like to discuss the topic of "Minor Girls' Marriage" and the consequences of that marriage at multiple levels starting from the psychological level and the social level. Even after separation, the consequence is incurable in many of the cases.

I think the only way to eradicate such types of unfair marriages is to raise awareness among young people and their families. I also wish that we saw more girls have the courage to narrate their stories in public, so the lesson could be taken. Today, as a victim, I share my story. I wish that at least five girls could listen to my story and benefit from my mistake, or at least, they could stand up to anyone wanting to turn their lives that way.

Journalism is still one of the instruments and main factors to make a significant change. However, the journalism operating in the region is still careful when dealing with such sensitive topics relating to religion and costume.

As a journalist, I have worked on such issues, unfortunately I have faced so many problems: do you want to liberate our women and girls, do you want them to stay out on the street? Their thought on liberty is to be perverted and to stay on the street!

I wish that we could really witness a true illumination in the region to illustrate the core of freedom to those people who think that freedom is chaos.

Regarding me becoming an influential woman in my tribe, I would say that I have proved for them many things, I have proved that I exist in society. In the past, I would cry myself to sleep, after any voluntary activity I had done like cleaning and so on. I would cry because of the bad things being said about me.

How could I work with men on the street? You are a woman whose place is the house. You can only work as a nurse or teacher. They didn't want to believe that women can operate as civil activists.

Today, the city of Mosul has changed dramatically. I have seen so many women working as civil activists; it has become normal to work in the organisations. In the past, such work was taboo.

Today, I would like to talk about myself. Being a divorced woman was the biggest problem I had to encounter. Even when I had to travel somewhere, it wasn't easy to do it alone because of my marital status. My mobility has been bogged down a lot until now, but I managed to get over it, because I am a confident woman. I was able to reconstruct myself until reaching a level of independence; no one can influence my decisions anymore. However, I am still exhausted from exerting a lot of my energy to repel such issues. For how long should I keep facing such obstacles? I want to get rid of the estranging glare of people. I want to normalise the topic of a divorced woman.

I would like to find a chance to work on this topic in the town. I would like to get the support to work on (divorced women). I don't want people to feel pity when they know I am divorced.

People could exclaim: "Oh my god, you are a divorced woman who has scored all that success!"

I would say: "What is wrong with the divorced woman?"

Due to my strong personality, I can resist. Other women have been stricken hard by the social torrent. Other women have been exploited a lot by other people, they broke their confidence and made them feel that they are nothing, she needs someone, a second-class woman.

I scored a significant victory for myself and against my family. I had been a student returning from school when I was informed that my engagement party would take place next week. I didn't know anything, I was only a 13-year-old girl, I didn't know what to say or what to answer. I didn't have the capacity to discuss. In 2006, we were a different generation compared to the current generation. In that time, the internet wasn't so prevalent in the town, no social media and so on. I didn't know anything, my life revolved around my school and family.

I would reveal this information for the first time. When my family escorted me to the court, the judge looked at me and said, "I can't make a marriage contract with this girl. Why? Because she doesn't look like an adult" (physically).

I didn't have a women's menstrual cycle yet! He asked my family to bring him a medical report obtained by a doctor that I was an adult.

They took me to a doctor who was a friend of the family of my ex. So, she just gave them a fake report that I was an adult; she wouldn't even check me up. They felt so happy after getting the report, and I felt odd, I couldn't tell what was going on; I thought that was part of the normal, any girl must go through what I was going through now.

I got married to a man who didn't have confidence in himself. That has impacted my life. I have never thought that there was something wrong with me. The marriage experience has helped to grow and to see things that I couldn't have seen before. I began to see myself as a victim. My father was sick at the time I got married. He really thought that he could secure his daughter's life in case he passed away.

For five years I lived distant from my family. I hadn't told them anything. I have lived a dramatic life; I was avoiding any escalation. That was the reason why I had to bear everything on my own shoulders, until I reached a level: No, I couldn't stand more than that! I thought of ending my life to get rid of all the situations. I tried to commit suicide, but I failed. I went to my family's house thereafter, then my family knew what I had been going through, the sufferings I concealed, the pain I couldn't reveal.

Marwa - life after separation

I thought my life would be better after detaching myself from the source of my sorrow and distress but the following happened: people started to keep an eye on me and monitoring everything I did. If I listened to a song or put on new clothes, people wanted to know if I had a lover or something. I wouldn't have said such private things to anyone, but I would like such stories to be in the mainstream so moms could listen, and everyone might benefit from it. I would say that I was fortunate that I didn't have children, because it could double the problem.

Everywhere I went, I needed to be accompanied by my mother and brothers.

My father had been careful, he knew that as a divorced woman, people can fabricate any story they want about me. My father trusted me a lot, but also tried to maintain my reputation in society.

Marwa - women and financial independence

When I found a job, I started to be a self-dependent person. I felt that I have built my entity, but there is a main point among all this: my past and my vulnerability are still impacting my life up to the present day; influencing the way I think and the way I make my choices. There is a psychological part of me that would look for people's reaction when hearing that I am a divorced woman. I wish to get rid of that part of myself, I am seeking psychological help. Sometimes, I feel that my steps are bogged down by the past. I couldn't tread smoothly when the ghosts of my marriage experience were pulling me backwards. People might think that after divorce everything is over, but that is not the case. Now I started to feel where I was, I started to deal with the trauma of the past. People deal with the crisis according to their awareness, and when I grew up, I started to discover new parts of the pain that I must deal with, regarding marriage and divorce, my life that had been lost and everything.

When I got divorced, I just felt that it was a great relief to escape that type of life, slipping into a new type of life. Yes, I would say that I have attained so many achievements which helped me to balance between my loss and my gain, however everything I have scored now, couldn't compensate for my childhood and my teenage years.

I am always saying: I didn't live as a teenager. My family ruined my life in the name of society, thinking that they were doing good for me. But until my last breath I have, I will do my best to change this society.

Mosul - A Better Tomorrow

Mosul is slowly recovering from the horrors inflicted by ISIS, and hope is beginning to reemerge in the hearts of its residents.

Despite the war's poisonous fumes
A better tomorrow begins to loom
Beyond the hills and valleys, the sun rises –
dancing in the foam that
oozes from the beautiful stream.

Ahmed Zaidan

After a deadly war has cost a large number of innocent lives, and left many suffering from permanent injuries and post-war trauma, we begin to catch the fragrance of hope drifting on the breeze.

We discover the new Mosul through poetry and then through photos sent by its inhabitants of life returning to its veins. The city that was ruthlessly bombed will rise like a Phoenix from the ashes of war to soar aloft in the sky of humanity casting its story as a lesson that may stand as a wall to repel the torrent of ugliness brought by hate and ignorance: for what happened not to happen again.

Nor should it happen again elsewhere either. The people of Mosul realised more than ever that we are all connected, living on the same vessel so that we learn either to live together or to perish.

Back in the past, I lived in the city under the title "It is none of my business!" In that time, people trusted no one, not even what were supposed to be the competent authorities. They knew moles were everywhere and if they had reported about a terror activity or somebody suspicious, their information would be revealed to the terrorists, and I don't want to give rise to the bloody scenes that would accompany this scenario.

Currently people of Mosul have come to a conclusion that security is the result of mutual work between the state and locals. I would not exaggerate when I say that nearly every family in Mosul had lost someone, either killed or forcibly disappeared, however the families of those who weren't confirmed killed, are still living in hope that their absent children are still alive. Most of them were \taken a few days before the battle of liberation from Wadi Hajar neighbourhood; as I mentioned in previous chapters, Wadi Hajar was called by ISIS "the neighbourhood of apostates."

Abu Omar - Mosul is reclaiming its spirit

Abu Omar, whose testimony we shared in the section on ISIS occupying Mosul, reflects on the unimaginable peace that has settled over the eastern neighbourhoods since the city's liberation:

Despite the immense challenges and losses suffered, Mosul is gradually reclaiming its spirit, and the uncovering of these documents serves as a reminder that the true nature of ISIS has been exposed. The road to recovery will be long and arduous, but with the strength and resilience of its people, Mosul will continue to rebuild and move forward.

Um Umar – now feeling optimistic

Um Umar, like many people, had witnessed the development of the events post-2003 right up to the peak of turmoil that led to the city's swift downfall in 2014. Like them, she believed the city was sliding in that direction and it was impossible to stop the tumbling ball. She doesn't want to reveal her identity for fear of any attempts by Iranian-affiliate militias that imposed their grip on the city after the era of ISIS.

During Ramadan, I used to send a plate of what we had cooked for Iftar to Ameena; our Christian old lady and on Eid, I would send her sweet dumplings and she did the same. But after 2003, everything changed. Terrorists found the Old Town to be the best den to hide in among people and tighten our way of living. Many Christians had left for fear, only a few had stayed until the conquest in 2014, later they were forced to leave everything behind and leave.

At some point we wondered if we should have left as well. Who would want to stay in a city that had become a battlefield. If we'd known what was going to happen, we would have left with the Christians. However, in the second year of the conquest, ISIS had barred the people of Mosul from leaving."

Now however, Um Umar is optimistic and sees that what had happened would not happen again, since people of Mosul have come to a conclusion that the only way to live in peace is to fortify the pillars of coexistence and acceptance.

A Gleam of Hope

The blow which doesn't break your back, will definitely make you stronger! This is exactly what is happening in Mosul nowadays. Youth movements are leading the city. Voluntary work is a remarkable phenomenon functioning in the city's favour.

Co-existence came as a popular reaction to what ISIS had tried to do with Mosul identity, the identity of diversity, the biggest home for Christians in Iraq, in addition to other minorities that lived peacefully alongside to Muslims for centuries.

Today Mosul has managed to change its corrupt governor and restore what he embezzled. This is quite a rare occurrence in Iraq; a youth-led civilised demonstration ousting a governor! People were just totally fed up following the infamous Mosul ferry incident, leaving over 200 dead.

Today, the following campaign could tell us a lot. It is entitled "we have started" referring to the local people, deployed on the streets of the city, cleaning the city of garbage in a bid to implant new values: that when you clean your city yourself it is an act that doesn't detract from your worth but enhances your sense of self respect as a good citizen. Today Mosul has been chosen as "the capital of voluntary work in Iraq."

Mosul's rehabilitation went swiftly, and the university central library was reconstructed. It looks better now than before. Thanks to UNESCO who made it possible for the main hall of the theatre to open its doors again. Mosul is experiencing a new era in its history; being an open city, teeming with the international organisations that work persistently to keep Mosul as a beautiful part of the world.

However, it's important that we don't forget what happened to bring us to this rebirth so that it doesn't happen again.

Poem: Story of Hope

Hope permeates the air,
The Tigris River refuses to halt
Chamomile blooms over the hills,
washing away the stench of death with the morning breeze.

We are the exhalation of war,
children of the merciful god,
scattered overseas.

We are the olive tree's trunk, travelling into the souls of enemies,
enduring a thousand slaps on the other cheek,
until the tyrant perishes.
Will the victims ever enjoy a day of peace?

We are the loneliness of the burnt palm tree in the battlefield.

*"War has never been here.
I stood taller than the folk of trenches, crawling to despair.
O folk of imminent tombs, I see a sunrise looming in the end.
I see the colours wrapping the edge of no man's land.
I sniff the scent of hope amidst the smoke and clutter of sand.
I see a group of women making a wall of rejection,
advancing steadily towards the oppressors, holding hands.
I see warships vanishing, one by one,
while lovers begin to spill out onto the southern strand."*

*I know the speech of the burnt palm tree was hard for them to understand.
She cast over the besieged all types of wonders,
as a magic wand, or river of miracles splitting the desert sand,
resurrecting their dying homeland, their tattered homeland.
In the last chapter, the impish power decided to put in a wistful end.
The standing palm tree said: "I see what you cannot believe,
I see Adam making love to Eve.
I see spring weaving a dress of hope.
Eventually, the shivering trees will be endowed with leaves.
I see pollen disseminate around the ominous globe.
It is a message from eternity,
that Mosul is truly a story of hope.*

*I see the flyers in the form of poems,
flaking like feathers of wisdom on our strife.*

*I see the message of women from the recent chapters:
That in the middle of bombing, there is a spot of life.
On the mountains' slopes, the Edelweiss thrive.*

Ahmed Zaidan

A New Era

In recent years, the city of Mosul has undergone a new era of "coexistence." Despite the hardships and tragedy that the people endure, the city has achieved a level of prosperity.

Starting over was no easy feat. I recall telling my mother over the phone that it would take decades for the city to fully recover. However, she surprised me by informing me that the old market was being rehabilitated by locals who didn't wait for the Iraqi government to allocate funds for their work.

In the first month of liberation, a group of people decided to do voluntary work, making pages on social media, asking for more people to join them. Their call was swiftly responded to by people and in a matter of days the revolution of rebuilding the city started.

The first seeds of hope were planted when the international organisations were allowed to work inside the city, which had once been deemed the most unfriendly place to outsiders. However, this issue was understandable, as people in Mosul, like all Iraqis, had undergone three decades of dictatorship that had turned their country into a prison yard.

My first encounter with people from the West was after 2003 when well-equipped US soldiers, leaning on their military vehicles and dangling their M16's nozzles, answered the curious locals who approached them to test their English. I approached them gingerly and tried my first version of English, learned from school classes. At the time, I believed that we were studying English for a reason, and I remembered the famous proverb in Arabic (knowing the language of a tribe "nation" would bar their evil).

That was our experience with strangers, but I would say that the time of ISIS and the dark years that preceded the rise of the Islamic State and Militias has given people a clear vision of the essence of these fanatics' religious ideologies. This contributed to raising their awareness and resilience.

This crisis bestowed one good thing upon Iraqis - the chance to start their new journey towards the horizons of freedom. They are distancing themselves day by day from the gloomy past they were born into and the wounds they suffered. Since this part of the book is about hope, I have decided not to dwell on the days of despair and nights of fear. Instead, I want to wash myself in the flow of spring streams and sniff the morning breeze of April, the month in which the land wears a chamomile dress and grazing fields are full of life.

However, I remembered that the story of hope is like the pendulum of an old clock on the wall of knowledge, swinging in two directions to weave the fabric of time, ticking between life and death, day and night. This is a narrative of hope and despair intertwined together.

I decided to immerse myself in the darkest nights to bring the shine of the stars and to dive into the cold deep winter to bring the warmth of wisdom, endowed by endurance and cope. I resolved to sketch hope on the debris, knowing that it may bloom when the first light of morning looms, emerging from the dismal tombs.

Conclusion

Spanning the time Mosul was occupied by ISIS, I had been living a poor-quality life in Finland, with poetry being my sole hole in the wall of the siege. I wrote significant poems that become a poetry collection entitled "Aurora from Mosul", in which I tried to turn my torment into an aurora of beauty, taking place in the sky of the North. I believed that a great part of me had been trapped in Mosul with my beloved ones, trying to survive. I exerted an enormous effort to save my stuck self who refused to quit the city of Mosul, the places where my early memories were born on the banks of the Tigris River.

In Mosul, I witnessed the rotten values people wore as social accessories or medals of honour to win a social privilege, nothing more. But once the truth challenged the validity of those values, they proved to be a failure; they tore apart the natural fabric of the society and scattered individuals.

I used to try to be oblivious of Mosul and my remaining self in there, but I felt that I was betraying myself in Finland and also the society that I lived in. I felt compelled to share my story; the story of Mosul through poetry and prose, to give an idea of what was going on in that part of the globe. What happened in Mosul cast its shadow on the whole region, resulting in the biggest wave of asylum seekers, crossing the sea, drowning in the sea, striving on the way of salvation, attempting to ditch their prior life entitled an endless way of torment.

From there, I understood the core of the proverb: we are all connected, whether to survive or die together – that's one of the most important sayings that one should consider in life before posing any word and doing any deed.

Throughout my journey, I have sought to redefine my understanding of concepts based on the insights gained from my direct experiences, which enabled me to ditch outdated values, and embrace vibrant ones. In the course of life, we tend to believe in certain values inherited from our ancestors and promoted by the code of the group. We may live and die without having the chance to examine our values, to see how much they value in practice, how they can enhance our life without inflicting harm to others which would eventually affect us.

Author's Biography - Ahmed Zaidan

Ahmed Zaidan is a Finnish-Iraqi poet, writer and journalist. In 2009, he published his first poetry collection in Iraq. In 2013, he migrated to Finland, embarking on a new venture through publishing several works in Europe: *Aurora from Mosul*, *Kotimaa/Homeland* and the latest, *Double Vision* that was funded by Taike.

Palewell Press

Palewell Press is an independent publisher handling poetry, fiction and non-fiction with a focus on books that foster Justice, Equality and Sustainability. The Editor can be reached on enquiries@palewellpress.co.uk

www.ingramcontent.com/pod-product-compliance
Lightning Source LLC
Chambersburg PA
CBHW052016070526
44584CB00016B/1775